Selected Essays on the Gita

SELECTED ESSAYS ON THE GITA

Sri Aurobindo

hachette INDIA

First published in 2025 by Hachette India
(Registered name: Hachette Book Publishing India Pvt. Ltd)
An Hachette UK company

1

ISBN 978-93-5731-811-2

Hachette Book Publishing India Pvt. Ltd
4th/5th Floors, Corporate Centre,
Plot No. 94, Sector 44, Gurugram 122003, India

Typeset in Ibarra Real Nova
by Manmohan Kumar, Delhi

FSC
www.fsc.org
MIX
Paper | Supporting responsible forestry
FSC® C010615

Printed and bound in India
by Thomson Press India Ltd.

Contents

ESSAYS ON THE GITA: SECOND SERIES

Preface

Sri Aurobindo (1872–1950) was born as Aurobindo Ghose in Calcutta into a family of an Anglophile Brahmo surgeon who wished to distance his children from their native tongue and culture; therefore, he sent them to study in Britain. After being home-tutored by a Protestant reverend for five years in Manchester, Sri Aurobindo was enrolled in a prestigious St. Paul's School in London, and later in King's College, Cambridge.

During his studies in Britain, Sri Aurobindo learnt and developed a deep liking for French, Greek and Latin, and also picked up some German, Spanish and Italian due to his interest in European classical literature. He also had a considerable interest in English poetry and had an in-depth knowledge of the Christian tradition. While at Cambridge, Sri Aurobindo started rediscovering his Indian identity and became drawn towards the Indian freedom struggle. At the same time, he disqualified himself from the ICS examination, shattering his father's dream of seeing his son as a civil servant.

Sri Aurobindo was invited to join the State Service of Baroda by the enlightened prince Sayajirao Gaekwad III while the latter was travelling in Britain. He did that in 1893, occupying various positions, most notably that of the teacher of English Literature at the prestigious Baroda College.

During his Baroda years (1893–1907), Sri Aurobindo fully rediscovered his Indian identity, taught himself Sanskrit, learnt Bengali, Hindi, Marathi and Gujarati, and started intense yoga practice, both by himself and under the guidance of a guru. He expressed his experiences in his profoundly spiritual sonnets and penned a considerable number of poems based on Sanskrit classics and epics.

Simultaneously, Sri Aurobindo got involved in political activities, contributing to various magazines, delivering speeches, setting up political clubs, and developing links with several independence movement groups and revolutionaries in the Bengal Presidency. He was an active participant in the epochal Surat session of the Indian Congress (1907) that saw a clear rift between the moderates and the so-called extremists, the latter advocating complete independence for India. Sri Aurobindo was actively involved with the extremist wing of the Congress led by Bal Gangadhar Tilak and became the editor of its organ *Bande Mataram* (founded by Bipin Chandra Pal), which led to his first brief arrest in 1907. Believing in the need for truly national education in India, he accepted the position of the principal of the Bengal National College in Calcutta (1906).

Sri Aurobindo's second arrest, on the charges of taking part in the Alipore Bomb Case, resulted in his year-long imprisonment (1908–09), much of it solitary, which proved a turning point in his life. He spent his time intensively practising yoga and studying the Upanishads and the Gita. Although his acquittal and release from jail saw him start a new nationalist publication, *Karmayogin*, in cooperation with Sister Nivedita in Calcutta, Sri Aurobindo started to drift away from politics and devote himself entirely to yoga. He moved to Pondicherry, then a French possession in India, to escape the possible third arrest by the British colonial authorities, who never believed in his retirement from the independence movement and continued watching him closely.

Sri Aurobindo's first period of life in Pondicherry (1910–1926) saw him deepen his yoga practice and extensively write based on the resulting experience in the philosophical review *Arya* (1914–21). Several important books by Sri Aurobindo were serialized in this publication: *Essays on the Gita*, *The Synthesis of Yoga*, *The Ideal of Human Unity*, *The Secret of the Veda,* to name a few. This magazine was published with the help of Sri Aurobindo's spiritual equal and collaborator from France, Mirra Alfassa (1878–1973), known as The Mother, who later on became the head of Sri Aurobindo Ashram in Pondicherry.

During his second period of life in Pondicherry (1926–50), Sri Aurobindo retreated into seclusion in his room in the Ashram building and maintained direct contact only with the Mother and a few closest disciples. Over the years, he developed and extensively wrote on the system of Integral Yoga, radically different from all the previous spiritual practices and yogas in that it attempted to divinize the matter rather than help one escape from it. During these years, Sri Aurobindo penned his magnum opus, *The Life Divine*, and a spiritual epic, *Savitri*, both of which are rightly considered his testament. He also maintained correspondence with his disciples, discussing with them the complex issues of his thought and practice.

Sri Aurobindo's literary output is enormous: his collected works run into more than thirty volumes. He authored a great number of long and short poems, several plays, reflected on the value of national art and education, offered a deeply psychological interpretation of the Veda, discussed the value of poetry and developed new meters, interpreted the Gita and the Upanishads, researched the questions of human evolution, and aimed for the spiritual renaissance of India and the world.

Essays on the Gita
First Series

Our Demand and Need from the Gita

The world abounds with scriptures sacred and profane, with revelations and half-revelations, with religions and philosophies, sects and schools and systems. To these the many minds of a half-ripe knowledge or no knowledge at all attach themselves with exclusiveness and passion and will have it that this or the other book is alone the eternal Word of God and all others are either impostures or at best imperfectly inspired, that this or that philosophy is the last word of the reasoning intellect and other systems are either errors or saved only by such partial truth in them as links them to the one true philosophical cult. Even the discoveries of physical Science have been elevated into a creed and in its name religion and spirituality banned as ignorance and superstition, philosophy as frippery and moonshine. And to these bigoted exclusions and vain wranglings even the wise have often lent themselves, misled by some spirit of darkness that has mingled with their light and overshadowed it with some cloud of intellectual egoism or spiritual pride. Mankind seems now indeed inclined to grow a little modester and wiser; we no longer slay our fellows in the name of God's truth or because they have minds differently trained or differently constituted from ours; we are less ready to curse and revile our neighbour because he is wicked or presumptuous enough to differ from us in opinion; we are ready even to admit that Truth is everywhere and cannot be our sole monopoly; we are beginning to look at other religions and philosophies for the truth and help they contain and no longer merely in order to damn them as false or criticise what we conceive to be their errors. But we are still apt to declare that our truth gives us *the* supreme knowledge which other religions or philosophies have missed or only imperfectly grasped so that they deal either with subsidiary and inferior aspects of the truth of things or can merely prepare less evolved minds for the heights to which we have arrived. And we are still prone to force upon ourselves or others the whole sacred mass of the book or gospel we admire, insisting that all shall be accepted as eternally valid truth and no iota or underline or diaeresis denied its part of the plenary inspiration.

It may therefore be useful in approaching an ancient Scripture, such as the Veda, Upanishads or Gita, to indicate precisely the spirit in which we approach it and what exactly we think we may derive from it that is of value to humanity and its future. First of all, there is undoubtedly a Truth one and eternal which we are seeking, from which all other truth derives, by the light of which all other truth finds its right place, explanation and relation to the scheme of knowledge. But precisely for that reason it cannot be shut up in a single trenchant formula, it is not likely to be found in its entirety or in all its bearings in any single philosophy or scripture or uttered altogether and forever by any one teacher, thinker, prophet or Avatar. Nor has it been wholly found by us if our view of it necessitates the intolerant exclusion of the truth underlying other systems; for when we reject passionately, we mean simply that we cannot appreciate and explain. Secondly, this Truth, though it is one and eternal, expresses itself in Time and through the mind of man; therefore, every Scripture must necessarily contain two elements, one temporary, perishable, belonging to the ideas of the period and country in which it was produced, the other eternal and imperishable and applicable in all ages and countries. Moreover, in the statement of the Truth the actual form given to it, the system and arrangement, the metaphysical and intellectual mould, the precise expression used must be largely subject to the mutations of Time and cease to have the same force; for the human intellect modifies itself always; continually dividing and putting together it is obliged to shift its divisions continually and to rearrange its syntheses; it is always leaving old expression and symbol for new or, if it uses the old, it so changes its connotation or at least its exact content and association that we can never be quite sure of understanding an ancient book of this kind precisely in the sense and spirit it bore to its contemporaries. What is of entirely permanent value is that which besides being universal has been experienced, lived and seen with a higher than the intellectual vision.

I hold it therefore of small importance to extract from the Gita its exact metaphysical connotation as it was understood by the men of the time, even if that were accurately possible. That it is not possible, is shown by the divergence of the original commentaries which have been and are still being written upon it; for they all agree in each disagreeing with all the others, each finds in the Gita its own system of metaphysics and trend of religious thought. Nor will even the most painstaking and disinterested scholarship and the most luminous theories of the historical development of Indian philosophy save us from inevitable error. But what we can do with profit is to seek in the Gita for the actual living truths it contains, apart from their metaphysical form, to extract from it what can help us or the world at large and to put it in the most natural and vital form and expression we can find that will be suitable to the mentality and helpful to the spiritual needs of our present-day humanity. No doubt in this attempt we may mix a good deal of error born of our own individuality and of the ideas in which we live, as did greater men before us, but if we steep ourselves in the spirit of this great Scripture and, above all, if we have tried to live in that spirit, we may be sure of finding in it as much real truth as we are capable of receiving as well as the spiritual influence and actual help that, personally, we were intended to derive from it. And that is after all what Scriptures were written to give; the rest is academical disputation or theological dogma.

Only those Scriptures, religions, philosophies which can be thus constantly renewed, relived, their stuff of permanent truth constantly reshaped and developed in the inner thought and spiritual experience of a developing humanity, continue to be of living importance to mankind. The rest remain as monuments of the past but have no actual force or vital impulse for the future.

In the Gita, there is very little that is merely local or temporal, and its spirit is so large, profound and universal that even this little can easily be universalised without the sense of the teaching suffering any diminution or violation; rather, by giving an ampler scope to it than belonged to the country and epoch, the teaching gains in depth, truth and power. Often indeed, the Gita itself suggests the wider scope that can in this way be given to an idea in itself local or limited. Thus, it dwells on the ancient Indian system and idea of sacrifice as an interchange between gods and men—a system and idea which have long been practically obsolete in India itself and are no longer real to the general human mind; but we find here a sense so entirely subtle, figurative and symbolic given to the word 'sacrifice,' and the conception of the gods is so little local or mythological, so entirely cosmic and philosophical that we can easily accept both as expressive of a practical fact of psychology and general law of Nature and so apply them to the modern conceptions of interchange between life and life and of ethical sacrifice and self-giving as to widen and deepen these and cast over them a more spiritual aspect and the light of a profounder and more far-reaching Truth. Equally, the idea of action according to the Shastra, the fourfold order of society, the allusion to the relative position of the four orders or the comparative spiritual disabilities of Shudras and women seem at first sight local and temporal, and, if they are too much pressed in their literal sense, narrow so much at least of the teaching, deprive it of its universality and spiritual depth and limit its validity for mankind at large. But if we look behind to the spirit and sense and not at the local name and temporal institution, we see that here too the sense is deep and true and the spirit philosophical, spiritual and universal. By Shastra we perceive that the Gita means the law imposed on itself by humanity as a substitute for the purely egoistic action of the natural unregenerate man and a control on his tendency to seek in the satisfaction of his desire the standard and aim of his life. We see too that the fourfold order of society is merely the concrete form of a spiritual truth which is itself independent of the form; it rests on the conception of right works as a rightly ordered expression of the nature of the individual being through whom the work is done, that nature assigning him his line and scope in life according to his inborn quality and his self-expressive function. Since this is the spirit in which the Gita advances its most local and particular instances, we are justified in pursuing always the same principle and looking always for the deeper general truth, which is sure to underlie whatever seems at first sight merely local and of the time. For we shall find always that the deeper truth and principle is implied in the grain of the thought even when it is not expressly stated in its language.

Nor shall we deal in any other spirit with the element of philosophical dogma or religious creed which either enters into the Gita or hangs about it owing to its use of the philosophical terms and religious symbols current at the time. When the Gita speaks of Sankhya and Yoga, we shall not discuss beyond the limits of what is just essential for our statement, the relations of the Sankhya of the Gita with its one Purusha and strong Vedantic colouring to the non-theistic or 'atheistic' Sankhya that has come down to us bringing with it its scheme of many Purushas and one Prakriti, nor of the Yoga of the Gita, many-sided, subtle, rich and flexible to the theistic doctrine and the fixed, scientific, rigorously defined and graded system of the Yoga of Patanjali. In the Gita, the Sankhya and Yoga are evidently only two convergent parts of the same Vedantic truth or rather two concurrent ways of approaching its realisation, the one philosophical, intellectual, analytic the other intuitional, devotional, practical, ethical, synthetic, reaching knowledge through experience. The Gita recognises no real difference in their teachings. Still less need we discuss the theories which regard the Gita as the fruit of some particular religious system or tradition. Its teaching is universal, whatever may have been its origins.

The philosophical system of the Gita, its arrangement of truth, is not that part of its teaching which is the most vital, profound, eternally durable; but most of the material of which the system is composed, the principal ideas suggestive and penetrating which are woven into its complex harmony, are eternally valuable and valid; for they are not merely the luminous ideas or striking speculations of a philosophic intellect, but rather enduring truths of spiritual experience, verifiable facts of our highest psychological possibilities which no attempt to read deeply the mystery of existence can afford to neglect. Whatever the system may be, it is not, as the commentators strive to make it, framed or intended to support any exclusive school of philosophical thought or to put forward predominantly the claims of any one form of Yoga. The language of the Gita, the structure of thought, the combination and balancing of ideas belong neither to the temper of a sectarian teacher nor to the spirit of a rigorous analytical dialectics cutting off one angle of the truth to exclude all the others; but rather, there is a wide, undulating, encircling movement of ideas which is the manifestation of a vast synthetic mind and a rich synthetic experience. This is one of those great syntheses in which Indian spirituality has been as rich as in its creation of the more intensive, exclusive movements of knowledge and religious realisation that follow out with an absolute concentration one clue, one path to its extreme issues. It does not cleave asunder but reconciles and unifies.

The thought of the Gita is not pure Monism although it sees in one unchanging, pure, eternal Self the foundation of all cosmic existence, nor Mayavada although it speaks of the Maya of the three modes of Prakriti omnipresent in the created world; nor is it qualified Monism although it places in the One his eternal supreme Prakriti manifested in the form of the Jiva and lays most stress on dwelling in God rather than dissolution as the supreme state of spiritual consciousness; nor is it Sankhya although it explains the created world by the double principle of Purusha and Prakriti; nor is it Vaishnava Theism although it presents to us Krishna, who is the Avatara of Vishnu according to the Puranas, as the supreme Deity and allows no essential difference nor any actual superiority of the status of the indefinable relationless Brahman over that of this Lord of beings who is the Master of the universe and the Friend of all creatures. Like the earlier spiritual synthesis of the Upanishads, this later synthesis, at once spiritual and intellectual, avoids naturally every such rigid determination as would injure its universal comprehensiveness. Its aim is precisely the opposite to that of the polemist commentators who found this Scripture established as one of the three highest Vedantic authorities and attempted to turn it into a weapon of offence and defence against other schools and systems. The Gita is not a weapon for dialectical warfare; it is a gate opening on the whole world of spiritual truth and experience and the view it gives us embraces all the provinces of that supreme region. It maps out, but it does not cut up or build walls or hedges to confine our vision.

Our object, then, in studying the Gita will not be a scholastic or academical scrutiny of its thought, nor to place its philosophy in the history of metaphysical speculation, nor shall we deal with it in the manner of the analytical dialectician. We approach it for help and light and our aim must be to distinguish its essential and living message, that in it on which humanity has to seize for its perfection and its highest spiritual welfare.

The Divine Teacher

The peculiarity of the Gita among the great religious books of the world is that it does not stand apart as a work by itself, the fruit of the spiritual life of a creative personality like Christ, Mahomed or Buddha or of an epoch of pure spiritual searching like the Veda and Upanishads, but is given as an episode in an epic history of nations and their wars and men and their deeds and arises out of a critical moment in the soul of one of its leading personages face to face with the crowning action of his life, a work terrible, violent and sanguinary, at the point when he must either recoil from it altogether or carry it through to its inexorable completion. It matters little whether or no, as modern criticism supposes, the Gita is a later composition inserted into the mass of the Mahabharata by its author in order to invest its teaching with the authority and popularity of the great national epic. There seem to me to be strong grounds against this supposition for which, besides, the evidence, extrinsic or internal, is in the last degree scanty and insufficient. But even if it be sound, there remains the fact that the author has not only taken pains to interweave his work inextricably into the vast web of the larger poem, but is careful again and again to remind us of the situation from which the teaching has arisen; he returns to it prominently, not only at the end, but in the middle of his profoundest philosophical disquisitions. We must accept the insistence of the author and give its full importance to this recurrent preoccupation of the Teacher and the disciple. The teaching of the Gita must therefore be regarded not merely in the light of a general spiritual philosophy or ethical doctrine, but as bearing upon a practical crisis in the application of ethics and spirituality to human life. For what that crisis stands, what is the significance of the battle of Kurukshetra and its effect on Arjuna's inner being, we have first to determine if we would grasp the central drift of the ideas of the Gita.

There are indeed three things in the Gita which are spiritually significant, almost symbolic, typical of the profoundest relations and problems of the spiritual life and of human existence at its roots; they are the divine personality of the Teacher, his characteristic relations with his disciple and the occasion of his teaching.

India has from ancient times held strongly a belief in the reality of the Avatara, the descent into form, the revelation of the Godhead in humanity. In the West, this belief has never really stamped itself upon the mind because it has been presented through exoteric Christianity as a theological dogma without any roots in the reason and general consciousness and attitude towards life. But in

India, it has grown up and persisted as a logical outcome of the Vedantic view of life and taken firm root in the consciousness of the race. All existence is a manifestation of God because He is the only existence and nothing can be except as either a real figuring or else a figment of that one reality. Therefore, every conscious being is in part or in some way a descent of the Infinite into the apparent finiteness of name and form. But it is a veiled manifestation and there is a gradation between the supreme being[1] of the Divine and the consciousness shrouded partly or wholly by ignorance of self in the finite. The conscious embodied soul[2] is the spark of the divine Fire and that soul in man opens out to self-knowledge as it develops out of ignorance of self into self-being. The Divine also, pouring itself into the forms of the cosmic existence, is revealed ordinarily in an efflorescence of its powers, in energies and magnitudes of its knowledge, love, joy, developed force of being,[3] and in degrees and faces of its divinity. But when the divine Consciousness and Power, taking upon itself the human form and the human mode of action, possesses it not only by powers and magnitudes, by degrees and outward faces of itself but out of its eternal self-knowledge, when the Unborn knows itself and acts in the frame of the mental being and the appearance of birth, that is the height of the conditioned manifestation; it is the full and conscious descent of the Godhead, it is the Avatara. The Vaishnava form of Vedantism, which has laid most stress upon

[1] *para bhāva*

[2] *dehī*

[3] *vibhūti*

this conception, expresses the relation of God in man to man in God by the double figure of Nara-Narayana, associated historically with the origin of a religious school very similar in its doctrines to the teaching of the Gita. Nara is the human soul which, eternal companion of the Divine, finds itself only when it awakens to that companionship and begins, as the Gita would say, to live in God. Narayana is the divine Soul always present in our humanity, the secret guide, friend and helper of the human being, the 'Lord who abides within the heart of creatures' of the Gita; when within us the veil of that secret sanctuary is withdrawn and man speaks face to face with God, hears the divine voice, receives the divine light, acts in the divine power, then becomes possible the supreme uplifting of the embodied human conscious-being into the unborn and eternal. He becomes capable of that dwelling in God and giving up of his whole consciousness into the Divine which the Gita upholds as the best or highest secret of things, *uttamaṁ rahasyam*. When this eternal divine Consciousness always present in every human being, this God in man, takes possession partly[4] or wholly of the human consciousness and becomes in visible human shape the guide, teacher, leader of the world, not as those who living in their humanity yet feel something of the power or light or love of the divine Gnosis informing and conducting them, but out of that divine Gnosis itself, direct from its central force and plenitude, then we have the manifest Avatar. The inner Divinity is the

[4] Chaitanya, the Avatar of Nadiya, is said to have been thus partly or occasionally occupied by the divine Consciousness and Power.

eternal Avatar in man; the human manifestation is its sign and development in the external world.

When we thus understand the conception of Avatarhood, we see that whether for the fundamental teaching of the Gita, our present subject, or for spiritual life generally, the external aspect has only a secondary importance. Such controversies as the one that has raged in Europe over the historicity of Christ, would seem to a spiritually minded Indian largely a waste of time; he would concede to it a considerable historical, but hardly any religious importance; for what does it matter in the end whether a Jesus son of the carpenter Joseph was actually born in Nazareth or Bethlehem, lived and taught and was done to death on a real or trumped-up charge of sedition, so long as we can know by spiritual experience the inner Christ, live uplifted in the light of his teaching and escape from the yoke of the natural Law by that atonement of man with God of which the crucifixion is the symbol? If the Christ, God made man, lives within our spiritual being, it would seem to matter little whether or not a son of Mary physically lived and suffered and died in Judea. So too the Krishna who matters to us is the eternal incarnation of the Divine and not the historical teacher and leader of men.

In seeking the kernel of the thought of the Gita we need, therefore, only concern ourselves with the spiritual significance of the human-divine Krishna of the Mahabharata who is presented to us as the teacher of Arjuna on the battlefield of Kurukshetra. The historical Krishna, no doubt, existed. We meet the name first in the

Chhandogya Upanishad where all we can gather about him is that he was well known in spiritual tradition as a knower of the Brahman, so well-known indeed in his personality and the circumstances of his life that it was sufficient to refer to him by the name of his mother as Krishna son of Devaki for all to understand who was meant. In the same Upanishad we find mention of King Dhritarashtra son of Vichitravirya, and since tradition associated the two together so closely that they are both of them leading personages in the action of the Mahabharata, we may fairly conclude that they were actually contemporaries and that the epic is to a great extent dealing with historical characters and in the war of Kurukshetra with a historical occurrence imprinted firmly on the memory of the race. We know too that Krishna and Arjuna were the object of religious worship in the pre-Christian centuries; and there is some reason to suppose that they were so in connection with a religious and philosophical tradition from which the Gita may have gathered many of its elements and even the foundation of its synthesis of knowledge, devotion and works, and perhaps also that the human Krishna was the founder, restorer or at the least one of the early teachers of this school. The Gita may well in spite of its later form represent the outcome in Indian thought of the teaching of Krishna and the connection of that teaching with the historical Krishna, with Arjuna and with the war of Kurukshetra may be something more than a dramatic fiction. In the Mahabharata, Krishna is represented both as the historical character and the Avatar; his worship and Avatarhood must therefore have been well established by the time – apparently from the fifth to the first centuries B.C. – when the old story and poem or epic tradition of the Bharatas took its present form. There is a hint also in the poem of the story or legend of the Avatar's early life in Vrindavan which, as developed by the Puranas into an intense and powerful spiritual symbol, has exercised so profound an influence on the religious mind of India. We have also in the Harivansha an account of the life of Krishna, very evidently full of legends, which perhaps formed the basis of the Puranic accounts.

But all this, though of considerable historical importance, has none whatever for our present purpose. We are concerned only with the figure of the divine Teacher as it is presented to us in the Gita and with the Power for which it there stands in the spiritual illumination of the human being. The Gita accepts the human Avatarhood; for the Lord speaks of the repeated, the constant[5] manifestation of the Divine in humanity, when He the eternal Unborn assumes by his Maya, by the power of the infinite Consciousness to clothe itself apparently in finite forms, the conditions of becoming which we call birth. But it is not this upon which stress is laid, but on the transcendent, the cosmic and the internal Divine; it is on the Source of all things and the Master of all and on the Godhead secret in man. It is this internal divinity who is meant when the Gita speaks of the doer of violent Asuric austerities troubling the God within or of the sin of those who despise the Divine lodged in the human

[5] *bahūni me vyatītāni janmāni . . . sambhavāmi yuge yuge*

body or of the same Godhead destroying our ignorance by the blazing lamp of knowledge. It is then the eternal Avatar, this God in man, the divine Consciousness always present in the human being who manifested in a visible form speaks to the human soul in the Gita, illumines the meaning of life and the secret of divine action and gives it the light of the divine knowledge and guidance and the assuring and fortifying word of the Master of existence in the hour when it comes face to face with the painful mystery of the world.

Secondly, there is the typical, almost the symbolic significance of the human Krishna who stands behind the great action of the Mahabharata, not as its hero, but as its secret centre and hidden guide. That action is the action of a whole world of men and nations, some of whom have come as helpers of an effort and result by which they do not personally profit, and to these he is a leader, some as its opponents and to them he also is an opponent, the baffler of their designs and their slayer and he seems even to some of them an instigator of all evil and destroyer of their old order and familiar world and secure conventions of virtue and good; some are representatives of that which has to be fulfilled and to them he is counsellor, helper, friend. Where the action pursues its natural course or the doers of the work have to suffer at the hands of its enemies and undergo the ordeals which prepare them for mastery, the Avatar is unseen or appears only for occasional comfort and aid, but at every crisis his hand is felt, yet in such a way that all imagine themselves to be the protagonists and even Arjuna, his nearest friend and chief instrument, does not perceive that he is an instrument and has to confess at last that all the while he did not really know his divine Friend. He has received counsel from his wisdom, help from his power, has loved and been loved, has even adored without understanding his divine nature; but he has been guided like all others through his own egoism and the counsel, help and direction have been given in the language and received by the thoughts of the Ignorance. Until the moment when all has been pushed to the terrible issue of the struggle on the field of Kurukshetra and the Avatar stands at last, still not as fighter, but as the charioteer in the battle-car which carries the destiny of the fight, he has not revealed Himself even to those whom he has chosen.

Thus, the figure of Krishna becomes, as it were, the symbol of the divine dealings with humanity. Through our egoism and ignorance we are moved, thinking that we are the doers of the work, vaunting of ourselves as the real causes of the result, and that which moves us we see only occasionally as some vague or even some human and earthly fountain of knowledge, aspiration, force, some Principle or Light or Power which we acknowledge and adore without knowing what it is until the occasion arises that forces us to stand arrested before the Veil.

And the action in which this divine figure moves is the whole wide action of man in life, not merely the inner life, but all this obscure course of the world which we can judge only by the twilight of the human reason as it opens up dimly before our uncertain advance the little span in front. This is the distinguishing feature of the Gita that it is the culmination of such an action which gives rise to its teaching and assigns that prominence and bold relief to the gospel of works which it enunciates with an emphasis and force we do not find in other Indian Scriptures. Not only in the Gita, but in other passages of the Mahabharata we meet with Krishna declaring emphatically the necessity of action, but it is here that he reveals its secret and the divinity behind our works.

The symbolic companionship of Arjuna and Krishna, the human and the divine soul, is expressed elsewhere in Indian thought, in the heavenward journey of Indra and Kutsa seated in one chariot, in the figure of the two birds upon one tree in the Upanishad, in the twin figures of Nara and Narayana, the seers who do *tapasyā* together for the knowledge. But in all three, it is the idea of the divine knowledge in which, as the Gita says, all action culminates that is in view; here it is instead the action which leads to that knowledge and in which the divine Knower figures himself. Arjuna and Krishna, this human and this divine, stand together not as seers in the peaceful hermitage of meditation, but as fighter and holder of the reins in the clamorous field, in the midst of the hurtling shafts, in the chariot of battle. The Teacher of the Gita is therefore not only the God in man who unveils himself in the word of knowledge, but the God in man who moves our whole world of action, by and for whom all our humanity exists and struggles and labours, towards whom all human life travels and progresses. He is the secret Master of works and sacrifice and the Friend of the human peoples.

The Core of the Teaching

We know the divine Teacher, we see the human disciple; it remains to form a clear conception of the doctrine. A clear conception fastening upon the essential idea, the central heart of the teaching is especially necessary here because the Gita with its rich and many-sided thought, its synthetical grasp of different aspects of the spiritual life and the fluent winding motion of its argument lends itself, even more than other scriptures, to one-sided misrepresentations born of a partisan intellectuality. The unconscious or half-conscious wresting of fact and word and idea to suit a preconceived notion or the doctrine or principle of one's preference is recognised by Indian logicians as one of the most fruitful sources of fallacy; and it is perhaps the one which it is most difficult for even the most conscientious thinker to avoid. For the human reason is incapable of always playing the detective upon itself in this respect; it is its very nature to seize upon some partial conclusion, idea, principle, become its partisan and make it the key to all truth, and it has an infinite faculty of doubling upon itself so as to avoid detecting in its operations this necessary and cherished weakness. The Gita lends itself easily to this kind of error, because it is easy, by throwing particular emphasis on one of its aspects or even on some salient and emphatic text and putting all the rest of the eighteen chapters into the background or making them a subordinate and auxiliary teaching, to turn it into a partisan of our own doctrine or dogma.

Thus, there are those who make the Gita teach, not works at all, but a discipline of preparation for renouncing life and works: the indifferent performance of prescribed actions or of whatever task may lie ready to the hands, becomes the means, the discipline; the final renunciation of life and works is the sole real object. It is quite easy to justify this view by citations from the book and by a certain arrangement of stress in following out its argument, especially if we shut our eyes to the peculiar way in which it uses such a word as *sannyāsa*, renunciation; but it is quite impossible to persist in this view on an impartial reading in face of the continual assertion to the very end that action should be preferred to inaction and that superiority lies with the true, the inner renunciation of desire by equality and the giving up of works to the supreme Purusha.

Others again speak of the Gita as if the doctrine of devotion were its whole teaching and put in the background its monistic elements and the high place it gives to quietistic immergence in the one self of all. And undoubtedly its emphasis on devotion, its insistence on the aspect of the Divine as Lord and Purusha and its doctrine of the Purushottama, the Supreme Being who is superior both to the mutable Being and to the Immutable and who is what in His relation to the world we know as God, are the most striking and among the most vital elements of the Gita. Still, this Lord is the Self in whom all knowledge culminates and the Master of sacrifice to whom all works lead as well as the Lord of Love into whose being the heart of devotion enters, and the Gita preserves a perfectly equal balance, emphasising now knowledge, now works, now devotion, but for the purposes of the immediate trend of the thought, not with any absolute separate preference of one over the others. He in whom all three meet and become one, He is the Supreme Being, the Purushottama.

But at the present day, since in fact the modern mind began to recognise and deal at all with the Gita, the tendency is to subordinate its elements of knowledge and devotion, to take advantage of its continual insistence on action and to find in it a scripture of the Karmayoga, a Light leading us on the path of action, a Gospel of Works. Undoubtedly, the Gita is a Gospel of Works, but of works which culminate in knowledge, that is, in spiritual realisation and quietude, and of works motived by devotion, that is, a conscious surrender of one's whole self first into the hands and then into the being of the Supreme, and not at all of works as they are understood by the modern mind, not at all an action dictated by egoistic and altruistic, by personal, social, humanitarian motives, principles, ideals. Yet this is what present-day interpretations seek to make of the Gita. We are told continually by many authoritative voices that the Gita, opposing in this the ordinary ascetic and quietistic tendency of Indian thought and spirituality, proclaims with no uncertain sound the gospel of human action, the ideal of disinterested performance of social duties, nay, even, it would seem, the quite modern ideal of social service. To all this I can only reply that very patently and even on the very surface of it the Gita does nothing of the kind and that this is a modern misreading, a reading of the modern mind into an ancient book, of the present-day European or Europeanised intellect into a thoroughly antique, a thoroughly Oriental and Indian teaching. That which the Gita teaches is not a human, but a divine action; not the performance of social duties, but the abandonment of all other standards of duty or conduct for a selfless performance of the divine will working through our nature; not social service, but the action of the Best, the God-possessed, the Master-men done impersonally for the sake of the world and as a sacrifice to Him who stands behind man and Nature.

In other words, the Gita is not a book of practical ethics, but of the spiritual life.

We must remember that duty is an idea which in practice rests upon social conceptions. We may extend the term beyond its proper connotation and talk of our duty to ourselves or we may, if we like, say in a transcendent sense that it was Buddha's duty to abandon all, or even that it is the ascetic's duty to sit motionless in a cave! But this is obviously to play with words. Duty is a relative term and depends upon our relation to others. It is a father's duty, as a father, to nurture and educate his children; a lawyer's to do his best for his client even if he knows him to be guilty and his defence to be a lie; a soldier's to fight and shoot to order even if he kill his own kin and countrymen; a judge's to send the guilty to prison and hang the murderer. And so long as these positions are accepted, the duty remains clear, a practical matter of course even when it is not a point of honour or affection and overrides the absolute religious or moral law. But what if the inner view is changed, if the lawyer is the lawyer is awakened to the absolute sinfulness of falsehood, the judge becomes convinced that capital punishment is a crime against humanity, the man called upon to the battlefield feels, like the conscientious objector of today or as a Tolstoy would feel, that in no circumstances is it permissible to take human life any more than to eat human flesh? It is obvious that here the moral law which is above all relative duties must prevail; and that law depends on no social relation or conception of duty but on the awakened inner perception of man, the moral being.

What the great, the supreme word of the Gita is, its *mahāvākya*, we have not to seek; for the Gita itself declares it in its last utterance, the crowning note of the great diapason. 'With the Lord in thy heart take refuge with all thy being; by His grace thou shalt attain to the supreme peace and the eternal status. So have I expounded to thee a knowledge more secret than that which is hidden. Further hear the most secret, the supreme word that I shall speak to thee. Become my-minded, devoted to Me, to Me do sacrifice and adoration; infallibly, thou shalt come to Me, for dear to me art thou. Abandoning all laws of conduct seek refuge in Me alone. I will release thee from all sin; do not grieve.'

Sankhya, Yoga and Vedanta

The whole object of the first six chapters of the Gita is to synthetise in a large frame of Vedantic truth the two methods, ordinarily supposed to be diverse and even opposite, of the Sankhyas and the Yogins. The Sankhya is taken as the starting-point and the basis; but it is from the beginning and with a progressively increasing emphasis permeated with the ideas and methods of Yoga and remoulded in its spirit. The practical difference, as it seems to have presented itself to the religious minds of that day, lay first in this that Sankhya proceeded by knowledge and through the Yoga of the intelligence, while Yoga proceeded by works and the transformation of the active consciousness and, secondly – a corollary of this first distinction – that Sankhya led to entire passivity and the renunciation of works, *sannyāsa*, while Yoga held to be quite sufficient the inner renunciation of desire, the purification of the subjective principle which leads to action and the turning of works Godwards, towards the divine existence and towards liberation. Yet both had the same aim, the transcendence of birth and of this terrestrial existence and the union of the human soul with the Highest. This at least is the difference as it is presented to us by the Gita.

The difficulty which Arjuna feels in understanding any possible synthesis of these oppositions is an indication of the hard line that was driven in between these two systems in the normal ideas of the time. The Teacher sets out by reconciling works and the Yoga of the intelligence: the latter, he says, is far superior to mere works; it is by the Yoga of the Buddhi, by knowledge raising man out of the ordinary human mind and its desires into the purity and equality of the Brahmic condition free from all desire that works can be made acceptable. Yet are works a means of salvation but works thus purified by knowledge.

Filled with the notions of the then prevailing culture, misled by the emphasis which the Teacher lays upon the ideas proper to Vedantic Sankhya, conquest of the senses, withdrawal from mind into the Self, ascent into the Brahmic condition, extinction of our lower personality in the Nirvana of impersonality – for the ideas proper to Yoga are as yet subordinated and largely held back – Arjuna is perplexed and asks, 'If thou holdest the intelligence to be greater than works, why then dost thou appoint me to a terrible work? Thou seemest to bewilder my intelligence with a confused and mingled speech; tell me then decisively that one thing by which I may attain to my soul's weal.'

In answer, Krishna affirms that the Sankhya goes by knowledge and renunciation, the Yoga by works; but the real renunciation is impossible without Yoga, without works done as a sacrifice, done with equality and without desire of the fruit, with the perception that it is Nature which does the actions and not the soul; but immediately afterwards he declares that the sacrifice of knowledge is the highest, all work finds its consummation in knowledge, by the fire of knowledge all works are burnt up; therefore, by Yoga, works are renounced and their bondage overcome for the man who is in possession of his Self. Again, Arjuna is perplexed; here are desireless works, the principle of Yoga, and renunciation of works, the principle of Sankhya, put together side by side as if part of one method, yet there is no evident reconciliation between them. For the kind of reconciliation which the Teacher has already given – in outward inaction to see action still persisting and in apparent action to see a real inaction since the soul has renounced its illusion of the worker and given up works into the hands of the Master of sacrifice – is for the practical mind of Arjuna too slight, too subtle and expressed almost in riddling words; he has not caught their sense or at least not penetrated into their spirit and reality. Therefore, he asks again, 'Thou declarest to me the renunciation of works, O Krishna, and again thou declarest to me Yoga; which one of these is the better way, that tell me with a clear decisiveness.'

The answer is important, for it puts the whole distinction very clearly and indicates though it does not develop entirely the line of reconciliation. 'Renunciation and Yoga of works both bring about the soul's salvation, but of the two the Yoga of works is distinguished above the renunciation of works. He should be known as always a Sannyasin (even when he is doing action) who neither dislikes nor desires; for free from the dualities he is released easily and happily from the bondage. Children speak of Sankhya and Yoga apart from each other, not the wise; if a man applies himself integrally to one, he gets the fruit of both,' because in their integrality each contains the other. 'The status which is attained by the Sankhya, to that the men of the Yoga also arrive; who sees Sankhya and Yoga as one, he sees. But renunciation is difficult to attain without Yoga; the sage who has Yoga attains soon to the Brahman; his self becomes the self of all existences (of all things that have become), and even though he does works, he is not involved in them.' He knows that the actions are not his, but Nature's and by that very knowledge he is free; he has renounced works, does no actions, though actions are done through him; he becomes the Self, the Brahman, *brahmabhūta*, he sees all existences as becomings (*bhūtāni*) of that self-existent Being, his own only one of them, all their actions as only the development of cosmic Nature working through their individual nature and his own actions also as a part of the same cosmic activity. This is not the whole teaching of the Gita; for as yet there is only the idea of the immutable self or Purusha, the Akshara Brahman, and of Nature, Prakriti, as that which is responsible for the cosmos and not yet the idea, clearly expressed, of the Ishwara, the Purushottama; as yet only the synthesis of works and knowledge and not yet, in spite of certain hints, the introduction of the supreme element of devotion which becomes so important afterwards; as yet only the one inactive Purusha and the lower Prakriti and not yet the distinction of the triple Purusha and the double Prakriti. It is true the Ishwara is spoken of, but his relation to the self and nature is not yet made definite. The first six chapters only carry the synthesis so far as it can be carried without the clear expression and decisive entrance of these all-important truths which, when they come in, must necessarily enlarge and modify, though without abolishing, these first reconciliations.

Twofold, says Krishna, is the self-application of the soul by which it enters into the Brahmic condition: 'that of the Sankhyas by the Yoga of knowledge, that of the Yogins by the Yoga of works.' This identification of Sankhya with Jnanayoga and of Yoga with the way of works is interesting; for it shows that quite a different order of ideas prevailed at that time from those we now possess as the result of the great Vedantic development of Indian thought, subsequent evidently to the composition of the Gita, by which the other Vedic philosophies fell into desuetude as practical methods of liberation. To justify the language of the Gita we must suppose that at that time it was the Sankhya method which was very commonly[1] adopted by those who followed the path of knowledge. Subsequently, with the spread of Buddhism, the Sankhya method of knowledge must have

[1] The systems of the Puranas and Tantras are full of the ideas of the Sankhya, though subordinated to the Vedantic idea and mingled with many others.

been much overshadowed by the Buddhistic. Buddhism, like the Sankhya non-Theistic and anti-Monistic, laid stress on the impermanence of the results of the cosmic energy, which it presented not as Prakriti but as Karma because the Buddhists admitted neither the Vedantic Brahman nor the inactive Soul of the Sankhyas, and it made the recognition of this impermanence by the discriminating mind its means of liberation. When the reaction against Buddhism arrived, it took up not the old Sankhya notion, but the Vedantic form popularised by Shankara who replaced the Buddhistic impermanence by the cognate Vedantic idea of illusion, Maya, and the Buddhistic idea of Non-Being, indefinable Nirvana, a negative Absolute, by the opposite and yet cognate Vedantic idea of the indefinable Being, Brahman, an ineffably positive Absolute in which all feature and action and energy cease because in That they never really existed and are mere illusions of the mind. It is the method of Shankara based upon these concepts of his philosophy, it is the renunciation of life as an illusion of which we ordinarily think when we speak now of the Yoga of knowledge. But in the time of the Gita, Maya was evidently not yet quite the master word of the Vedantic philosophy, nor had it, at least with any decisive clearness, the connotation which Shankara brought out of it with such a luminous force and distinctness; for in the Gita there is little talk of Maya and much of Prakriti and, even, the former word is used as little more than an equivalent of the latter but only in its inferior status; it is the lower Prakriti of the three gunas, *traiguṇyamayīmāyā*. Prakriti, not illusive Maya, is in the teaching of the Gita the effective cause of cosmic existence.

Still, whatever the precise distinctions of their metaphysical ideas, the practical difference between the Sankhya and Yoga as developed by the Gita is the same as that which now exists between the Vedantic Yogas of knowledge and of works, and the practical results of the difference are also the same. The Sankhya proceeded like the Vedantic Yoga of knowledge by the Buddhi, by the discriminating intelligence; it arrived by reflective thought, *vicāra*, at right discrimination, *viveka*, of the true nature of the soul and of the imposition on it of the works of Prakriti through attachment and identification, just as the Vedantic method arrives by the same means at the right discrimination of the true nature of the Self and of the imposition on it of cosmic appearances by mental illusion which leads to egoistic identification and attachment. In the Vedantic method, Maya ceases for the soul by its return to its true and eternal status as the one Self, the Brahman, and the cosmic action disappears; in the Sankhya method the working of the *guṇas* falls to rest by the return of the soul to its true and eternal status as the inactive Purusha and the cosmic action ends. The Brahman of the Mayavadins is silent, immutable and inactive; so too is the Purusha of the Sankhya; therefore, for both ascetic renunciation of life and works is a necessary means of liberation. But for the Yoga of the Gita, as for the Vedantic Yoga of works, action is not only a preparation but itself the means of liberation; and it is the justice of this view which the Gita seeks to bring out with such an unceasing force and insistence – an insistence, unfortunately, which could not prevail in India against the tremendous tide of Buddhism,[2] was lost afterwards in the intensity of ascetic illusionism and the fervour of world-shunning saints and devotees and is only now beginning to exercise its real and salutary influence on the Indian mind. Renunciation is indispensable, but the true renunciation is the inner rejection of desire and egoism; without that the outer physical abandoning of works is a thing unreal and ineffective, with it, it ceases even to be necessary, although it is not forbidden. Knowledge is essential, there is no higher force for liberation, but works with knowledge are also needed; by the union of knowledge and works the soul dwells entirely in the Brahmic status not only in repose and inactive calm, but in the very midst and stress and violence of action. Devotion is all-important, but works with devotion are also important; by the union of knowledge, devotion and works, the soul is taken up into the highest status of the Ishwara to dwell there in the Purushottama, who is master at once of the eternal spiritual calm and the eternal cosmic activity. This is the synthesis of the Gita.

But, apart from the distinction between the Sankhya way of knowledge and the Yoga way of works, there was

[2] At the same time the Gita seems to have largely influenced Mahayanist Buddhism and texts are taken bodily from it into the Buddhist Scriptures. It may therefore have helped largely to turn Buddhism, originally a school of quietistic and illuminated ascetics, into that religion of meditative devotion and compassionate action which has so powerfully influenced Asiatic culture.

another and similar opposition in the Vedanta itself, and this also the Gita has to deal with, to correct and to fuse into its large restatement of the Aryan spiritual culture. This was the distinction between Karmakanda and Jnanakanda, between the original thought that led to the philosophy of the Purva Mimansa, the Vedavada, and that which led to the philosophy of the Uttara Mimansa,[3] the Brahmavada, between those who dwelt in the tradition of the Vedic hymns and the Vedic sacrifice and those who put these aside as a lower knowledge and laid stress on the lofty metaphysical knowledge which emerges from the Upanishads.

For the pragmatic mind of the Vedavadins the Aryan religion of the Rishis meant the strict performance of the Vedic sacrifices and the use of the sacred Vedic mantras in order to possess all human desires in this world, wealth, progeny, victory, every kind of good fortune and the joys of immortality in Paradise beyond. For the idealism of the Brahmavadins this was only a preliminary preparation and the real object of man, true *purusārtha*, began with his turning to the knowledge of the Brahman which would give him the true immortality of an ineffable spiritual bliss far beyond the lower joys of this world or of any inferior heaven. Whatever may have been the true and original sense of the Veda, this was the distinction which had long established itself and with which therefore the Gita has to deal.

[3] Jaimini's idea of liberation is the eternal Brahmaloka in which the soul that has come to know Brahman still possesses a divine body and divine enjoyments. For the Gita the Brahmaloka is not liberation; the soul must pass beyond to the supracosmic status.

Works and Sacrifice

The Yoga of the intelligent will and its culmination in the Brahmic status, which occupies all the close of the second chapter, contains the seed of much of the teaching of the Gita – its doctrine of desireless works, of equality, of the rejection of outward renunciation, of devotion to the Divine; but as yet all this is slight and obscure. What is most strongly emphasised as yet is the withdrawal of the will from the ordinary motive of human activities, desire, from man's normal temperament of the sense-seeking thought and will with its passions and ignorance, and from its customary habit of troubled many-branching ideas and wishes to the desireless calm unity and passionless serenity of the Brahmic poise. The intelligence withdrawing from sense and desire and human action and turning to the Highest, to the One, to the actionless Purusha, to the immobile, to the featureless Brahman, that surely is the eternal seed of knowledge. That is the orthodox philosophical doctrine, and Krishna seems quite to admit it when he says that works are far inferior to the Yoga of the intelligence. Here then is an unreconciled contradiction. Arjuna complains that he has been given a contradictory and confusing doctrine, not the clear, strenuously single road by which the human intelligence can move straight and trenchantly to the supreme good. It is in answer to this objection that the Gita begins at once to develop more clearly its positive and imperative doctrine of Works.

The Teacher first makes a distinction between the two means of salvation on which in this world men can concentrate separately, the Yoga of knowledge, the Yoga of works, the one implying, it is usually supposed, renunciation of works as an obstacle to salvation, the other accepting works as a means of salvation. He does not yet insist strongly on any fusion of them, on any reconciliation of the thought that divides them, but begins by showing that the renunciation of the Sankhyas, the physical renunciation, Sannyasa, is neither the only way, nor at all the better way. *Naiṣkarmya*, a calm voidness from works, is no doubt that to which the soul, the Purusha has to attain; for it is Prakriti which does the work and the soul has to rise above involution in the activities of the being and attain to a free serenity and poise watching over the operations of Prakriti, but not affected by them. That, and not cessation of the works of Prakriti, is what is really meant by the soul's *naiṣkarmya*. 'Not by abstention from works does a man enjoy actionlessness, nor by mere renunciation (of works) does he attain to his perfection,' – to *siddhi*, the accomplishment of the aims of his self-discipline by Yoga.

But at least it must be one necessary means, indispensable, imperative? For how, if the works of Prakriti continue, can the soul help being involved in them? How can I fight and yet in my soul not think or feel that I the individual am fighting, not desire victory nor be inwardly touched by defeat? This is the teaching of the Sankhyas that the intelligence of the man who engages in the activities of Nature, is entangled in egoism, ignorance and desire and therefore drawn to action; on the contrary, if the intelligence draws back, then the action must cease with the cessation of the desire and the ignorance. Therefore, the giving up of life and works is a necessary part, an inevitable circumstance and an indispensable last means of the movement to liberation. This objection of a current logic – it is not expressed by Arjuna, but it is in his mind as the turn of his subsequent utterances shows – the Teacher immediately anticipates. No, he says, such renunciation, far from being indispensable, is not even possible. 'For none stands even for a moment not doing work; everyone is made to do action helplessly by the modes born of Prakriti.' The strong perception of the great cosmic action and the eternal activity and power of the cosmic energy which was so much emphasised afterwards by the teaching of the Tantric Shaktas who even made Prakriti or Shakti superior to Purusha, is a very remarkable feature of the Gita. Although here an undertone, it is still strong enough, coupled with what we might call the theistic and devotional elements of its thought, to bring in that activism which so strongly modifies in its scheme of Yoga the quietistic tendencies of the old metaphysical Vedanta. Man embodied in the natural world cannot cease from action, not for a moment, not for a second; his very existence here is an action; the whole universe is an act of God, mere living even is His movement.

Our physical life, its maintenance, its continuance is a journey, a pilgrimage of the body, *śarīra-yātrā*, and that cannot be effected without action. But even if a man could leave his body unmaintained, otiose, if he could stand still always like a tree or sit inert like a stone, *tiṣṭhati*, that vegetable or material immobility would not save him from the hands of Nature; he would not be liberated from her workings. For it is not our physical movements and activities alone which are meant by works, by karma; our mental existence also is a great complex action, it is even the greater and more important part of the works of the unresting energy – subjective cause and determinant of the physical. We have gained nothing if we repress the effect but retain the activity of the subjective cause. The objects of sense are only an occasion for our bondage, the mind's insistence on them is the means, the instrumental cause. A man may control his organs of action and refuse to give them their natural play, but he has gained nothing if his mind continues to remember and dwell upon the objects of sense. What is vital is the mighty energy of Nature which will have her way and her play in her great field of mind and life and body; what is dangerous in her is the power of her three gunas, modes or qualities to confuse and bewilder the intelligence and so obscure the soul.

The real goal of the Yoga is then a living and self-completing union with the divine Purushottama and is not merely a self-extinguishing immergence in the impersonal Being. To raise our whole existence to the Divine Being, to dwell in him (*mayyeva nivasiṣyasi*), to be at one with him, unify our consciousness with his, to make our fragmentary nature a reflection of his perfect nature, to be inspired in our thought and sense wholly by the divine knowledge, to be moved in will and action utterly and faultlessly by the divine will, to lose desire in his love and delight, is man's perfection; it is that which the Gita describes as the highest secret. It is the true goal and the last sense of human living and the highest step in our progressive sacrifice of works. For he remains to the end the master of works and the soul of sacrifice.

The Divine Birth and Divine Works

The work for which the Avatar descends has like his birth a double sense and a double form. It has an outward side of the divine force acting upon the external world in order to maintain there and to reshape the divine law by which the Godward effort of humanity is kept from decisive retrogression and instead decisively carried forward in spite of the rule of action and reaction, the rhythm of advance and relapse by which Nature proceeds. It has an inward side of the divine force of the Godward consciousness acting upon the soul of the individual and the soul of the race, so that it may receive new forms of revelation of the Divine in man and may be sustained, renewed and enriched in its power of upward self-unfolding. The Avatar does not descend merely for a great outward action, as the pragmatic sense in humanity is too often tempted to suppose. Action and event have no value in themselves but only take their value from the force which they represent and the idea which they symbolise and which the force is there to serve.

The crisis in which the Avatar appears, though apparent to the outward eye only as a crisis of events and great material changes, is always in its source and real meaning a crisis in the consciousness of humanity when it has to undergo some grand modification and effect some new development. For this action of change a divine force is needed; but the force varies always according to the power of consciousness which it embodies; hence the necessity of a divine consciousness manifesting in the mind and soul of humanity. Where, indeed, the change is mainly intellectual and practical, the intervention of the Avatar is not needed; there is a great uplifting of consciousness, a great manifestation of power in which men are for the time being exalted above their normal selves, and this surge of consciousness and power finds its wave-crests in certain exceptional individuals, *vibhūtis*, whose action leading the general action is sufficient for the change intended. The Reformation in Europe and the French Revolution were crises of this character; they were not great spiritual events, but intellectual and practical changes, one in religious, the other in social and political ideas, forms and motives, and the modification of the general consciousness brought about was a mental and dynamic, but not a spiritual modification. But when the crisis has a spiritual seed or intention, then a complete or a partial manifestation of the God-consciousness in a human mind and soul comes as its originator or leader. That is the Avatar.

The outward action of the Avatar is described in the Gita as the restoration of the Dharma; when from age to age the Dharma fades, languishes, loses force and its opposite arises, strong and oppressive, then the Avatar comes and raises it again to power; and as these things in idea are always represented by things in action and by human beings who obey their impulsion, his mission is, in its most human and outward terms, to relieve the seekers of the Dharma who are oppressed by the reign of the reactionary darkness and to destroy the wrong-doers who seek to maintain the denial of the Dharma. But the language used can easily be given a poor and insufficient connotation which would deprive Avatarhood of all its spiritual depth of meaning. Dharma is a word which has an ethical and practical, a natural and philosophical and a religious and spiritual significance, and it may be used in any of these senses exclusive of the others, in a purely ethical, a purely philosophical or a purely religious sense. Ethically, it means the law of righteousness, the moral rule of conduct, or in a still more outward and practical significance social and political justice, or even simply the observation of the social law. If used in this sense we shall have to understand that when unrighteousness, injustice and oppression prevail, the Avatar descends to deliver the good and destroy the wicked, to break down injustice and oppression and restore the ethical balance of mankind.

Thus, the popular and mythical account of the Krishna avatar is that the unrighteousness of the Kurus as incarnated in Duryodhana and his brothers became so great a burden to the earth that she had to call upon God to descend and lighten her load; accordingly, Vishnu incarnated as Krishna, delivered the oppressed Pandavas and destroyed the unjust Kauravas. A similar account is given of the descent of the previous Vishnu avatars, of Rama to destroy the unrighteous oppression of Ravana, of Parashurama to destroy the unrighteous license of the military and princely caste, the Kshatriyas, of the dwarf Vamana to destroy the rule of the Titan Bali. But obviously the purely practical, ethical or social and political mission of the Avatar which is thus thrown into popular and mythical form, does not give a right account of the phenomenon of Avatarhood. It does not cover its spiritual sense, and if this outward utility were all, we should have to exclude Buddha and Christ whose mission was not at all to destroy evil-doers and deliver the good, but to bring to all men a new spiritual message and a new law of divine growth and spiritual realisation. On the other hand, if we give to the word dharma only its religious sense, in which it means a law of religious and spiritual life, we shall indeed get to the kernel of the matter, but we shall be in danger of excluding a most important part of the work done by the Avatar. Always we see in the history of the divine incarnations the double work, and inevitably, because the Avatar takes up the workings of God in human life, the way of the divine Will and Wisdom in the world, and that always fulfils itself externally as well as internally, by inner progress in the soul and by an outer change in the life.

The Avatar may descend as a great spiritual teacher and saviour, the Christ, the Buddha, but always his work leads, after he has finished his earthly manifestation, to a profound and powerful change not only in the ethical, but in the social and outward life and ideals of the race. He may, on the other hand, descend as an incarnation of the divine life, the divine personality and power in its characteristic action, for a mission ostensibly social, ethical and political, as is represented in the story of Rama or Krishna; but always then this descent becomes in the soul of the race a permanent power for the inner living and the spiritual rebirth. It is indeed curious to note that the permanent, vital, universal effect of Buddhism and Christianity has been the force of their ethical, social and practical ideals and their influence even on the men and the ages which have rejected their religious and spiritual beliefs, forms and disciplines; later Hinduism which rejected Buddha, his *saṅgha* and his *dharma*, bears the ineffaceable imprint of the social and ethical influence of Buddhism and its effect on the ideas and the life of the race, while in modern Europe, Christian only in name, humanitarianism is the translation into the ethical and social sphere and the aspiration to liberty, equality and fraternity the translation into the social and political sphere of the spiritual truths of Christianity, the latter especially being effected by men who aggressively rejected the Christian religion and spiritual discipline and by an age which in its intellectual effort of emancipation tried to get rid of Christianity as a creed. On the other hand the life of Rama and Krishna belongs to the prehistoric past which has come down only in poetry and legend and may even be regarded as myths;

but it is quite immaterial whether we regard them as myths or historical facts, because their permanent truth and value lie in their persistence as a spiritual form, presence, influence in the inner consciousness of the race and the life of the human soul. Avatarhood is a fact of divine life and consciousness which may realise itself in an outward action, but must persist, when that action is over and has done its work, in a spiritual influence; or may realise itself in a spiritual influence and teaching, but must then have its permanent effect, even when the new religion or discipline is exhausted, in the thought, temperament and outward life of mankind.

The Divine Worker

To attain to the divine birth – a divinising new birth of the soul into a higher consciousness – and to do divine works both as a means towards that before it is attained and as an expression of it after it is attained, is then all the Karmayoga of the Gita. The Gita does not try to define works by any outward signs through which it can be recognisable to an external gaze, measurable by the criticism of the world; it deliberately renounces even the ordinary ethical distinctions by which men seek to guide themselves in the light of the human reason. The signs by which it distinguishes divine works are all profoundly intimate and subjective; the stamp by which they are known is invisible, spiritual, supraethical.

They are recognisable only by the light of the soul from which they come. For, it says, 'what is action and what is inaction, as to this even the sages are perplexed and deluded,' because, judging by practical, social, ethical, intellectual standards, they discriminate by accidentals and do not go to the root of the matter; 'I will declare to thee that action by the knowledge of which thou shalt be released from all ills. One has to understand about action as well as to understand about wrong action and about inaction one has to understand; thick and tangled is the way of works.' Action in the world is like a deep forest, *gahana*, through which man goes stumbling as best he can, by the light of the ideas of his time, the standards of his personality, his environment, or rather of many times, many personalities, layers of thought and ethics from many social stages all inextricably confused together, temporal and conventional amidst all their claim to absoluteness and immutable truth, empirical and irrational in spite of their aping of right reason. And finally, the sage seeking in the midst of it all a highest foundation of fixed law and an original truth finds himself obliged to raise the last supreme question, whether all action and life itself are not a delusion and a snare and whether cessation from action, *akarma*, is not the last resort of the tired and disillusioned human soul. But, says Krishna, in this matter even the sages are perplexed and deluded. For by action, by works, not by inaction comes the knowledge and the release.

What then is the solution? what is that type of works by which we shall be released from the ills of life, from this doubt, this error, this grief, from this mixed, impure and baffling result even of our purest and best-intentioned acts, from these million forms of evil and suffering? No outward distinctions need be made, is the reply; no work the world needs, be shunned; no limit or hedge set round our human activities; on the contrary, all actions should be done, but from a soul in Yoga with the Divine, *yuktaḥ kṛtsna-karma-kṛt*. *Akarma*, cessation from action is not the way; the man who has attained to the insight of the highest reason, perceives that such inaction is itself a constant action, a state subject to the workings of Nature and her qualities. The mind that takes refuge in physical inactivity, is still under the delusion that it and not Nature is the doer of works; it has mistaken inertia for liberation; it does not see that even in what seems absolute inertia greater than that of the stone or clod, Nature is at work, keeps unimpaired her hold. On the contrary in the full flood of action the soul is free from its works, is not the doer, not bound by what is done, and he who lives in the freedom of the soul, not in the bondage of the modes of Nature, alone has release from works. This is what the Gita clearly means when it says that he who in action can see inaction and can see action still continuing in cessation from works, is the man of true reason and discernment among men. This saying hinges upon the Sankhya distinction between Purusha and Prakriti, between the free inactive soul, eternally calm, pure and unmoved in the midst of works, and ever active Nature operative as much in inertia and cessation as in the overt turmoil of her visible hurry of labour. This is the knowledge which the highest effort of the discriminating reason, the *buddhi*, gives to us, and therefore whoever possesses it is the truly rational and discerning man, *sabuddhimān manuṣyeṣu* – not the perplexed thinker who judges life and works by the external, uncertain and impermanent distinctions of the lower reason. Therefore, the liberated man is not afraid of action, he is a large and universal doer of all works, *kṛtsna-karma-kṛt*; not as others do them in subjection to Nature, but poised in the silent calm of the soul, tranquilly in Yoga with the Divine. The Divine is the lord of his works, he is only their channel through the instrumentality of his nature conscious of and subject to her Lord. By the flaming intensity and purity of this knowledge all his works are burned up as in a fire and his mind remains without any stain or disfiguring mark from them, calm, silent, unperturbed, white and clean and pure. To do all in this liberating knowledge, without the personal egoism of the doer, is the first sign of the divine worker.

The second sign is freedom from desire; for where there is not the personal egoism of the doer, desire becomes impossible; it is starved out, sinks for want of a support, dies of inanition. Outwardly the liberated man seems to undertake works of all kinds like other men, on a larger scale perhaps with a more powerful will and driving-force, for the might of the divine will works in his active nature; but from all his inceptions and undertakings the inferior concept and nether will of desire is entirely banished, *sarve samārambhāḥ kāmasaṅkalpavarjitāḥ*. He has abandoned all attachment to the fruits of his works, and where one does not work for the fruit, but solely as an impersonal instrument of the Master of works, desire can find no place – not even the desire to serve successfully, for the fruit is the Lord's and determined by him and not by the personal will and effort, or to serve with credit and to the

Master's satisfaction, for the real doer is the Lord himself and all glory belongs to a form of his Shakti missioned in the nature and not to the limited human personality. The human mind and soul of the liberated man does nothing, *na kiñcit karoti*; even though through his nature he engages in action, it is the Nature, the executive Shakti, it is the conscious Goddess governed by the divine Inhabitant who does the work.

It does not follow that the work is not to be done perfectly, with success, with a right adaptation of means to ends; on the contrary, a perfect working is easier to action done tranquilly in Yoga than to action done in the blindness of hopes and fears, lamed by the judgments of the stumbling reason, running about amidst the eager trepidations of the hasty human will; Yoga, says the Gita elsewhere, is the true skill in works, *yogaḥ karmasu kauśalam*. But all this is done impersonally by the action of a great universal light and power operating through the individual nature. The Karmayogin knows that the power given to him will be adapted to the fruit decreed, the divine thought behind the work equated with the work he has to do, the will in him – which will not be wish or desire, but an impersonal drive of conscious power directed towards an aim not his own – subtly regulated in its energy and direction by the divine wisdom. The result may be success, as the ordinary mind understands it, or it may seem to that mind to be defeat and failure; but to him it is always the success intended, not by him, but by the all-wise manipulator of action and result, because he does not seek for victory, but only for the fulfilment of the divine will and wisdom which works out its ends through apparent failure as well as and often with greater force than through apparent triumph. Arjuna, bidden to fight, is assured of victory; but even if certain defeat were before him, he must still fight because that is the present work assigned to him as his immediate share in the great sum of energies by which the divine will is surely accomplished.

Equality and Knowledge

Yoga and knowledge are, in this early part of the Gita's teaching, the two wings of the soul's ascent. By Yoga is meant union through divine works done without desire, with equality of soul to all things and all men, as a sacrifice to the Supreme, while knowledge is that on which this desirelessness, this equality, this power of sacrifice is founded. The two wings indeed assist each other's flight; acting together, yet with a subtle alternation of mutual aid, like the two eyes in a man which see together because they see alternately, they increase one another mutually by interchange of substance. As the works grow more and more desireless, equal-minded, sacrificial in spirit, the knowledge increases; with the increase of the knowledge the soul becomes firmer in the desireless, sacrificial equality of its works. The sacrifice of knowledge, says the Gita therefore, is greater than any material sacrifice. 'Even if thou art the greatest doer of sin beyond all sinners, thou shalt cross over all the crookedness of evil in the ship of knowledge. There is nothing in the world equal in purity to knowledge.' By knowledge, desire and its first-born child, sin, are destroyed. The liberated man is able to do works as a sacrifice because he is freed from attachment through his mind, heart and spirit being firmly founded in self-knowledge, *gata-saṅgasya jñānāvasthita-cetasaḥ*. All his work disappears completely as soon as done, suffers *laya*, as one might say, in the being of the Brahman, *pravilīyate*; it has no reactionary consequence on the soul of the apparent doer. The work is done by the Lord through his Nature, it is no longer personal to the human instrument. The work itself becomes but power of the nature and substance of the being of the Brahman.

It is in this sense that the Gita is speaking when it says that all the totality of work finds its completion, culmination, end in knowledge, *sarvaṁ karmākhilaṁ jñāne parisamāpyate*. 'As a fire kindled turns to ashes its fuel, so the fire of knowledge turns all works to ashes.' By this it is not at all meant that when knowledge is complete, there is cessation from works. What is meant is made clear by the Gita when it says that he who has destroyed all doubt by knowledge and has by Yoga given up all works and is in possession of the Self is not bound by his works, *yoga-sannyasta-karmāṇam ātmavantaṃ na karmāṇi nibadhnanti*, and that he whose self has become the self of all existences, acts and yet is not affected by his works, is not caught in them, receives from them no soul-ensnaring reaction, *kurvann api na lipyate*. Therefore, it says, the Yoga of works is better than the physical renunciation of works, because, while Sannyasa is difficult for embodied beings who must do works so long as they are in the body, Yoga of works is entirely sufficient and it rapidly and easily brings the soul to Brahman. That Yoga of works is, we have seen, the offering of all action to the Lord, which induces as its culmination an inner and not an outer, a spiritual, not a physical giving up of works into the Brahman, into the being of the Lord, *brahmaṇi ādhāya karmāṇi,*, *mayi sannyasya*. When works are thus 'reposed on the Brahman,' the personality of the instrumental doer ceases; though he acts, he does nothing; for he has given up not only the fruits of his works, but the works themselves and the doing of them to the Lord. The Divine then takes the burden of works from him; the Supreme becomes the doer and the act and the result.

This knowledge of which the Gita speaks, is not an intellectual activity of the mind; it is a luminous growth into the highest state of being by the outshining of the light of the divine sun of Truth, 'that Truth, the Sun lying concealed in the darkness' of our ignorance of which the Rigveda speaks, *tat satyaṁ sūryaṁ tamasi kṣiyantam*. The immutable Brahman is there in the spirit's skies above this troubled lower nature of the dualities, untouched either by its virtue or by its sin, accepting neither our sense of sin nor our self-righteousness, untouched by its joy and its sorrow, indifferent to our joy in success and our grief in failure, master of all, supreme, all-pervading, *prabhu vibhu*, calm, strong, pure, equal in all things, the source of Nature, not the direct doer of our works, but the witness of Nature and her works, not imposing on us either the illusion of being the doer, for that illusion is the result of the ignorance of this lower Nature. But this freedom, mastery, purity we cannot see; we are bewildered by the natural ignorance which hides from us the eternal self-knowledge of the Brahman secret within our being. But knowledge comes to its persistent seeker and removes the natural self-ignorance; it shines out like a long-hidden sun and lights up to our vision that self-being supreme beyond the dualities of this lower existence, *ādityavat prakāśayati tat param*. By a long whole-hearted endeavour, by directing our whole conscious being to that, by making that our whole aim, by turning it into the whole object of our discerning mind and so seeing it not only in ourselves but everywhere, we become one thought and self with that, *tad-buddhayas tad-ātmānaḥ*, we are washed clean of all the darkness and suffering of the lower man by the waters of knowledge,[1] *jñāna-nirdhūta-kalmaṣāḥ*.

The result is, says the Gita, a perfect equality to all things and all persons; and then only can we repose our works completely in the Brahman. For the Brahman is equal, *samaṁ brahma*, and it is only when we have this perfect equality, *sāmye sthitaḥ manaḥ*, 'seeing with an equal eye the learned and cultured Brahmin, the cow, the elephant, the dog, the outcaste' and knowing all as one Brahman, that we can, living in that oneness, see like the

[1] The Rigveda so speaks of the streams of the Truth, the waters that have perfect knowledge, the waters that are full of the divine sunlight, *ṛtasya dhārāḥ, āpo vicetasaḥ, svarvatīr apaḥ*. What are here metaphors, are there concrete symbols.

Brahman our works proceeding from the nature freely without any fear of attachment, sin or bondage. Sin and stain then cannot be; for we have overcome that creation full of desire and its works and reactions which belongs to the ignorance, *tair jitaḥ sargaḥ*, and living in the supreme and divine Nature there is no longer fault or defect in our works; for these are created by the inequalities of the ignorance. The equal Brahman is faultless, *nirdoṣaṁ hi samaṁ brahma*, beyond the confusion of good and evil, and living in the Brahman we too rise beyond good and evil; we act in that purity, stainlessly, with an equal and single purpose of fulfilling the welfare of all existences, *kṣīṇa-kalmaṣāḥ sarvabhūta-hite ratāḥ*. The Lord in our hearts is in the ignorance also the cause of our actions, but through his Maya, through the egoism of our lower nature which creates the tangled web of our actions and brings back upon our egoism the recoil of their tangled reactions affecting us inwardly as sin and virtue, affecting us outwardly as suffering and pleasure, evil fortune and good fortune, the great chain of Karma. When we are freed by knowledge, the Lord, no longer hidden in our hearts but manifest as our supreme self, takes up our works and uses us as faultless instruments, *nimitta-mātram*, for the helping of the world. Such is the intimate union between knowledge and equality; knowledge here in the *buddhi* reflected as equality in the temperament; above, on a higher plane of consciousness, knowledge as the light of the Being, equality as the stuff of the Nature.

The Determinism of Nature

The passages in which the Gita lays stress on the subjection of the ego-soul to Nature, have by some been understood as the enunciation of an absolute and a mechanical determinism which leaves no room for any freedom within the cosmic existence. Certainly, the language it uses is emphatic and seems very absolute. But we must take, here as elsewhere, the thought of the Gita as a whole and not force its affirmations in their solitary sense quite detached from each other – as indeed every truth, however true in itself, yet, taken apart from others which at once limit and complete it, becomes a snare to bind the intellect and a misleading dogma; for in reality each is one thread of a complex weft and no thread must be taken apart from the weft. Everything in the Gita is even so interwoven and must be understood in its relation to the whole. The Gita itself makes a distinction between those who have not the knowledge of the whole, *akṛtsnavidaḥ*, and are misled by the partial truths of existence, and the Yogin who is called upon to rise. A certain absolute freedom is one aspect of the soul's relations with Nature at one pole of our complex being; a certain absolute determinism by Nature is the opposite aspect at its opposite pole; and there is also a partial and apparent, therefore an unreal eidolon of liberty which the soul receives by a contorted reflection of these two opposite truths in the developing mentality. It is the latter to which we ordinarily give, more or less inaccurately, the name of free will; but the Gita regards nothing as freedom which is not a complete liberation and mastery.

We speak of the soul being subject to Nature; but on the other hand, the Gita in distinguishing the properties of the soul and Nature affirms that while Nature is the executrix, the soul is always the lord, *īśvara*. It speaks here of the self being bewildered by egoism, but the real Self to the Vedantin is the divine, eternally free and self-aware. What then is this self that is bewildered by Nature, this soul that is subject to her? The answer is that we are speaking here in the common parlance of our lower or mental view of things; we are speaking of the apparent self, of the apparent soul, not of the real self, not of the true Purusha. It is really the ego which is subject to Nature, inevitably, because it is itself part of Nature, one functioning of her machinery; but when the self-awareness in the mind-consciousness identifies itself with the ego, it creates the appearance of a lower self, an ego-self. And so too what we think of ordinarily as the soul is really the natural personality, not the true Person, the Purusha, but the desire-soul in us which is a reflection of the consciousness of the Purusha in the workings of Prakriti: it is, in fact, itself only an action of the three modes and therefore a part of Nature. Thus, there are, we may say, two souls in us, the apparent or desire-soul, which changes with the mutations of the gunas and is entirely constituted and determined by them, and the free and eternal Purusha not limited by Nature and her gunas. We have two selves, the apparent self, which is only the ego, that mental centre in us which takes up this mutable action of Prakriti, this mutable personality, and which says 'I am this personality, I am this natural being who am doing these works,' – but the natural being is simply Nature, a composite of the gunas – and the true self which is, indeed, the upholder, the possessor and the lord of Nature and figured in her, but is not itself the mutable natural personality. The way to be free must then be to get rid of the desires of this desire-soul and the false self-view of this ego. 'Having become free from desire and egoism,' cries the Teacher, 'fight with all the fever of thy soul passed away from thee,' – *nirāśīr nirmamo bhūtvā.*

This view of our being starts from the Sankhya analysis of the dual principle in our nature, Purusha and Prakriti. Purusha is inactive, *akartā*; Prakriti is active, *kartrī*: Purusha is the being full of the light of consciousness; Prakriti is the Nature, mechanical, reflecting all her works in the conscious witness, the Purusha. Prakriti works by the inequality of her three modes, gunas, in perpetual collision and intermixture and mutation with each other; and by her function of ego-mind she gets the Purusha to identify himself with all this working and so creates the sense of active, mutable, temporal personality in the silent eternity of the Self. The impure natural consciousness overclouds the pure soul-consciousness; the mind forgets the Person in the ego and the personality; we suffer the discriminating intelligence to be carried away by the sense-mind and its outgoing functions and by the desire of the life and the body. So long as the Purusha sanctions this action, ego and desire and ignorance must govern the natural being.

But if this were all, then the only remedy would be to withdraw altogether the sanction, suffer or compel all our nature by this withdrawal to fall into a motionless equilibrium of the three gunas and so cease from all action. But this is precisely the remedy – though it is undoubtedly a remedy, one which abolishes, we might say, the patient along with the disease – which the Gita constantly discourages. Especially, to resort to a tamasic inaction is just what the ignorant will do if this truth is thrust upon them; the discriminating mind in them will fall into a false division, a false opposition, *buddhibheda*; their active nature and their intelligence will be divided against each other and produce a disturbance and confusion without true issue, a false and self-deceiving line of action, *mithyācāra*, or else a mere tamasic inertia, cessation of works, diminution of the will to life and action, not therefore a liberation, but rather a subjection to the lowest of the three gunas, to *tamas*, the principle of ignorance and of inertia. Or else they will not be able to understand at all, they will find fault with this higher teaching, assert against it their present mental experience, their ignorant idea of free will and, yet more confirmed by the plausibility of their logic in their bewilderment and the deception of ego and desire, lose their chance of liberation in a deeper, more obstinate confirmation of the ignorance.

In fact, these higher truths can only be helpful, because there only they are true to experience and can be lived, on a higher and vaster plane of consciousness and being. To view these truths from below is to mis-see, misunderstand and probably to misuse them. It is a higher truth that the distinction of good and evil is indeed a practical fact and law valid for the egoistic human life which is the stage of transition from the animal to the divine, but on a higher plane we rise beyond good and evil, are above their duality even as the Godhead is above it. But the unripe mind, seizing on this truth without rising from the lower consciousness where it is not practically valid, will simply make it a convenient excuse for indulging its Asuric propensities, denying the distinction between good and evil altogether and falling by self-indulgence deeper into the morass of perdition, *sarva-jñāna-vimūḍhān naṣṭān acetasaḥ*. So too with this truth of the determinism of Nature; it will be mis-seen and misused, as those misuse it who declare that a man is what his nature has made him and cannot do otherwise than as his nature compels him. It is true in a sense, but not in the sense which is attached to it, not in the sense that the ego-self can claim irresponsibility and impunity for itself in its works; for it has will and it has desire and so long as it acts according to its will and desire, even though that be its nature, it must bear the reactions of its Karma. It is in a net, if you will, a snare which may well seem perplexing, illogical, unjust, terrible to its present experience, to its limited self-knowledge, but a snare of its own choice, a net of its own weaving.

The Gita says, indeed, 'All existences follow their nature and what shall coercing it avail?' which seems, if we take it by itself, a hopelessly absolute assertion of the omnipotence of Nature over the soul; 'even the man of knowledge acts according to his own nature.' And on this it founds the injunction to follow faithfully in our action the law of our nature. 'Better is one's own law of works, *svadharma*, though in itself faulty than an alien law well wrought out; death in one's own law of being is better, perilous is it to follow an alien law.' What is precisely meant by this *svadharma* we have to wait to see until we get to the more elaborate disquisition in the closing chapters about Purusha and Prakriti and the gunas; but certainly it does not mean that we are to follow any impulse, even though evil, which what we call our nature dictates to us. For between these two verses the Gita throws in this further injunction, 'In the object of this or that sense liking and disliking are set in ambush; fall not into their power, for they are the besetters of the soul in its path.' And immediately after this, in answer to Arjuna's objection who asks him, if there is no fault in following our Nature, what are we then to say of that in us which drives a man to sin, as if by force, even against his own struggling will, the Teacher replies that this is desire and its companion wrath, children of rajas, the second guna, the principle of passion, and this desire is the soul's great enemy and has to be slain. Abstention from evil-doing it declares to be the first condition for liberation, and always it enjoins self-mastery, self-control, *saṁyama*, control of the mind, senses, all the lower being.

There is therefore a distinction to be made between what is essential in the nature, its native and inevitable action, which it avails not at all to repress, suppress, coerce, and what is accidental to it, its wanderings, confusions, perversions, over which we must certainly get control. There is a distinction implied too between coercion and suppression, *nigraha*, and control with right use and right guidance, *saṁyama*. The former is a violence done to the nature by the will, which in the end depresses the natural powers of the being, *ātmānam avasādayet*; the latter is the control of the lower by the higher self, which successfully gives to those powers their right action and their maximum efficiency – *yogaḥ karmasu kauśalam*. This nature of *saṁyama* is made very clear by the Gita in the opening of its sixth chapter, 'By the self thou shouldst deliver the self, thou shouldst not depress and cast down the self (whether by self-indulgence or suppression); for the self is the friend of the self and the self is the enemy. To the man is his self a friend in whom the (lower) self has been conquered by the (higher) self, but to him who is not in possession of his (higher) self, the (lower) self is as if an enemy and it acts as an enemy.' When one has conquered one's self and attained to the calm of a perfect self-mastery and self-possession, then is the supreme self in a man founded and poised even in his outwardly conscious human being, *samāhita*. In other words, to master the lower self by the higher, the natural self by the spiritual is the way of man's perfection and liberation. Here then is a very great qualification of the determinism of Nature, a precise limitation of its meaning and scope. How the passage from subjection to mastery works out is best seen if we observe the working of the gunas in the scale of Nature from the bottom to the top. At the bottom are the existences in which the principle of tamas is supreme, the beings who have not yet attained to the light of self-consciousness and are utterly driven by the current of Nature. There is a will even in the atom, but we see clearly enough that it is not free will, because it is mechanical and the atom does not possess the will, but is possessed by it. Here the *buddhi*, the element of intelligence and will in Prakriti, is actually and plainly what the Sankhya asserts it to be, *jaḍa*, a mechanical, even an inconscient principle in which the light of the conscious Soul has not at all struggled to the surface: the atom is not conscious of an intelligent will; tamas, the inert and ignorant principle, has its grip on it, contains *rajas*, conceals *sattva* within itself and holds a high holiday of mastery, Nature compelling this form of existence to act with a stupendous force indeed, but as a mechanical instrument, *yantrārūḍhaṁ māyayā.*

Next, in the plant the principle of *rajas* has struggled to the surface, with its power of life, with its capacity of the nervous reactions which in us are recognisable as pleasure and suffering, but *sattva* is quite involved, has not yet emerged to awaken the light of a conscious intelligent will;

all is still mechanical, subconscient or half-conscient, tamas stronger than rajas, both gaolers of the imprisoned sattwa.

In the animal, though tamas is still strong, though we may still describe him as belonging to the tamasic creation, *tāmasa sarga*, yet rajas prevails much more against tamas, brings with it its developed power of life, desire, emotion, passion, pleasure, suffering, while sattwa, emerging, but still dependent on the lower action, contributes to these the first light of the conscious mind, the mechanical sense of ego, conscious memory, a certain kind of thought, especially the wonders of instinct and animal intuition. But as yet the buddhi, the intelligent will, has not developed the full light of consciousness; therefore, no responsibility can be attributed to the animal for its actions. The tiger can be no more blamed for killing and devouring than the atom for its blind movements, the fire for burning and consuming or the storm for its destructions. If it could answer the question, the tiger would indeed say, like man, that it had free will, it would have the egoism of the doer, it would say, 'I kill, I devour'; but we can see clearly enough that it is not really the tiger, but Nature in the tiger that kills, it is Nature in the tiger that devours; and if it refrains from killing or devouring, it is from satiety, from fear or from indolence, from another principle of Nature in it, from the action of the guna called tamas. As it was Nature in the animal that killed, so it is Nature in the animal that refrained from killing. Whatever soul is in it, sanctions passively the action of Nature, is as much passive in its passion and activity as in its indolence or inaction. The animal like the atom acts according to the mechanism of its Nature, and not otherwise, *sadṛśaṁ ceṣṭate svasyāḥ prakṛteḥ*, as if mounted on a machine, *yantrārūḍho māyayā*.

Well, but in man at least there is another action, a free soul, a free will, a sense of responsibility, a real doer other than Nature, other than the mechanism of Maya? So it seems, because in man there is a conscious intelligent will; *buddhi* is full of the light of the observing Purusha, who through it, it seems, observes, understands, approves or disapproves, gives or withholds the sanction, seems indeed at last to begin to be the lord of his nature. Man is not like the tiger or the fire or the storm; he cannot kill and say as a sufficient justification, 'I am acting according to my nature,' and he cannot do it, because he has not the nature and not, therefore, the law of action, *svadharma*, of the tiger, storm or fire. He has a conscious intelligent will, a *buddhi*, and to that he must refer his actions. If he does not do so, if he acts blindly according to his impulses and passions, then the law of his being is not rightly worked out, *svadharmaḥsu-anuṣṭhitaḥ*, he has not acted according to the full measure of his humanity, but even as might the animal. It is true that the principle of *rajas* or the principle of *tamas* gets hold of his *buddhi* and induces it to justify any and every action he commits or any avoidance of action; but still, the justification or at least the reference to the buddhi must be there either before or after the action is committed. And, besides, in man *sattva* is awake and acts not only as intelligence and intelligent will, but as a seeking for light, for right knowledge and right action according to that knowledge, as a sympathetic perception of the existence and claims of others, as an attempt to know the higher law of his own nature, which the sattwic principle in him creates, and to obey it, and as a conception of the greater peace and happiness which virtue, knowledge and sympathy bring in their train. He knows more or less imperfectly that he has to govern his rajasic and tamasic by his sattwic nature and that thither tends the perfection of his normal humanity.

But is the condition of the predominantly sattwic nature freedom and is this will in man a free will? That the Gita from the standpoint of a higher consciousness in which alone is true freedom, denies. The buddhi or conscious intelligent will is still an instrument of Nature and when it acts, even in the most sattwic sense, it is still Nature which acts and the soul which is carried on the wheel by Maya. At any rate, at least ninetenths of our freedom of will is a palpable fiction; that will is created and determined not by its own self-existent action at a given moment, but by our past, our heredity, our training, our environment, the whole tremendous complex thing we call Karma, which is, behind us, the whole past action of Nature on us and the world converging in the individual, determining what he is, determining what his will shall be at a given moment and determining, as far as analysis can see, even its action at that moment. The ego associates itself always with its Karma and it says 'I did' and 'I will' and 'I suffer,' but if it looks at itself and sees how it was made, it is obliged to say of man as of the animal, 'Nature did this in me, Nature wills in me,' and if it qualifies by saying 'my Nature,' that only means 'Nature as self-determined in this individual creature.' It was the strong perception of this aspect of existence which compelled the Buddhists to declare that all is Karma and that there is no self in existence, that the idea of self is only a delusion of the ego-mind. When the ego thinks 'I choose and will this virtuous and not that evil action,' it is simply associating itself, somewhat like the fly on the wheel, or rather as might a cog or other part of a mechanism if it were conscious, with a predominant wave or a formed current of the sattwic principle by which Nature chooses through the buddhi one type of action in preference to another. Nature forms itself in us and wills in us, the Sankhya would say, for the pleasure of the inactive observing Purusha.

But even if this extreme statement has to be qualified, and we shall see hereafter in what sense, still the freedom of our individual will, if we choose to give it that name, is very relative and almost infinitesimal, so much is it mixed up with other determining elements. Its strongest power does not amount to mastery. It cannot be relied upon to resist the strong wave of circumstance or of other nature which either overbears or modifies or mixes up with it or at the best subtly deceives and circumvents it. Even the most sattwic will is so overborne or mixed up with or circumvented by the rajasic and tamasic gunas as to be only in part sattwic, and thence arises that sufficiently strong element of self-deception, of a quite involuntary and even innocent make-believe and hiding from oneself which the merciless eye of the psychologist detects even in the best human action. When we think that we are acting quite freely, powers are concealed behind our action which escape the most careful self-introspection; when we think that we are free from ego, the ego is there, concealed, in the mind of the saint as in that of the sinner. When our eyes are really opened on our action and its springs, we are obliged to say with the Gita '*guṇā guṇeṣu vartante*,' 'it was the modes of Nature that were acting upon the modes.'

For this reason, even a high predominance of the sattwic principle does not constitute freedom. For, as the Gita points out, the sattwa binds, as much as the other gunas, and binds just in the same way, by desire, by ego; a nobler desire, a purer ego – but so long as in any form these two hold the being, there is no freedom. The man of virtue, of knowledge, has his ego of the virtuous man, his ego of knowledge, and it is that sattwic ego which he seeks to satisfy; for his own sake he seeks virtue and knowledge. Only when we cease to satisfy the ego, to think and to will from the ego, the limited 'I' in us, then is there a real freedom. In other words, freedom, highest self-mastery begins when above the natural self we see and hold the supreme Self of which the ego is an obstructing veil and a blinding shadow. And that can only be when we see the one Self in us seated above Nature and make our individual being one with it in being and consciousness and in its individual nature of action only an instrument of a supreme Will, the one Will that is really free. For that we must rise high above the three gunas, become *triguṇātīta*; for that Self is beyond even the sattwic principle. We have to climb to it through the sattwa, but we attain to it only when we get beyond sattwa; we reach out to it from the ego, but only reach it by leaving the ego. We are drawn towards it by the highest, most passionate, most stupendous and ecstatic of all desires; but we can securely live in it only when all desire drops away from us. We have at a certain stage to liberate ourselves even from the desire of our liberation.

Nirvana and Works in the World

The union of the soul with the Purushottama by a Yoga of the whole being is the complete teaching of the Gita and not only the union with the immutable Self as in the narrower doctrine which follows the exclusive way of knowledge. That is why the Gita subsequently, after it has effected the reconciliation of knowledge and works, is able to develop the idea of love and devotion, unified with both works and knowledge, as the highest height of the way to the supreme secret. For if the union with the immutable Self were the sole secret or the highest secret, that would not at all be possible; for then at a given point our inner basis for love and devotion, no less than our inner foundation of works, would crumble away and collapse. Union utter and exclusive with the immutable Self alone means the abolition of the whole point of view of the mutable being, not only in its ordinary and inferior action but in its very roots, in all that makes its existence possible, not only in the works of its ignorance, but in the works of its knowledge. It would mean the abolition of all that difference in conscious poise and activity between the human soul and the Divine which makes possible the play of the Kshara; for the action of the Kshara would become then entirely a play of the ignorance without any root or basis of divine reality in it. On the contrary, union by Yoga with the Purushottama means the knowledge and enjoyment of our oneness with him in our self-existent being and of a certain differentiation in our active being. It is the persistence of the latter in a play of divine works which are urged by the motive power of divine love and constituted by a perfected divine Nature, it is the vision of the Divine in the world harmonised with a realisation of the Divine in the self which makes action and devotion possible to the liberated man, and not only possible but inevitable in the perfect mode of his being.

But the direct way to union lies through the firm realisation of the immutable Self, and it is the Gita's insistence on this as a first necessity, after which alone works and devotion can acquire their whole divine meaning, that makes it possible for us to mistake its drift. For if we take the passages in which it insists most rigorously upon this necessity and neglect to observe the whole sequence of thought in which they stand, we may easily come to the conclusion that it does really teach actionless absorption as the final state of the soul and action only as a preliminary means towards stillness in the motionless Immutable. It is in the close of the fifth and throughout the sixth chapter that this insistence is strongest and most comprehensive.

There we get the description of a Yoga which would seem at first sight to be incompatible with works and we get the repeated use of the word Nirvana to describe the status to which the Yogin arrives.

The mark of this status is the supreme peace of a calm self-extinction, *śāntiṁ nirvāṇa-paramām*, and, as if to make it quite clear that it is not the Buddhist's Nirvana in a blissful negation of being, but the Vedantic loss of a partial in a perfect being that it intends, the Gita uses always the phrase *brahma-nirvāṇa*, extinction in the Brahman; and the Brahman here certainly seems to mean the Immutable, to denote primarily at least the inner timeless Self withdrawn from active participation even though immanent in the externality of Nature. We have to see then what is the drift of the Gita here, and especially whether this peace is the peace of an absolute inactive cessation, whether the self-extinction in the Akshara means the absolute excision of all knowledge and consciousness of the Kshara and of all action in the Kshara. We are accustomed indeed to regard Nirvana and any kind of existence and action in the world as incompatible and we might be inclined to argue that the use of the word is by itself sufficient and decides the question. But if we look closely at Buddhism, we shall doubt whether the absolute incompatibility really existed even for the Buddhists; and if we look closely at the Gita, we shall see that it does not form part of this supreme Vedantic teaching.

The Gita after speaking of the perfect equality of the Brahman-knower who has risen into the Brahman-consciousness, *brahmavid brahmaṇi sthitaḥ*, develops in nine verses that follow its idea of Brahmayoga and of Nirvana in the Brahman. 'When the soul is no longer attached to the touches of outward things,' it begins, 'then one finds the happiness that exists in the Self; such a one enjoys an imperishable happiness, because his self is in Yoga, *yukta*, by Yoga with the Brahman.' The non-attachment is essential, it says, in order to be free from the attacks of desire and wrath and passion, a freedom without which true happiness is not possible. That happiness and equality are to be gained entirely by man in the body: he is not to suffer any least remnant of the subjection to the troubled lower nature to remain in the idea that the perfect release will come by a putting off of the body; a perfect spiritual freedom is to be won here upon earth and possessed and enjoyed in the human life, *prāk śarīravimokṣaṇāt*. It then continues, 'He who has the inner happiness and the inner ease and repose and the inner light, that Yogin becomes the Brahman and reaches self-extinction in the Brahman, *brahma-nirvāṇam*.' Here, very clearly, Nirvana means the extinction of the ego in the higher spiritual, inner Self, that which is for ever timeless, spaceless, not bound by the chain of cause and effect and the changes of the world-mutation, self-blissful, self-illumined and for ever at peace. The Yogin ceases to be the ego, the little person limited by the mind and the body; he becomes the Brahman; he is unified in consciousness with the immutable divinity of the eternal Self which is immanent in his natural being.

But is this a going in into some deep sleep of samadhi away from all world-consciousness, or is it the preparatory movement for a dissolution of the natural being and the individual soul into some absolute Self who is utterly and for ever beyond Nature and her works, *laya*, *mokṣa*? Is that withdrawal necessary before we can enter into Nirvana, or is Nirvana, as the context seems to suggest, a state which can exist simultaneously with world-consciousness and even in its own way include it? Apparently the latter, for in the succeeding verse the Gita goes on to say, 'Sages win Nirvana in the Brahman, they in whom the stains of sin are effaced and the knot of doubt is cut asunder, masters of their selves, who are occupied in doing good to all creatures, *sarvabhūta-hite ratāḥ*.' That would almost seem to mean that to be thus is to be in Nirvana. But the next verse is quite clear and decisive, '*Yatis* (those who practise self-mastery by Yoga and austerity) who are delivered from desire and wrath and have gained self-mastery, for them Nirvana in the Brahman exists all about them, encompasses them, they already live in it because they have knowledge of the Self.' That is to say, to have knowledge and possession of the self is to exist in Nirvana. This is clearly a large extension of the idea of Nirvana. Freedom from all stain of the passions, the self-mastery of the equal mind on which that freedom is founded, equality to all beings, *sarvabhūteṣu*, and beneficial love for all, final destruction of that doubt and obscurity of the ignorance which keeps us divided from the all-unifying Divine and the knowledge of the One Self within us and in all are evidently the conditions of Nirvana which are laid down in these verses of the Gita, go to constitute it and are its spiritual substance.

Thus, Nirvana is clearly compatible with world-consciousness and with action in the world. For the sages who possess it are conscious of and in intimate relation by works with the Divine in the mutable universe; they are occupied with the good of all creatures, *sarvabhūta-hite*. They have not renounced the experiences of the Kshara Purusha, they have divinised them; for the Kshara, the Gita tells us, is all existences, *sarvabhūtāni*, and the doing universal good to all is a divine action in the mutability of Nature. This action in the world is not inconsistent with living in Brahman, it is rather its inevitable condition and outward result because the Brahman in whom we find Nirvana, the spiritual consciousness in which we lose the separative ego-consciousness, is not only within us but within all these existences, exists not only above and apart from all these universal happenings, but pervades them, contains them and is extended in them. Therefore, by Nirvana in the Brahman must be meant a destruction or extinction of the limited separative consciousness, falsifying and dividing, which is brought into being on the surface of existence by the lower Maya of the three gunas, and entry into Nirvana is a passage into this other true unifying consciousness which is the heart of existence and its continent and its whole containing and supporting, its whole original and eternal and final truth. Nirvana when we gain it, enter into it, is not only within us, but all around, *abhito vartate*, because this is not only the Brahman-consciousness which lives secret within us, but the Brahman-consciousness in which we live. It is the Self which we are within, the supreme Self of our individual being but also the Self which we are without, the supreme Self of the universe, the self of all existences. By living in that self, we live in all, and no longer in our egoistic being alone; by oneness with that self a steadfast oneness with all in the universe becomes the very nature of our being and the root status of our active consciousness and root motive of all our action.

But again, we get immediately afterwards two verses which might seem to lead away from this conclusion. 'Having put outside of himself all outward touches and concentrated the vision between the eyebrows and made equal the *prāṇa* and the *apāna* moving within the nostrils, having controlled the senses, the mind and the understanding, the sage devoted to liberation, from whom desire and wrath and fear have passed away is ever free.' Here we have a process of Yoga that brings in an element which seems quite other than the Yoga of works and other even than the pure Yoga of knowledge by discrimination and contemplation; it belongs in all its characteristic features to the system, introduces the psychophysical askesis of Rajayoga. There is the conquest of all the movements of the mind, *cittavṛttinirodha*; there is the control of the breathing, Pranayama; there is the drawing in of the sense and the vision. All of them are processes which lead to the inner trance of Samadhi, the object of all of them *mokṣa*, and *mokṣa* signifies in ordinary parlance the renunciation not only of the separative ego-consciousness, but of the whole active consciousness, a dissolution of our being into the highest Brahman. Are we to suppose that the Gita gives this process in that sense as the last movement of a release by dissolution or only as a special means and a strong aid to overcome the outward-going mind? Is this the finale, the climax, the last word? We shall find reason to regard it as both a special means, an aid, and at least one gate of a final departure, not by dissolution, but by an uplifting to the supracosmic existence. For even here in this passage this is not the last word; the last word, the finale, the climax comes in a verse that follows and is the last couplet of the chapter. 'When a man has known Me as the Enjoyer of sacrifice and tapasya (of all askesis and energisms), the mighty lord of all the worlds, the friend of all creatures, he comes by the peace.' The power of the Karmayoga comes in again; the knowledge of the active Brahman, the cosmic supersoul, is insisted on among the conditions of the peace of Nirvana.

We get back to the great idea of the Gita, the idea of the Purushottama – though that name is not given till close upon the end, it is always that which Krishna means by his 'I' and 'Me,' the Divine who is there as the one self in our timeless immutable being, who is present too in the world, in all existences, in all activities, the master of the silence and the peace, the master of the power and the action, who is here incarnate as the divine charioteer of the stupendous conflict, the Transcendent, the Self, the All, the master of every individual being. He is the enjoyer of all sacrifice and of all tapasya, therefore shall the seeker of liberation do works as a sacrifice and as a tapasya; he is the lord of all the worlds, manifested in Nature and in these beings, therefore shall the liberated man still do works for the right government and leading on of the peoples in these worlds, *loka saṅgraha*; he is the friend of all existences, therefore is the sage who has found Nirvana within him and all around, still and always occupied with the good of all creatures – even as the Nirvana of Mahayana Buddhism took for its highest sign the works of a universal compassion. Therefore too, even when he has found oneness with the Divine in his timeless and immutable self, is he still capable, since he embraces the relations also of the play of Nature, of divine love for man and of love for the Divine, of bhakti.

That this is the drift of the meaning, becomes clearer when we have fathomed the sense of the sixth chapter which is a large comment on and a full development of the idea of these closing verses of the fifth, that shows the importance which the Gita attaches to them. We shall therefore run as briefly as possible through the substance of this sixth chapter. First the Teacher emphasises – and this is very significant – his often-repeated asseveration about the real essence of Sannyasa, that it is an inward, not an outward renunciation. 'Whoever does the work to be done without resort to its fruits, he is the Sannyasin and the Yogin, not the man who lights not the sacrificial fire and does not the works. What they have called renunciation

(Sannyasa), know to be in truth Yoga; for none becomes a Yogin who has not renounced the desire-will in the mind.' Works are to be done, but with what purpose and in what order? They are first to be done while ascending the hill of Yoga, for then works are the cause, *kāraṇam*. The cause of what? The cause of self-perfection, of liberation, of nirvana in the Brahman; for by doing works with a steady practice of the inner renunciation this perfection, this liberation, this conquest of the desire-mind and the ego-self and the lower nature, are easily accomplished.

But when one has got to the top? Then works are no longer the cause; the calm of self-mastery and self-possession gained by works becomes the cause. Again, the cause of what? Of fixity in the Self, in the Brahman-consciousness and of the perfect equality in which the divine works of the liberated man are done. 'For when one does not get attached to the objects of sense or to works and has renounced all will of desire in the mind, then is he said to have ascended to the top of Yoga.' That, as we know already, is the spirit in which the liberated man does works; he does them without desire and attachment, without the egoistic personal will and the mental seeking which is the parent of desire. He has conquered his lower self, reached the perfect calm in which his highest self is manifest to him, that highest self always concentrated in its own being, *samāhita*, in Samadhi, not only in the trance of the inward-drawn consciousness, but always, in the waking state of the mind as well, in exposure to the causes of desire and of the disturbance of calm, to grief and pleasure, heat and cold, honour and disgrace, all the dualities, *śītoṣṇa-sukhaduḥkheṣu tathā mānāpamānayoḥ*. This higher self is the Akshara, *kūṭastha*, which stands above the changes and the perturbations of the natural being; and the Yogin is said to be in Yoga with it when he also is like it, *kūṭastha*, when he is superior to all appearances and mutations, when he is satisfied with self-knowledge, when he is equal-minded to all things and happenings and persons.

But this Yoga is after all no easy thing to acquire, as Arjuna indeed shortly afterwards suggests, for the restless mind is always liable to be pulled down from these heights by the attacks of outward things and to fall back into the strong control of grief and passion and inequality. Therefore, it would seem, the Gita proceeds to give us in addition to its general method of knowledge and works a special process of Rajayogic meditation also, a powerful method of practice, *abhyāsa*, a strong way to the complete control of the mind and all its workings. In this process the Yogin is directed to practise continually union with the Self so that that may become his normal consciousness. He is to sit apart and alone, with all desire and idea of possession banished from his mind, self-controlled in his whole being and consciousness. 'He should set in a pure spot his firm seat, neither too high, nor yet too low, covered with a cloth, with a deer-skin, with sacred grass, and there seated with a concentrated mind and with the workings of the mental consciousness and the senses under control he should practise Yoga for self-purification, *ātma-viśuddhaye*.' The posture he takes must be the motionless erect posture proper to the practice of Rajayoga; the vision should be drawn in and fixed between the eye-brows, 'not regarding the regions.' The mind is to be kept calm and free from fear and the vow of Brahmacharya observed; the whole controlled mentality must be devoted and turned to the Divine so that the lower action of the consciousness shall be merged in the higher peace. For the object to be attained is the still peace of Nirvana. 'Thus, always putting himself in Yoga by control of his mind the Yogin attains to the supreme peace of Nirvana which has its foundation in Me, *śāntiṁ nirvāṇa-paramāṁ matsaṁsthām*.'

This peace of Nirvana is reached when all the mental consciousness is perfectly controlled and liberated from desire and remains still in the Self, when, motionless like the light of a lamp in a windless place, it ceases from its restless action, shut in from its outward motion, and by the silence and stillness of the mind the Self is seen within, not disfigured as in the mind, but in the Self, seen, not as it is mistranslated falsely or partially by the mind and represented to us through the ego, but self-perceived by the Self, *svaprakāśa*. Then the soul is satisfied and knows its own true and exceeding bliss, not that untranquil happiness which is the portion of the mind and the senses, but an inner and serene felicity in which it is safe from the mind's perturbations and can no longer fall away from the spiritual truth of its being. Not even the fieriest assault of mental grief can disturb it; for mental grief comes to us from outside, is a reaction to external touches, and this is the inner, the self-existent happiness of those who no longer accept the slavery of the unstable mental reactions to external touches. It is the putting away of the contact with pain, the divorce of the mind's marriage with grief, *duḥkha-saṁyoga-viyogam*. The firm winning of this inalienable spiritual bliss is Yoga, it is the divine union; it is the greatest of all gains and the treasure beside which all others lose their value. Therefore, is this Yoga to be resolutely practised without yielding to any discouragement by difficulty or failure until the release, until the bliss of Nirvana is secured as an eternal possession.

The main stress here has fallen on the stilling of the emotive mind, the mind of desire and the senses which are the recipients of outward touches and reply to them with our customary emotional reactions; but even the mental thought has to be stilled in the silence of the self-existent being. First, all the desires born of the desire-will have to be wholly abandoned without any exception or residue and the senses have to be held in by the mind so that they shall not run out to all sides after their usual disorderly and restless habit; but next the mind itself has to be seized by the buddhi and drawn inward. One should slowly cease from mental action by a buddhi held in the grasp of fixity and having fixed the mind in the higher self, one should not think of anything at all. Whenever the restless and unquiet mind goes forth, it should be controlled and brought into subjection in the Self. When the mind is thoroughly quieted, then there comes upon the Yogin the highest, stainless, passionless bliss of the soul that has become the Brahman. 'Thus, freed from stain of passion and putting himself constantly into Yoga, the Yogin easily and happily enjoys the touch of the Brahman which is an exceeding bliss.'

And yet the result is not, while one yet lives, a Nirvana which puts away every possibility of action in the world, every relation with beings in the world. It would seem at first that it ought to be so. When all the desires and passions have ceased, when the mind is no longer permitted to throw itself out in thought, when the practice of this silent and solitary Yoga has become the rule, what farther action or relation with the world of outward touches and mutable appearances is any longer possible? No doubt, the Yogin for a time still remains in the body, but the cave, the forest, the mountain-top seem now the fittest, the only possible scene of his continued living and constant trance of Samadhi his sole joy and occupation. But, first, while this solitary Yoga is being pursued, the renunciation of all other action is not recommended by the Gita. This Yoga, it says, is not for the man who gives up sleep and food and play and action, even as it is not for those who indulge too much in these things of the life and the body; but the sleep and waking, the food, the play, the putting forth of effort in works should all be *yukta*. This is generally interpreted as meaning that all should be moderate, regulated, done in fit measure, and that may indeed be the significance. But at any rate when the Yoga is attained, all this has to be *yukta* in another sense, the ordinary sense of the word everywhere else in the Gita. In all states, in waking and in sleeping, in food and play and action, the Yogin will then be in Yoga with the Divine, and all will be done by him in the consciousness of the Divine as the self and as the All and as that which supports and contains his own life and his action. Desire and ego and personal will and the thought of the mind are the motives of action only in the lower nature; when the ego is lost and the Yogin becomes Brahman, when he lives in and is, even, a transcendent and universal consciousness, action comes spontaneously out of that, luminous knowledge higher than the mental thought comes out of that, a power other and mightier than the personal will comes out of that to do for him his works and bring its fruits:[1] personal action has ceased, all has been taken up into the Brahman and assumed by the Divine, *mayi sannyasya karmāṇi*.

For when the Gita describes the nature of this self-realisation and the result of the Yoga which comes by Nirvana of the separative ego-mind and its motives of thought and feeling and action into the Brahman-consciousness, it includes the cosmic sense, though lifted into a new kind of vision. 'The man whose self is in Yoga, sees the self in all beings and all beings in the self, he sees all with an equal vision.' All that he sees is to him the Self, all is his self, all is the Divine. But is there no danger, if he dwells at all in the mutability of the Kshara, of his losing all the results of this difficult Yoga, losing the Self and falling back into the mind, of the Divine losing him and the world getting him, of his losing the Divine and getting back in its place

[1] *yoga-kṣemaṁ vahāmyaham*

the ego and the lower nature? No, says the Gita; 'he who sees Me everywhere and sees all in Me, to him I do not get lost, nor does he get lost to Me.' For this peace of Nirvana, though it is gained through the Akshara, is founded upon the being of the Purushottama, *mat-saṁsthām*, and that is extended, the Divine, the Brahman is extended too in the world of beings and, though transcendent of it, not imprisoned in its own transcendence. One has to see all things as He and live and act wholly in that vision; that is the perfect fruit of the Yoga.

But why act? Is it not safer to sit in one's solitude looking out upon the world, if you will, seeing it in Brahman, in the Divine, but not taking part in it, not moving in it, not living in it, not acting in it, living rather ordinarily in the inner Samadhi? Should not that be the law, the rule, the dharma of this highest spiritual condition? No, again; for the liberated Yogin there is no other law, rule, dharma than simply this, to live in the Divine and love the Divine and be one with all beings; his freedom is an absolute and not a contingent freedom, self-existent and not dependent any longer on any rule of conduct, law of life or limitation of any kind. He has no longer any need of a process of Yoga, because he is now perpetually in Yoga. 'The Yogin who has taken his stand upon oneness and loves Me in all beings, however and in all ways he lives and acts, lives and acts in Me.' The love of the world spiritualised, changed from a sense-experience to a soul-experience, is founded on the love of God and in that love there is no peril and no shortcoming. Fear and disgust of the world may often be necessary for the recoil from the lower nature, for it is really the fear and disgust of our own ego which reflects itself in the world. But to see God in the world is to fear nothing, it is to embrace all in the being of God; to see all as the Divine is to hate and loathe nothing, but love God in the world and the world in God.

But at least the things of the lower nature will be shunned and feared, the things which the Yogin has taken so much trouble to surmount? Not this either; all is embraced in the equality of the self-vision. 'He, O Arjuna, who sees with equality everything in the image of the Self, whether it be grief or it be happiness, him I hold to be the supreme Yogin.' And by this, it is not meant at all that he himself shall fall from the griefless spiritual bliss and feel again worldly unhappiness, even in the sorrow of others, but seeing in others the play of the dualities which he himself has left and surmounted, he shall still see all as himself, his self in all, God in all and, not disturbed or bewildered by the appearances of these things, moved only by them to help and heal, to occupy himself with the good of all beings, to lead men to the spiritual bliss, to work for the progress of the world Godwards, he shall live the divine life, so long as days upon earth are his portion. The God-lover who can do this, can thus embrace all things in God, can look calmly on the lower nature and the works of the Maya of the three gunas and act in them and upon them without perturbation or fall or disturbance from the height and power of the spiritual oneness, free in the largeness of the God-vision, sweet and great and luminous in the strength of the God-nature, may well be declared to be the supreme Yogin. He indeed has conquered the creation, *jitaḥ sargaḥ*.

The Gita brings in here as always bhakti as the climax of the Yoga, *sarvabhūtasthitaṁ yo māṁ bhajati ekatvam āsthitaḥ*; that may almost be said to sum up the whole final result of the Gita's teaching – whoever loves God in all and his soul is founded upon the divine oneness, however he lives and acts, lives and acts in God. And to emphasise it still more, after an intervention of Arjuna and a reply to his doubt as to how so difficult a Yoga can be at all possible for the restless mind of man, the divine Teacher returns to this idea and makes it his culminating utterance. 'The Yogin is greater than the doers of askesis, greater than the men of knowledge, greater than the men of works; become then the Yogin, O Arjuna,' the Yogin, one who seeks for and attains, by works and knowledge and askesis or by whatever other means, not even spiritual knowledge or power or anything else for their own sake, but the union with God alone; for in that all else is contained and in that lifted beyond itself to a divinest significance. But even among Yogins the greatest is the Bhakta. 'Of all Yogins he who with all his inner self given up to Me, for Me has love and faith, *śraddhāvān bhajate*, him I hold to be the most united with Me in Yoga.' It is this that is the closing word of these first six chapters and contains in itself the seed of the rest, of that which still remains unspoken and is nowhere entirely spoken; for it is always and remains something of a mystery and a secret, *rahasyam*, the highest spiritual mystery and the divine secret.

The Gist of the Karmayoga

The first six chapters of the Gita form a sort of preliminary block of the teaching; all the rest, all the other twelve chapters are the working out of certain unfinished figures in this block which here are seen only as hints behind the large-size execution of the main motives, yet are in themselves of capital importance and are therefore reserved for a yet larger treatment on the other two faces of the work. If the Gita were not a great written Scripture which must be carried to its end, if it were actually a discourse by a living teacher to a disciple which could be resumed in good time, when the disciple was ready for farther truth, one could conceive of his stopping here at the end of the sixth chapter and saying, 'Work this out first, there is plenty for you to do to realise it and you have the largest possible basis; as difficulties arise, they will solve themselves or I will solve them for you. But at present live out what I have told you; work in this spirit.' True, there are many things here which cannot be properly understood except in the light thrown on them by what is to come after. In order to clear up immediate difficulties and obviate possible misunderstandings, I have had myself to anticipate a good deal, to bring in repeatedly, for example, the idea of the Purushottama, for without that it would have been impossible to clear up certain obscurities about the Self and action and the Lord of action, which the Gita deliberately accepts so that it may not disturb the firmness of the first steps by reaching out prematurely to things too great as yet for the mind of the human disciple.

Arjuna, himself, if the Teacher were to break off his discourse here, might well object: 'You have spoken much of the destruction of desire and attachment, of equality, of the conquest of the senses and the stilling of the mind, of passionless and impersonal action, of the sacrifice of works, of the inner as preferable to the outer renunciation, and these things I understand intellectually, however difficult they may appear to me in practice. But you have also spoken of rising above the gunas, while yet one remains in action, and you have not told me how the gunas work, and unless I know that, it will be difficult for me to detect and rise above them. Besides, you have spoken of bhakti as the greatest element in Yoga, yet you have talked much of works and knowledge, but very little or nothing of bhakti. And to whom is bhakti, this greatest thing, to be offered? Not to the still impersonal Self, certainly, but to you, the Lord. Tell me, then, what you are, who, as bhakti is greater even than this self-knowledge, are greater than the immutable Self, which is yet itself greater than mutable Nature and the world of action, even as knowledge is greater than works. What is the relation between these three things? between works and knowledge and divine love? between the soul in Nature and the immutable Self and that which is at once the changeless Self of all and the Master of knowledge and love and works, the supreme Divinity who is here with me in this great battle and massacre, my charioteer in the chariot of this fierce and terrible action?' It is to answer these questions that the rest of the Gita is written, and in a complete intellectual solution they have indeed to be taken up without delay and resolved. But in actual *sādhanā*, one has to advance from stage to stage, leaving many things, indeed the greatest things to arise subsequently and solve themselves fully by the light of the advance we have made in spiritual experience. The Gita follows to a certain extent this curve of experience and puts first a sort of large preliminary basis of works and knowledge which contains an element leading up to bhakti and to a greater knowledge, but not yet fully arriving. The six chapters present us with that basis.

We may then pause to consider how far they have carried the solution of the original problem with which the Gita started. The problem in itself, it may be useful again to remark, need not necessarily have led up to the whole question of the nature of existence and of the replacement of the normal by the spiritual life. It might have been dealt with on a pragmatical or an ethical basis or from an intellectual or an ideal standpoint or by a consideration of all of these together; that in fact would have been our modern method of solving the difficulty. By itself it raises in the first instance just this question, whether Arjuna should be governed by the ethical sense of personal sin in slaughter or by the consideration equally ethical of his public and social duty, the defence of the Right, the opposition demanded by conscience from all noble natures to the armed forces of injustice and oppression? That question has been raised in our own time and the present hour, and it can be solved, as we solve it now, by one or other of very various solutions, but all from the standpoint of our normal life and our normal human mind. It may be answered as a question between the personal conscience and our duty to the society and the State, between an ideal and a practical morality, between 'soul-force' and the recognition of the troublesome fact that life is not yet at least all soul and that to take up arms for the right in a physical struggle is sometimes inevitable. All these solutions are, however, intellectual, temperamental, emotional; they depend upon the individual standpoint and are at the best our own proper way of meeting the difficulty offered to us, proper because suitable to our nature and the stage of our ethical and intellectual evolution, the best we can, with the light we have, see and do; it leads to no final solution. And this is so because it proceeds from the normal mind which is always a tangle of various tendencies of our being and can only arrive at a choice or an accommodation between them, between our reason, our ethical being, our dynamic needs, our life-instincts, our emotional being and those rarer movements which we may perhaps call soul-instincts or psychical preferences. The Gita recognises that from this standpoint there can be no absolute, only an immediate practical solution and, after offering to Arjuna from the highest ideals of his age just such a practical solution, which he is in no mood to accept and indeed is evidently not intended to accept, it proceeds to quite a different standpoint and to quite another answer.

The Gita's solution is to rise above our natural being and normal mind, above our intellectual and ethical perplexities into another consciousness with another law of being and therefore another standpoint for our action; where personal desire and personal emotions no longer govern it; where the dualities fall away; where the action is no longer our own and where therefore the sense of personal virtue and personal sin is exceeded; where the universal, the impersonal, the divine spirit works out through us its purpose in the world; where we are ourselves by a new and divine birth changed into being of that Being, consciousness of that Consciousness, power of that Power, bliss of that Bliss, and, living no longer in our lower nature, have no works to do of our own, no personal aim to pursue of our own, but if we do works at all – and that is the one real problem and difficulty left – do only the divine works, those of which our outward nature is only a passive instrument and no longer the cause, no longer provides the motive; for the motive-power is above us in the will of the Master of our works. And this is presented to us as the true solution, because it goes back to the real truth of our being and to live according to the real truth of our being is evidently the highest solution and the sole entirely true solution of the problems of our existence. Our mental and vital personality is a truth of our natural existence, but a truth of the ignorance, and all that attaches itself to it is also truth of that order, practically valid for the works of the ignorance, but no longer valid when we get back to the real truth of our being. But how can we actually be sure that this is the truth? We cannot so long as we remain satisfied with our ordinary mental experience; for our normal mental experience is wholly that of this lower nature full of the ignorance. We can only know this greater truth by living it, that is to say, by passing beyond the mental into the spiritual experience, by Yoga. For the living out of spiritual experience until we cease to be mind and become spirit, until, liberated from the imperfections of our present nature, we are able to live entirely in our true and divine being is what in the end we mean by Yoga.

This upward transference of our centre of being and the consequent transformation of our whole existence and consciousness, with a resultant change in the whole spirit and motive of our action, the action often remaining precisely the same in all its outward appearances, makes the gist of the Gita's Karmayoga. Change your being, be reborn into the spirit and by that new birth proceed with the action to which the Spirit within has appointed you, may be said to be the heart of its message. Or again, put otherwise, with a deeper and more spiritual import – make the work you have to do here your means of inner spiritual rebirth, the divine birth, and, having become divine, do still divine works as an instrument of the Divine for the leading of the peoples. Therefore, there are here two things which have to be clearly laid down and clearly grasped, the way to the change, to this upward transference, this new divine birth, and the nature of the work or rather the spirit in which it has to be done, since the outward form of it need not at all change, although really its scope and aim become quite different. But these two things are practically the same, for the elucidation of one elucidates the other. The spirit of our action arises from the nature of our being and the inner foundation it has taken, but also this nature is itself affected by the trend and spiritual effect of our action; a very great change in the spirit of our works changes the nature of our being and alters the foundation it has taken; it shifts the centre of conscious force from which we act. If life and action were entirely illusory, as some would have it, if the Spirit had nothing to do with works or life, this would not be so; but the soul in us develops itself by life and works and, not indeed so much the action itself, but the way of our soul's inner force of working determines its relations to the Spirit. This is, indeed, the justification of Karmayoga as a practical means of the higher self-realisation.

We start from this foundation that the present inner life of man, almost entirely dependent as it is upon his vital and physical nature, only lifted beyond it by a limited play of mental energy, is not the whole of his possible existence, not even the whole of his present real existence. There is within him a hidden Self, of which his present nature is either only an outer appearance or is a partial dynamic result. The Gita seems throughout to admit its dynamic reality and not to adopt the severer view of the extreme Vedantists that it is only an appearance, a view which strikes at the very roots of all works and action. Its way of formulating this element of its philosophical thought – it might be done in a different way – is to admit the Sankhya distinction between the Soul and Nature, the power that knows, supports and informs and the power that works, acts, provides all the variations of instrument, medium and process. Only it takes the free and immutable Soul of the Sankhyas, calls it in Vedantic language the one immutable omnipresent Self or Brahman, and distinguishes it from this other soul involved in Nature, which is our mutable and dynamic being, the multiple soul of things, the basis of variation and personality. But in what then consists this action of Nature?

It consists in a power of process, Prakriti, which is the interplay of three fundamental modes of its working, three qualities, gunas. And what is the medium? It is the complex system of existence created by a graded evolution of the instruments of Prakriti, which, as they are reflected here in the soul's experience of her workings, we may call successively the reason and the ego, the mind, the senses and the elements of material energy which are the basis of its forms. These are all mechanical, a complex engine of Nature, *yantra*; and from our modern point of view we may say that they are all involved in material energy and manifest themselves in it as the soul in Nature becomes aware of itself by an upward evolution of each instrument, but in the inverse order to that which we have stated, matter first, then sensation, then mind, next reason, last spiritual consciousness. Reason, which is at first only preoccupied with the workings of Nature, may then detect their ultimate character, may see them only as a play of the three gunas in which the soul is entangled, may distinguish between the soul and these workings; then the soul gets a chance of disentangling itself and of going back to its original freedom and immutable existence. In Vedantic language, it sees the spirit, the being; it ceases to identify itself with the instruments and workings of Nature, with its becoming; it identifies itself with its true Self and being and recovers its immutable spiritual self-existence. It is then from this spiritual self-existence, according to the Gita, that it can freely and as the master of its being, the Ishwara, support the action of its becoming.

Looking only at the psychological facts on which these philosophical distinctions are founded – philosophy is only a way of formulating to ourselves intellectually in their essential significance the psychological and physical facts of existence and their relation to any ultimate reality that may exist – we may say that there are two lives we can lead, the life of the soul engrossed in the workings of its active nature, identified with its psychological and physical instruments, limited by them, bound by its personality, subject to Nature, and the life of the Spirit, superior to these things, large, impersonal, universal, free, unlimited, transcendent, supporting with an infinite equality its natural being and action, but exceeding them by its freedom and infinity. We may live in what is now our natural being or we may live in our greater and spiritual being. This is the first great distinction on which the Karmayoga of the Gita is founded.

The whole question and the whole method lie then in the liberation of the soul from the limitations of our present natural being. In our natural life the first dominating fact is our subjection to the forms of material Nature, the outward touches of things. These present themselves to our life through the senses, and the life through the senses immediately returns upon these objects to seize upon them and deal with them, desires, attaches itself, seeks for results. The mind in all its inner sensations, reactions, emotions, habitual ways of perceiving, thinking and feeling obeys this action of the senses; the reason too carried away by the mind gives itself up to this life of the senses, this life in which the inner being is subject to the externality of things and cannot for a moment really get above it or outside the circle of its action upon us and its psychological results and reactions within us. It cannot get beyond them because there is the principle of ego by which the reason differentiates the sum of the action of Nature upon our mind, will, sense, body from her action in other minds, wills, nervous organisms, bodies; and life to us means only the way she affects our ego and the way our ego replies to her touches. We know nothing else, we seem to be nothing else; the soul itself seems then only a separate mass of mind, will, emotional and nervous reception and reaction. We may enlarge our ego, identify ourselves with the family, clan, class, country, nation, humanity even, but still the ego remains in all these disguises the root of our actions, only it finds a larger satisfaction of its separate being by these wider dealings with external things.

What acts in us is still the will of the natural being seizing upon the touches of the external world to satisfy the different phases of its personality, and the will in this seizing is always a will of desire and passion and attachment to our works and their results, the will of Nature in us; our personal will, we say, but our ego personality is a creation of Nature, it is not and cannot be our free self, our independent being. The whole is the action of the modes of Nature. It may be a tamasic action, and then we have an inert personality subject to and satisfied with the mechanical round of things, incapable of any strong effort at a freer action and mastery. Or it may be the rajasic action, and then we have the restless active personality which throws itself upon Nature and tries to make her serve its needs and desires, but does not see that its apparent mastery is a servitude, since its needs and desires are those of Nature, and while we are subject to them, there can be for us no freedom. Or it may be a sattwic action, and then we have the enlightened personality which tries to live by reason or to realise some preferred ideal of good, truth or beauty; but this reason is still subject to the appearances of Nature and these ideals are only changing phases of our personality in which we find in the end no sure rule or permanent satisfaction. We are still carried on a wheel of mutation, obeying in our circlings through the ego some

Power within us and within all this, but not ourselves that Power or in union and communion with it. Still there is no freedom, no real mastery.

Yet freedom is possible. For that we have to get first away into ourselves from the action of the external world upon our senses; that is to say, we have to live inwardly and be able to hold back the natural running of the senses after their external objects. A mastery of the senses, an ability to do without all that they hanker after, is the first condition of the true soul-life; only so can we begin to feel that there is a soul within us which is other than the mutations of mind in its reception of the touches of outward things, a soul which in its depths goes back to something self-existent, immutable, tranquil, self-possessed, grandiose, serene and august, master of itself and unaffected by the eager runnings of our external nature. But this cannot be done so long as we are subject to desire. For it is desire, the principle of all our superficial life, which satisfies itself with the life of the senses and finds its whole account in the play of the passions. We must get rid then of desire and, that propensity of our natural being destroyed, the passions which are its emotional results will fall into quietude; for the joy and grief of possession and of loss, success and failure, pleasant and unpleasant touches, which entertain them, will pass out of our souls. A calm equality will then be gained. And since we have still to live and act in the world and our nature in works is to seek for the fruits of our works, we must change that nature and do works without attachment to their fruits, otherwise desire and all its results remain. But how can we change this nature of the doer of works in us? By dissociating works from ego and personality, by seeing through the reason that all this is only the play of the gunas of Nature, and by dissociating our soul from the play, by making it first of all the observer of the workings of Nature and leaving those works to the Power that is really behind them, the something in Nature which is greater than ourselves, not our personality, but the Master of the universe. But the mind will not permit all this; its nature is to run out after the senses and carry the reason and will with it. Then we must learn to still the mind. We must attain that absolute peace and stillness in which we become aware of the calm, motionless, blissful Self within us which is eternally untroubled and unaffected by the touches of things, is sufficient to itself and finds there alone its eternal satisfaction.

This Self is our self-existent being. It is not limited by our personal existence. It is the same in all existences, pervasive, equal to all things, supporting the whole universal action with its infinity, but unlimited by all that is finite, unmodified by the changings of Nature and personality. When this Self is revealed within us, when we feel its peace and stillness, we can grow into that; we can transfer the poise of our soul from its lower immergence in Nature and draw it back into the Self. We can do this by the force of the things we have attained, calm, equality, passionless impersonality. For as we grow in these things, carry them to their fullness, subject all our nature to them, we are growing into this calm, equal, passionless, impersonal, all-pervading Self. Our senses fall into that stillness and receive the touches of the world on us with a supreme tranquillity; our mind falls into stillness and becomes the calm, universal witness; our ego dissolves itself into this impersonal existence. All things we see in this self which we have become in ourself; and we see this self in all; we become one being with all beings in the spiritual basis of their existence. By doing works in this selfless tranquillity and impersonality, our works cease to be ours, cease to bind or trouble us with their reactions. Nature and her gunas weave the web of her works, but without affecting our griefless self-existent tranquillity. All is given up into that one equal and universal Brahman.

But here there are two difficulties. First, there seems to be an antinomy between this tranquil and immutable Self and the action of Nature. How then does the action at all exist or how can it continue once we have entered into the immutable Self-existence? Where in that is the will to works which would make the action of our nature possible? If we say with the Sankhya that the will is in Nature and not in the Self, still there must be a motive in Nature and the power in her to draw the soul into its workings by interest, ego and attachment, and when these things cease to reflect themselves in the soul-consciousness, her power ceases and the motive of works ceases with it. But the Gita does not accept this view, which seems indeed to necessitate the existence of many Purushas and not one universal Purusha, otherwise the separate experience of the soul and its separate liberation while millions of others are still involved, would not be intelligible. Nature is not a separate principle, but the power of the Supreme going forth in cosmic creation. But if the Supreme is only this immutable Self and the individual is only something that has gone forth from him in the Power, then the moment it returns and takes its poise in the self, everything must cease except the supreme unity and the supreme calm. Secondly, even if in some mysterious way action still continues, yet since the Self is equal to all things, it cannot matter whether works are done or, if they are done, it cannot matter what work is done. Why then this insistence on the most violent and disastrous form of action, this chariot, this battle, this warrior, this divine charioteer?

The Gita answers by presenting the Supreme as something greater even than the immutable Self, more comprehensive, one who is at once this Self and the Master of works in Nature. But he directs the works of Nature with the eternal calm, the equality, the superiority to works and personality which belong to the immutable. This, we may say, is the poise of being from which he directs works, and by growing into this we are growing into his being and into the poise of divine works. From this he goes forth as the Will and Power of his being in Nature, manifests himself in all existences, is born as Man in the world, is there in the heart of all men, reveals himself as the Avatar, the divine birth in man; and as man grows into his being, it is into the divine birth that he grows. Works must be done as a sacrifice to this Lord of our works, and we must by growing into the Self realise our oneness with him in our being and see our personality as a partial manifestation of him in Nature. One with him in being, we grow one with all beings in the universe and do divine works, not as ours, but as his workings through us for the maintenance and leading of the peoples.

This is the essential thing to be done, and once this is done, the difficulties which present themselves to Arjuna will disappear. The problem is no longer one of our personal actions, for that which makes our personality becomes a thing temporal and subordinate, the question is then only one of the workings of the divine Will through us in the universe. To understand that we must know what this supreme Being is in himself and in Nature, what the workings of Nature are and what they lead to, and the intimate relation between the soul in Nature and this supreme Soul, of which bhakti with knowledge is the foundation. The elucidation of these questions is the subject of the rest of the Gita.

Essays on the Gita
Second Series

PART I

THE SYNTHESIS OF WORKS, LOVE AND KNOWLEDGE

The Synthesis of Devotion and Knowledge[1]

The gita is not a treatise of metaphysical philosophy, in spite of the great mass of metaphysical ideas which arise incidentally in its pages; for here no metaphysical truth is brought into expression solely for its own sake. It seeks the highest truth for the highest practical utility, not for intellectual or even for spiritual satisfaction, but as the truth that saves and opens to us the passage from our present mortal imperfection to an immortal perfection. Therefore, after giving us in the first fourteen verses of this chapter a leading philosophical truth of which we stand in need, it hastens in the next sixteen verses to make an immediate application of it. It turns it into a first starting-point for the unification of works, knowledge and devotion – for the preliminary synthesis of works and knowledge by themselves has already been accomplished.

[1] Gita, VII. 15–28.

We have before us three powers, the Purushottama as the supreme truth of that into which we have to grow, the Self and the Jiva. Or, as we may put it, there is the Supreme, there is the impersonal spirit, and there is the multiple soul, timeless foundation of our spiritual personality, the true and eternal individual, *mamaivāṁśaḥ sanātanaḥ*. All these three are divine, all three are the Divine. The supreme spiritual nature of being, the Para Prakriti free from any limitation by the conditioning Ignorance, is the nature of the Purushottama. In the impersonal Self there is the same divine nature, but here it is in its state of eternal rest, equilibrium, inactivity, nivritti. Finally, for activity, for pravritti, the Para Prakriti becomes the multiple spiritual personality, the Jiva. But the intrinsic activity of this supreme Nature is always a spiritual, a divine working. It is force of the supreme divine Nature, it is the conscious will of the being of the Supreme that throws itself out in various essential and spiritual power of quality in the Jiva: that essential power is the swabhava of the Jiva. All act and becoming which proceed directly from this spiritual force are a divine becoming and a pure and spiritual action. Therefore it follows that in action the effort of the human individual must be to get back to his true spiritual personality and to make all his works flow from the power of its supernal Shakti, to develop action through the soul and the inmost intrinsic being, not through the mental idea and vital desire, and to turn all his acts into a pure outflowing of the will of the Supreme, all his life into a dynamic symbol of the Divine Nature.

But there is also this lower nature of the three gunas whose character is the character of the ignorance and whose action is the action of the ignorance, mixed, confused, perverted; it is the action of the lower personality, of the ego, of the natural and not of the spiritual individual. It is in order to recede from that false personality that we have to resort to the impersonal Self and make ourselves one with it. Then, freed so from the ego personality, we can find the relation of the true individual to the Purushottama. It is one with him in being, even though necessarily partial and determinative, because individual, in action and temporal manifestation of nature. Freed too from the lower nature we can realise the higher, the divine, the spiritual. Therefore, to act from the soul does not mean to act from the desire soul; for that is not the high intrinsic being, but only the lower natural and superficial appearance. To act in accordance with the intrinsic nature, the swabhava, does not mean to act out of the passions of the ego, to enact with indifference or with desire sin and virtue according to the natural impulses and the unstable play of the gunas. Yielding to passion, an active or an inert indulgence of sin is no way either to the spiritual quietism of the highest impersonality or to the spiritual activity of the divine individual who is to be a channel for the will of the supreme Person, a direct power and visible becoming of the Purushottama.

The Gita has laid it down from the beginning that the very first precondition of the divine birth, the higher existence is the slaying of rajasic desire and its children, and that means the exclusion of sin. Sin is the working of the lower nature for the crude satisfaction of its own ignorant, dull or violent rajasic and tamasic propensities in revolt against any high self-control and self-mastery of the nature by the spirit. And in order to get rid of this crude compulsion of the being by the lower Prakriti in its inferior modes we must have recourse to the highest mode of that Prakriti, the sattwic, which is seeking always for a harmonious light of knowledge and for a right rule of action. The Purusha, the soul within us which assents in Nature to the varying impulse of the gunas, has to give its sanction to that sattwic impulse and that sattwic will and temperament in our being which seeks after such a rule. The sattwic will in our nature has to govern us and not the rajasic and tamasic will. This is the meaning of all high reason in action as of all true ethical culture; it is the law of Nature in us striving to evolve from her lower and disorderly to her higher and orderly action, to act not in passion and ignorance with the result of grief and unquiet, but in knowledge and enlightened will with the result of inner happiness, poise and peace. We cannot get beyond the three gunas, if we do not first develop within ourselves the rule of the highest guna, sattwa.

'The evil-doers attain not to me,' says the Purushottama, 'souls bewildered, low in the human scale; for their knowledge is reft away from them by Maya and they resort to the nature of being of the Asura.' This bewilderment is a befooling of the soul in Nature by the deceptive ego. The evil-doer cannot attain to the Supreme because he is for ever trying to satisfy the idol ego on the lowest scale of human nature; his real God is this ego. His mind and will, hurried away in the activities of the Maya of the three gunas, are not instruments of the spirit, but willing slaves or self-deceived tools of his desires. He sees this lower nature only and not his supreme self and highest being or the Godhead within himself and in the world: he explains all existence to his will in the terms of ego and desire and serves only ego and desire. To serve ego and desire without aspiration to a higher nature and a higher law is to have the mind and the temperament of the Asura. A first necessary step upward is to aspire to a higher nature and a higher law, to obey a better rule than the rule of desire, to perceive and worship a nobler godhead than the ego or than any magnified image of the ego, to become a right thinker and a right doer. This too is not in itself enough; for even the sattwic man is subject to the bewilderment of the gunas, because he is still governed by wish and disliking, *icchā-dveṣa*. He moves within the circle of the forms of Nature and has not the highest, not the transcendental and integral knowledge. Still by the constant upward aspiration in his ethical aim he in the end gets rid of the obscuration of sin which is the obscuration of rajasic desire and passion and acquires a purified nature capable of deliverance from the rule of the triple Maya. By virtue alone, man cannot attain to the highest, but by virtue[2] he can develop a first

[2] Obviously, by the true inner *puṇya*, a sattwic clarity in thought, feeling, temperament, motive and conduct, not a merely conventional or social virtue.

capacity for attaining to it, *adhikāra*. For the crude rajasic or the dull tamasic ego is difficult to shake off and put below us; the sattwic ego is less difficult and at last, when it sufficiently subtilises and enlightens itself, becomes even easy to transcend, transmute or annihilate.

Man, therefore, has first of all to become ethical, *sukṛtī*, and then to rise to heights beyond any mere ethical rule of living, to the light, largeness and power of the spiritual nature, where he gets beyond the grasp of the dualities and its delusion, *dvandva-moha*. There he no longer seeks his personal good or pleasure or shuns his personal suffering or pain, for by these things he is no longer affected, nor says any longer, 'I am virtuous,' 'I am sinful,' but acts in his own high spiritual nature by the will of the Divine for the universal good.

It may be asked how is that devotion high and noble, *udāra*, which seeks God only for the worldly boons he can give or as a refuge in sorrow and suffering, and not the Divine for its own sake? Do not egoism, weakness, desire reign in such an adoration and does it not belong to the lower nature? Moreover, where there is not knowledge, the devotee does not approach the Divine in his integral all-embracing truth, *vāsudevaḥ sarvam iti*, but constructs imperfect names and images of the Godhead which are only reflections of his own need, temperament and nature, and he worships them to help or appease his natural longings. He constructs for the Godhead the name and form of Indra or Agni, of Vishnu or Shiva, of a divinised Christ or Buddha, or else some composite of natural qualities, an indulgent God of love and mercy, or a severe God of righteousness and justice, or an awe-inspiring God of wrath and terror and flaming punishments, or some amalgam of any of these, and to that he raises his altars without and in.

Thus by spiritual development devotion becomes one with knowledge. The Jiva comes to delight in the one Godhead – in the Divine known as all being and consciousness and delight and as all things and beings and happenings, known in Nature, known in the self, known for that which exceeds self and Nature. He is ever in constant union with him, nityayukta; his whole life and being are an eternal Yoga with the Transcendent than whom there is nothing higher, with the Universal besides whom there is none else and nothing else. On him is concentrated all his bhakti, *ekabhaktiḥ*, not on any partial godhead, rule or cult.

The Supreme Divine[1]

Already what has been said in the seventh chapter provides us with the starting-point of our new and fuller position and fixes it with sufficient precision. Substantially it comes to this that we are to move inwardly towards a greater consciousness and a supreme existence, not by a total exclusion of our cosmic nature, but by a higher, a spiritual fulfilment of all that we now essentially are. Only there is to be a change from our mortal imperfection to a divine perfection of being. The first idea on which this possibility is founded, is the conception of the individual soul in man as in its eternal essence and its original power a ray of the supreme Soul and Godhead, here a veiled manifestation of him, a being of his being, a consciousness of his consciousness, a nature of his nature, but in the obscurity of this mental and physical existence self-forgetful of its source, its reality, its true character. The second idea is that of the double nature of the Soul

[1] Gita, VII. 29–30, VIII.

in manifestation – the original nature in which it is one with its own true spiritual being, and the derived in which it is subject to the confusions of egoism and ignorance. The latter has to be cast away and the spiritual has to be inwardly recovered, fulfilled, made dynamic and active. Through an inner self-fulfilment, the opening of a new status, our birth into a new power, we return to the nature of the Spirit and re-become a portion of the Godhead from whom we have descended into this mortal figure of being.

There is here at once a departure from the general contemporary mind of Indian thought, a less negating attitude, a greater affirmation. In place of its obsessing idea of a self-annulment of Nature we get the glimpse of an ampler solution, the principle of a self-fulfilment in divine Nature. There is, even, at least a foreshadowing of the later developments of the religions of Bhakti. Our first experience of what is beyond our normal status, concealed behind the egoistic being in which we live, is still for the Gita the calm of a vast impersonal immutable self in whose equality and oneness we lose our petty egoistic personality and cast off in its tranquil purity all our narrow motives of desire and passion. But our second completer vision reveals to us a living Infinite, a divine immeasurable Being from whom all that we are proceeds and to which all that we are belongs, self and nature, world and spirit. When we are one with him in self and spirit, we do not lose ourselves but rather recover our true selves in him poised in the supremacy of this Infinite. And this is done at one and the same time by three simultaneous movements – an integral self-finding through works founded in his and our spiritual nature, an integral self-becoming through knowledge of the Divine Being in whom all exists and who is all, and – most sovereign and decisive movement of all – an integral self-giving through love and devotion of our whole being to this All and this Supreme, attracted to the Master of our works, to the Inhabitant of our hearts, to the continent of all our conscious existence. To him who is the source of all that we are, we give all that we are. Our persistent consecration turns into knowledge of him all our knowing and into light of his power all our action. The passion of love in our self-giving carries us up to him and opens the mystery of his deepest heart of being. Love completes the triple cord of the sacrifice, perfects the triune key of the highest secret, *uttamaṁ rahasyam*.

An integral knowledge in our self-giving is the first condition of its effective force. And therefore, we have first of all to know this Purusha in all the powers and principles of his divine existence, *tattvataḥ*, in the whole harmony of it, in its eternal essence and living process. But to the ancient thought all the value of this knowledge, *tattvajñāna*, lay in its power for release out of our mortal birth into the immortality of a supreme existence. The Gita therefore proceeds next to show how this liberation too in the highest degree is a final outcome of its own movement of spiritual self-fulfilment. The knowledge of the Purushottama, it says in effect, is the perfect knowledge of the Brahman. Those who have resort to Me as their refuge, *mām āśritya*, their divine light, their deliverer, receiver and harbourer of their souls, those who turn to Me in their spiritual effort towards release from age and death, from the mortal being and its limitations, says Krishna, come to know that Brahman and all the integrality of the spiritual nature and the entirety of Karma. And because they know Me and know at the same time the material and the divine nature of being and the truth of the Master of sacrifice, they keep knowledge of Me also in the critical moment of their departure from physical existence and have at that moment their whole consciousness in union with Me. Therefore, they attain to Me. No longer bound to the mortal existence, they reach the very highest status of the Divine quite as effectively as those who lose their separate personality in the impersonal and immutable Brahman. Thus, the Gita closes this important and decisive seventh chapter.

Here we have certain expressions which give us in their brief sum the chief essential truths of the manifestation of the supreme Divine in the cosmos. All the originative and effective aspects of it are there, all that concerns the soul in its return to integral self-knowledge. First there is that Brahman, *tad brahma*; *adhyātma*, second, the principle of the self in Nature; *adhibhūta* and *adhidaiva* next, the objective phenomenon and subjective phenomenon of being; *adhiyajña* last, the secret of the cosmic principle of works and sacrifice. I, the Purushottama (*māṁ viduḥ*), says in effect Krishna, I who am above all these things, must yet be sought and known through all together and by means of their relations, – that is the only complete way for the human consciousness which is seeking its path back towards Me.

But these terms in themselves are not at first quite clear or at least they are open to different interpretations, they have to be made precise in their connotation, and Arjuna the disciple at once asks for their elucidation. Krishna answers very briefly, nowhere does the Gita linger very long upon any purely metaphysical explanation; it gives only so much and in such a way as will make their truth just seizable for the soul to proceed on to experience. By that Brahman, a phrase which in the Upanishads is more than once used for the self-existent as opposed to the phenomenal being, the Gita intends, it appears, the immutable self-existence which is the highest self-expression of the Divine and on whose unalterable eternity all the rest, all that moves and evolves, is founded, *akṣaraṁ paramam*. By *adhyātma* it means *svabhāva*, the spiritual way and law of being of the soul in the supreme Nature. Karma, it says, is the name given to the creative impulse and energy, *visargaḥ*, which loses out things from this first essential self-becoming, this Swabhava, and effects, creates, works out under its influence the cosmic becoming of existences in Prakriti. By *adhibhūta* is to be understood all the result of mutable becoming, *kṣaro bhāvaḥ*. By *adhidaiva* is intended the Purusha, the soul in Nature, the subjective being who observes and enjoys as the object of his consciousness all that is this mutable becoming of his essential existence worked out here by Karma in Nature. By *adhiyajña*, the Lord of works and sacrifice, I mean, says Krishna, myself, the Divine, the Godhead, the Purushottama here secret in the body of all these embodied existences. All that is, therefore, falls within this formula.

The Gita immediately proceeds from this brief statement to work out the idea of the final release by knowledge which it has suggested in the last verse of the preceding chapter. It will return indeed upon its thought hereafter to give such ulterior light as is needed for action and inner realisation, and we may wait till then for a fuller knowledge of all that these terms indicate. But before we proceed farther, it is necessary to bring out as much of the connection between these things as we are justified in understanding from this passage itself and from what has gone before. For here is indicated the Gita's idea of the process of the cosmos. First there is the Brahman, the highest immutable self-existent being which all existences are behind the play of cosmic Nature in time and space and causality, *deśa-kalā-nimitta*. For by that self-existence alone time and space and causality are able to exist, and without that unchanging support omnipresent, yet indivisible they could not proceed to their divisions and results and measures. But of itself the immutable Brahman does nothing, causes nothing, determines nothing; it is impartial, equal, all-supporting, but does not select or originate. What then originates, what determines, what gives the divine impulsion of the Supreme? what is it that governs Karma and actively unrolls the cosmic becoming in Time out of the eternal being? It is Nature as Swabhava. The Supreme, the Godhead, the Purushottama is there and supports on his eternal immutability the action of his higher spiritual Shakti. He displays the divine Being, Consciousness, Will or Power, *yayedaṁ dhāryate jagat*: that is the Para Prakriti. The self-awareness of the Spirit in this supreme Nature perceives in the light of self-knowledge the dynamic idea, the authentic truth of whatever he separates in his own being and expresses it in the Swabhava, the spiritual nature of the Jiva. The inherent truth and principle of the self of each Jiva, that which works itself out in manifestation, the essential divine nature in all which remains constant behind all conversions, perversions, reversions, that is the Swabhava. All that is in the Swabhava is loosed out into cosmic Nature for her to do what she can with it under the inner eye of the Purushottama. Out of the constant *svabhāva*, out of the essential nature and self-principle of being of each becoming, she creates the varied mutations by which she strives to express it, unrolls all her changes in name and form, in time and space and those successions of condition developed one out of the other in time and space which we call causality, *nimitta*.

All this bringing out and continual change from state to state is Karma, is action of Nature, is the energy of Prakriti, the worker, the goddess of processes. It is first a loosing forth of the *svabhāva* into its creative action, *visargaḥ*. The creation is of existences in the becoming, *bhūta-karaḥ*, and of all that they subjectively or otherwise become, *bhāva-karaḥ*. All taken together, it is a constant birth of things in Time, *udbhava*, of which the creative energy of Karma is the principle. All this mutable becoming emerges by a combination of the powers and energies of Nature, *adhibhūta*, which constitutes the world and is the object of the soul's consciousness. In it all the soul is the enjoying and observing Deity in Nature; the divine powers of mind and will and sense, all the powers of its conscious being by which it reflects this working of Prakriti are its godheads, *adhidaiva*. This soul in Nature is therefore the *kṣara puruṣa*, it is the mutable soul, the eternal activity of the Godhead; the same soul in the Brahman drawn back from her is the *akṣara puruṣa*, the immutable self, the eternal silence of the Godhead. But in the form and body of the mutable being inhabits the supreme Godhead. Possessing at once the calm of the immutable existence and the enjoyment of the mutable action there dwells in man the Purushottama. He is not only remote from us in some supreme status beyond, but he is here too in the body of every being, in the heart of man and in Nature. There he receives the works of Nature as a sacrifice and awaits the conscious self-giving of the human soul: but always even in the human creature's ignorance and egoism he is the Lord of his swabhava and the Master of all his works, who presides over the law of Prakriti and Karma. From him the soul came forth into the play of Nature's mutations; to him the soul returns through immutable self-existence to the highest status of the Divine, *paraṁ dhāma*.

Man, born into the world, revolves between world and world in the action of Prakriti and Karma. Purusha in Prakriti is his formula: what the soul in him thinks, contemplates and acts, that always he becomes. All that he had been, determined his present birth; and all that he is, thinks, does in this life up to the moment of his death, determines what he will become in the worlds beyond and in lives yet to be. If birth is a becoming, death also is a becoming, not by any means a cessation. The body is abandoned, but the soul goes on its way, *tyaktvā kalevaram*. Much then depends on what he is at the critical moment of his departure. For whatever form of becoming his consciousness is fixed on at the time of death and has been full of that always in his mind and thought before death, to that form he must attain, since the Prakriti by Karma works out the soul's thoughts and energies and that is in real fact her whole business. Therefore, if the soul in the human being desires to attain to the status of the Purushottama, there are two necessities, two conditions which must be satisfied before that can be possible. He must have moulded towards that ideal his whole inner life in his earthly living; and he must be faithful to his aspiration and will in his departing. 'Whoever leaves his body and departs' says Krishna 'remembering me at his time of end, comes to my *bhāva*,' that of the Purushottama, my status of being. He is united with the original being of the Divine and that is the ultimate becoming of the soul, *paro bhāvaḥ*, the last result of Karma in its return upon itself and towards its source. The soul which has followed the play of cosmic evolution that veils here its essential spiritual nature, its original form of becoming, *svabhāva*, and has passed through all these other ways of becoming of its consciousness which are only its phenomena, *taṁ taṁbhāvam*, returns to that essential nature and, finding through this return its true self and spirit, comes to the original status of being which is from the point of view of the return a highest becoming, *mad-bhāvam*. In a certain sense we may say that it becomes God, since it unites itself with nature of the Divine in a last transformation of its own phenomenal nature and existence.

The Gita here lays a great stress on the thought and state of mind at the time of death, a stress which will with difficulty be understood if we do not recognise what may be called the self-creative power of the consciousness. What the thought, the inner regard, the faith, *śraddhā*, settles itself upon with a complete and definite insistence, into that our inner being tends to change. This tendency becomes a decisive force when we go to those higher spiritual and self-evolved experiences which are less dependent on external things than is our ordinary psychology, enslaved as that is to outward Nature. There we can see ourselves steadily becoming that on which we keep our minds fixed and to which we constantly aspire. Therefore, there any lapse of the thought, any infidelity of the memory means always a retardation of the change or some fall in its process and a going back towards what we were before – at least so long as we have not substantially and irrevocably fixed our new becoming. When we have done that, when we have made it normal to our experience, the memory of it remains self-existently because that now is the natural form of our consciousness. In the critical moment of passing from the mortal plane of living, the importance of our then state of consciousness becomes evident. But it is not a deathbed remembrance at variance with or insufficiently prepared by the whole tenor of our life and our past subjectivity that can have this saving power. The thought of the Gita here is not on a par with the indulgences and facilities of popular religion; it has nothing in common with the crude fancies that make the absolution and last unction of the priest, an edifying 'Christian' death after an unedifying profane life or the precaution or accident of a death in sacred Benares or holy Ganges a sufficient machinery of salvation. The divine subjective becoming on which the mind has to be fixed firmly in the moment of the physical death, *yaṁ smaran bhāvaṁ tyajati ante kalevaram*, must have been one into which the soul was at each moment growing inwardly during the physical life, *sadā tad-bhāva-bhāvitaḥ*. 'Therefore,' says the divine Teacher, 'at all times remember me and fight; for if thy mind and thy understanding are always fixed on and given up to Me, *mayi arpita-mano-buddhiḥ*, to Me thou shalt surely come. For it is by thinking always of him with a consciousness united with him in an undeviating Yoga of constant practice that one comes to the divine and supreme Purusha.'

We arrive here at the first description of this supreme Purusha – the Godhead who is even more and greater than the Immutable and to whom the Gita gives subsequently the name of Purushottama. He too in his timeless eternity is immutable and far beyond all this manifestation and here in Time there dawns on us only faint glimpses of his being conveyed through many varied symbols and disguises, *avyakto akṣaraḥ*. Still he is not merely a featureless or indiscernible existence, *anirdeśyam*; or he is indiscernible only because he is subtler than the last subtlety of which the mind is aware and because the form of the Divine is beyond our thought, *aṇor aṇīyāṁsam acintya-rūpam*. This supreme Soul and Self is the Seer, the Ancient of Days and in his eternal self-vision and wisdom the Master and Ruler of all existence who sets in their place in his being all things that are, *kaviṁ purāṇam anuśāsitāraṁ sarvasya dhātāram*. This supreme Soul is the immutable self-existent Brahman of whom the Veda-knowers speak, and this is that into which the doers of askesis enter when they have passed beyond the affections of the mind of mortality and for the desire of which they practise the control of the bodily passions.[2] That eternal reality is the highest step, place, foothold of being (*padam*); therefore, is it the supreme goal of the soul's movement in Time, itself no movement but a status original, sempiternal and supreme, *paraṁ sthānam ādyam*.

The Gita describes the last state of the mind of the Yogin in which he passes from life through death to this supreme divine existence. A motionless mind, a soul armed with the strength of Yoga, a union with God in bhakti – the union by love is not here superseded by the featureless unification through knowledge, it remains to the end a part of the supreme force of the Yoga – and the life-force entirely drawn up and set between the brows in the seat

[2] The language here is taken bodily from the Upanishads.

of mystic vision. All the doors of the sense are closed, the mind is shut in into the heart, the life-force taken up out of its diffused movement into the head, the intelligence concentrated in the utterance of the sacred syllable OM and its conceptive thought in the remembrance of the supreme Godhead, *mām anusmaran*. That is the established Yogic way of going, a last offering up of the whole being to the Eternal, the Transcendent. But still, that is only a process; the essential condition is the constant undeviating memory of the Divine in life, even in action and battle – *mām anusmara yudhya ca* – and the turning of the whole act of living into an uninterrupted Yoga, *nitya-yoga*. 'Whoever does that, finds Me easy to attain,' says the Godhead; he is the great soul who reaches the supreme perfection.

The condition to which the soul arrives when it thus departs from life is supracosmic. The highest heavens of the cosmic plan are subject to a return to rebirth; but there is no rebirth imposed on the soul that departs to the Purushottama. Therefore, whatever fruit can be had from the aspiration of knowledge to the indefinable Brahman, is acquired also by this other and comprehensive aspiration through knowledge, works and love to the self-existent Godhead who is the Master of works and the Friend of mankind and of all beings. To know him so and so to seek him does not bind to rebirth or to the chain of Karma; the soul can satisfy its desire to escape permanently from the transient and painful condition of our mortal being. And the Gita here, in order to make more precise to the mind this circling round of births and the escape from it, adopts the ancient theory of the cosmic cycles which became a fixed part of Indian cosmological notions. There is an eternal cycle of alternating periods of cosmic manifestation and non-manifestation, each period called respectively a day and a night of the creator Brahma, each of equal length in Time, the long aeon of his working which endures for a thousand ages, the long aeon of his sleep of another thousand silent ages. At the coming of the Day all manifestations are born into being out of the unmanifest, at the coming of the Night all vanish or are dissolved into it. Thus, all these existences alternate helplessly in the cycle of becoming and non-becoming; they come into the becoming again and again, *bhūtvā bhūtvā*, and they go back constantly into the unmanifest. But this unmanifest is not the original divinity of the Being; there is another status of his existence, *bhāvo 'nyo*, a supracosmic unmanifest beyond this cosmic non-manifestation, which is eternally self-seated, is not an opposite of this cosmic status of manifestation but far above and unlike it, changeless, eternal, not forced to perish with the perishing of all these existences. 'He is called the unmanifest immutable, him they speak of as the supreme soul and status, and those who attain to him return not; that is my supreme place of being, *paramaṁ dhāma*.' For the soul attaining to it has escaped out of the cycle of cosmic manifestation and non-manifestation.

Whether we entertain or we dismiss this cosmological notion – which depends on the value we are inclined to assign to the knowledge of 'the knowers of day and night,'

– the important thing is the turn the Gita gives to it. One might easily imagine that this eternally unmanifested Being whose status seems to have nothing to do with the manifestation or the non-manifestation, must be the ever undefined and indefinable Absolute, and the proper way to reach him is to get rid of all that we have become in the manifestation, not to carry up to it our whole inner consciousness in a combined concentration of the mind's knowledge, the heart's love, the Yogic will, the vital life-force. Especially, bhakti seems inapplicable to the Absolute who is void of every relation, *avyavahārya*. 'But' insists the Gita – although this condition is supracosmic and although it is eternally unmanifest – still 'that supreme Purusha has to be won by a bhakti which turns to him alone in whom all beings exist and by whom all this world has been extended in space.' In other words, the supreme Purusha is not an entirely relation-less Absolute aloof from our illusions, but he is the Seer, Creator and Ruler of the worlds, *kavim anuśāsitāram*, *dhātāram*, and it is by knowing and by loving Him as the One and the All, *vāsudevaḥ sarvam iti*, that we ought by a union with him of our whole conscious being in all things, all energies, all actions to seek the supreme consummation, the perfect perfection, the absolute release.

Then there comes a more curious thought which the Gita has adopted from the mystics of the early Vedanta. It gives the different times at which the Yogin has to leave his body according as he wills to seek rebirth or to avoid it. Fire and light and smoke or mist, the day and the night, the bright fortnight of the lunar month and the dark, the northern solstice and the southern, these are the opposites. By the first in each pair the knowers of the Brahman go to the Brahman; but by the second the Yogin reaches the 'lunar light' and returns subsequently to human birth. These are the bright and the dark paths, called the path of the gods and the path of the fathers in the Upanishads, and the Yogin who knows them is not misled into any error. Whatever psycho-physical fact or else symbolism there may be behind this notion[3] – it comes down from the age of the mystics who saw in every physical thing an effective symbol of the psychological and who traced everywhere an interaction and a sort of identity of the outward with the inward, light and knowledge, the fiery principle and the spiritual energy – we need observe only the turn by which the Gita closes the passage: 'Therefore, at all times be in Yoga.'

For that is after all the essential, to make the whole being one with the Divine, so entirely and in all ways one as to be naturally and constantly fixed in union, and thus to make all living, not only thought and meditation, but action, labour, battle, a remembering of God. 'Remember me and fight,' means not to lose the ever-present thought of the Eternal for one single moment in the clash of the temporal which normally absorbs our minds, and that

[3] Yogic experience shows in fact that there is a real psycho-physical truth, not indeed absolute in its application, behind this idea, viz., that in the inner struggle between the powers of the Light and the powers of the Darkness, the former tend to have a natural prevalence in the bright periods of the day or the year, the latter in the dark periods, and this balance may last until the fundamental victory is won.

seems sufficiently difficult, almost impossible. It is entirely possible indeed only if the other conditions are satisfied. If we have become in our consciousness oneself with all, one self which is always to our thought the Divine, and even our eyes and our other senses see and sense the Divine Being everywhere so that it is impossible for us at any time at all to feel or think of anything as that merely which the unenlightened sense perceives, but only as the Godhead at once concealed and manifested in that form, and if our will is one in consciousness with a supreme will and every act of will, of mind, of body is felt to come from it, to be its movement, instinct with it or identical, then what the Gita demands can be integrally done. The remembrance of the Divine Being becomes no longer an intermittent act of the mind, but the natural condition of our activities and in a way the very substance of the consciousness. The Jiva has become possessed of its right and natural, its spiritual relation to the Purushottama and all our life is a Yoga, an accomplished and yet an eternally self-accomplishing oneness.

The Secret of Secrets

All the truth that has developed itself at this length step by step, each bringing forward a fresh aspect of the integral knowledge and founding on it some result of spiritual state and action, has now to take a turn of immense importance. The Teacher therefore takes care first to draw attention to the decisive character of what he is about to say, so that the mind of Arjuna may be awakened and attentive. For he is going to open his mind to the knowledge and sight of the integral Divinity and lead up to the vision of the eleventh book, by which the warrior of Kurukshetra becomes conscious of the author and upholder of his being and action and mission, the Godhead in man and the world, whom nothing in man and the world limits or binds, because all proceeds from him, is a movement in his infinite being, continues and is supported by his will, is justified in his divine self-knowledge, has him always for its origin, substance and end. Arjuna is to become aware of himself as existing only in God and as acting only by the power within him, his workings only an instrumentality of the divine action, his egoistic consciousness only a veil and to his ignorance a misrepresentation of the real being within him which is an immortal spark and portion of the supreme Godhead.

This vision is to remove whatever doubt may still remain within his mind; it is to make him strong for the action from which he has shrunk, but to which he is irrevocably commanded and can no more recoil from it – for to recoil would be the negation and denial of the divine will and sanction within him already expressed in his individual consciousness but soon to assume the appearance of the greater cosmic sanction. For now, the world Being appears to him as the body of God ensouled by the eternal Time-spirit and with its majestic and dreadful voice missions him to the crash of the battle. He is called by it to the liberation of his spirit, to the fulfilment of his action in the cosmic mystery, and the two – liberation and action – are to be one movement. His intellectual doubts are clearing away as a greater light of self-knowledge and the knowledge of God and Nature is being unfolded before him. But intellectual clarity is not enough; he must see with the inner sight illumining his blind outward human vision, so that he may act with the consent of his whole being, with a perfect faith in all his members, *śraddhā*, with a perfect devotion to the Self of his self and the Master of his being and to the same Self of the world and Master of all being in the universe.

All that has gone before laid the foundations of the knowledge or prepared its first necessary materials or scaffolding, but now the full frame of the structure is to be placed before his unsealed vision. All that is to come after will have its great importance because it will analyse parts of this frame, show in what this or that in it consists; but in substance the integral knowledge of the Being who is speaking to him is to be now unveiled to his eyes so that he cannot choose but see. What has gone before showed him that he is not bound fatally to the knot of the ignorance and egoistic action in which he had hitherto remained contented till its partial solutions sufficed no longer to satisfy his mind bewildered by the conflict of opposite appearances that make up the action of the world and his heart troubled by the entanglement of his works from which he feels himself unable to escape except by renunciation of life and works. He has been shown that there are two opposed ways of working and living, one in the ignorance of the ego, one in the clear self-knowledge of a divine being. He may act with desire, with passion, an ego driven by the qualities of the lower Nature, subject to the balance of virtue and sin, joy and sorrow, preoccupied with the fruits and consequences of his works, success and defeat, good result and evil result, bound on the world machine, caught up in a great tangle of action and inaction and perverse action which perplex the heart and mind and soul of man with their changing and contrary masks and appearances. But he is not utterly tied down to the works of the ignorance; he may do if he will the works of knowledge. He may act here as the higher thinker, the knower, the Yogin, the seeker of freedom first and afterwards the liberated spirit. To perceive that great possibility and to keep his will and intelligence fixed on the knowledge and self-vision which will realise and make it effectual, is the path of escape from his sorrow and bewilderment, the way out of the human riddle.

There is a spirit within us calm, superior to works, equal, not bound in this external tangle, surveying it as its supporter, source, immanent witness, but not involved in it. Infinite, containing all, one self in all, it surveys impartially the whole action of nature and it sees that it is only the action of Nature, not its own action. It sees that the ego and its will and its intelligence are all a machinery of Nature and that all their activities are determined by the complexity of her triple modes and qualities. The eternal spirit itself is free from these things. It is free from them because it knows; it knows that Nature and ego and the personal being of all these creatures do not make up the whole of existence. For existence is not merely a glorious or a vain, a wonderful or a dismal panorama of a constant mutation of becoming. There is something eternal, immutable, imperishable, a timeless self-existence; that is not affected by the mutations of Nature. It is their impartial witness, neither affecting nor affected, neither acting nor acted upon, neither virtuous nor sinful, but always pure, complete, great and unwounded. Neither grieving nor rejoicing at all that afflicts and attracts the egoistic being, it is the friend of none, the enemy of none, but one equal self of all. Man is not now conscious of this self, because he is wrapped up in his outward-going mind, because he will not learn or has not learned to live within; he does not detach himself, draw back from his action and observe it as the work of Nature. Ego is the obstacle, the linchpin of the wheel of delusion, the loss of the ego in the soul's self the first condition of freedom. To become spirit, no longer merely a mind and ego, is the opening word of this message of liberation.

Arjuna has been therefore called upon first to give up all desire of the fruits of his works and become simply the desireless impartial doer of whatever has to be done – leaving the fruit to whatever power may be the master of the cosmic workings. For he very evidently is not the master; it is not for the satisfaction of his personal ego that Nature was set upon her ways, not for the fulfilment of his desires and preferences that the universal Life is living, not for the justification of his intellectual opinions, judgments and standards that the universal Mind is working, nor is it to that petty tribunal that it has to refer its cosmic aims or its terrestrial method and purposes. These claims can only be made by the ignorant souls who live in their personality and see everything from that poor and narrow standpoint. He must stand back first from his egoistic demand on the world and work only as one among the millions who contributes his share of effort and labour to a result determined not by himself, but by the universal action and purpose. But he has to do yet more, he has to give up the idea of being the doer and to see, freed from all personality, that it is the universal intelligence, will, mind, life that is at work in him and in all others. Nature is the universal worker; his works are hers, even as the fruits of her works in him are part of the grand sum of result guided by a greater Power than his own. If he can do these two things spiritually, then the tangle and bondage of his works will fall far away from him; for the whole knot of that bondage lay in his egoistic demand and participation. Passion and sin and personal joy and grief will fade away from his soul, which will now live within, pure, large, calm, equal to all persons and all things. Action will produce no subjective reaction and will leave no stain nor any mark on his spirit's purity and peace. He will have the inner joy, rest, ease and inalienable bliss of a free unaffected being. Neither within nor without will he have any more the old little personality, for he will feel consciously one self and spirit with all, even as his outer nature will have become to his consciousness an inseparable part of the universal mind, life and will. His separative egoistic personality will have been taken up and extinguished in the impersonality of spiritual being; his separative egoistic nature will be unified with the action of cosmic Nature.

But this liberation is dependent on two simultaneous, but not yet reconciled perceptions, the clear vision of spirit and the clear vision of Nature. This is not the scientific and intelligent detachment which is quite possible even to the materialistic philosopher who has some clear vision of Nature alone, but not the perception of his own soul and self-being. Nor is it the intellectual detachment of the idealistic sage who escapes from the more limiting and disturbing forms of his ego by a luminous use of the reason. This is a larger, more living, more perfect spiritual detachment which comes by a vision of the Supreme who is more than Nature and greater than mind and reason. But even this detachment is only the initial secret of freedom and of the clear vision of knowledge, it is not the whole clue to the divine mystery – for by itself it would leave Nature unexplained and the natural active part of being isolated from the spiritual and quietistic self-existence. The divine detachment must be the foundation for a divine participation in Nature which will replace the old egoistic participation, the divine quietism must support a divine activism and kinetism. This truth which the Teacher has had in view all along and therefore insisted on the sacrifice of works, the recognition of the Supreme as the master of our works and the doctrine of the Avatar and the divine birth, has yet been at first kept subordinate to the primary necessity of a quietistic liberation. Only the truths which lead to spiritual calm, detachment, equality and oneness, in a word, to the perception and becoming of the immutable self, have been fully developed and given their largest amplitude of power and significance. The other great and necessary truth, its complement, has been left in a certain obscurity of a lesser or relative light; it has been hinted at constantly, but not as yet developed. Now in these successive chapters it is being rapidly released into expression.

Throughout Krishna, the Avatar, the Teacher, the charioteer of the human soul in the world-action, has been preparing the revelation of the secret of himself, Nature's deepest secret. He has kept one note always sounding across his preparatory strain and insistently coming in as a warning and prelude of the larger ultimate harmony of his integral Truth. That note was the idea of a supreme Godhead which dwells within man and Nature, but is greater than man and Nature, is found by impersonality of the self, but of which impersonal self is not the whole significance. We now see the meaning of that strong recurring insistence. It was this one Godhead, the same in universal self and man and Nature who through the voice of the Teacher in the chariot was preparing for his absolute claim to the whole being of the awakened seer of things and doer of works. 'I who am within thee,' he was saying, 'I who am here in this human body, I for whom all exists, acts, strives, am at once the secret of the self-existent spirit and of the cosmic action. This 'I' is the greater I of whom the largest human personality is only a partial and fragmentary manifestation, Nature itself only an inferior working. Master of the soul, master of all the works of the cosmos, I am the one Light, the sole Power, the only Being. This Godhead within thee is the Teacher, the Sun, the lifter of the clear blaze of knowledge in which thou becomest aware of the difference between thy immutable self and thy mutable nature. But look beyond the light itself to its source; then shalt thou know the supreme Soul in which is recovered the spiritual truth of personality and Nature. See then the oneself in all beings that thou mayst see me in all beings; see all beings in one spiritual self and reality, because that is the way to see all beings in me; know one Brahman in all that thou mayst see God who is the supreme Brahman. Know thyself, be thyself that thou mayst be united with me of whom this timeless self is the clear light or the transparent curtain. I the Godhead am the highest truth of self and spirit.'

Arjuna has to see that the same Godhead is the higher truth too not only of self and spirit but of Nature and his own personality, the secret at once of the individual and the universe. That was the Will universal in Nature, greater than the acts of Nature which proceed from him, to whom belong her actions and man's and the fruits of them. Therefore, has he to do works as a sacrifice, because that is the truth of his works and of all works. Nature is the worker and not ego, but Nature is only a power of the Being who is the sole master of all her works and energisms and of all the aeons of the cosmic sacrifice. Therefore, since his works are that Being's, he has to give up all his actions to the Godhead in him and the world by whom they are done in the divine mystery of Nature. This is the double condition of the divine birth of the soul, of its release from the mortality of the ego and the body into the spiritual and eternal – knowledge first of one's timeless immutable self and union through it with the timeless Godhead, but knowledge too of that which lives behind the riddle of cosmos, the Godhead in all existences and their workings. Thus, only can we aspire through the offering of all our nature and being to a living union with the One who has become in Time and Space all that is. Here is the place of bhakti in the scheme of the Yoga of an integral self-liberation. It is an adoration and aspiration towards that which is greater than imperishable self or changing Nature. All knowledge then becomes an adoration and aspiration, but all works too become an adoration and aspiration. Works of nature and freedom of soul are unified in this adoration and become one self-uplifting to the one Godhead. The final release, a passing away from the lower nature to the source of the higher spiritual becoming, is not an extinction of the soul – only its form of ego becomes extinct – but a departure of our whole self of knowledge, will and love to dwell no longer in his universal, but in his supracosmic reality, a fulfilment, not an annullation.

Necessarily, to make this knowledge clear to the mind of Arjuna, the divine Teacher sets out by removing the source of two remaining difficulties, the antinomy between the impersonal self and the human personality and the antinomy between the self and Nature. While these two antinomies last, the Godhead in Nature and man remains obscure, irrational and unbelievable. Nature has been represented as the mechanical bondage of the gunas, the soul as the egoistic being subject to that bondage. But if that be all their truth, they are not and cannot be divine. Nature, ignorant and mechanical, cannot be a power of God; for divine Power must be free in its workings, spiritual in its origin, spiritual in its greatness. The soul bound and egoistic in Nature, mental, vital, physical only, cannot be a portion of the Divine and itself a divine being; for such a divine being must be itself of the very nature of the Divine, free, spiritual, self-developing, self-existent, superior to mind, life and body. Both these difficulties and the obscurities they bring in are removed by one illumining ray of truth. Mechanical Nature is only a lower truth; it is the formula of an inferior phenomenal action. There is a higher which is the spiritual and that is the nature of our spiritual personality, our true person. God is at once impersonal and personal. His impersonality is to our psychological realisation an infinite of timeless being, consciousness, bliss of existence; his personality represents itself here as a conscious power of being, a conscious centre of knowledge and will and the joy of multiple self-manifestation. We are that one impersonality in the static essence of our being; we are each of us the multitude of that essential power in our spiritual person. But the distinction is only for the purposes of self-manifestation; the divine impersonality is, when one goes behind it, at the same time infinite He, a supreme soul and spirit. It is the great 'I,' *so aham*, I am He, from which all personality and nature proceed and disport themselves here diversely in the appearance of an impersonal world. Brahman is all this that is, says the Upanishad, for Brahman is one self which sees itself in four successive positions of consciousness. Vasudeva, the eternal Being, is all, says the Gita. He is the Brahman, consciously supports and originates all from his higher spiritual nature, consciously here becomes all things in a nature of intelligence, mind, life and sense and objective phenomenon of material existence. The Jiva is he in that spiritual nature of the Eternal, his eternal multiplicity, his self-vision from many centres of conscious self-power. God, Nature and Jiva are the three terms of existence, and these three are one being.

How does this Being manifest himself in cosmos? First as the immutable timeless self-omnipresent and all-supporting which is in its eternity being and not becoming. Then, held in that being there is an essential power or spiritual principle of self-becoming, *svabhāva*, through which by spiritual self-vision it determines and expresses, creates by liberation all that is latent or contained in its own existence. The power or the energy of that self-becoming looses forth into universal action, Karma, all that is thus determined in the spirit. All creation is this action, is this working of the essential nature, is Karma. But it is developed here in a mutable Nature of intelligence, mind, life, sense and form-objectivity of material phenomenon actually cut off from the absolute light and limited by the Ignorance. All its workings become there a sacrifice of the soul in Nature to the supreme Soul secret within her, and the supreme Godhead dwells therefore in all as the Master of their sacrifice, whose presence and power govern it and whose self-knowledge and delight of being receive it. To know this is to have the right knowledge of the universe and the vision of God in the cosmos and to find out the door of escape from the Ignorance. For this knowledge, made effective for man by the offering up of his works and all his consciousness to the Godhead in all, enables him to return to his spiritual existence and through it to the supracosmic Reality eternal and luminous above this mutable Nature.

This truth is the secret of being which the Gita is now going to apply in its amplitude of result for our inner life and our outer works. What it is going to say is the most secret thing of all.[1] It is the knowledge of the whole Godhead, *samagraṁ mām*, which the Master of his being

[1] Gita, IX. 1–3

has promised to Arjuna, that essential knowledge attended with the complete knowledge of it in all its principles which will leave nothing yet to be known. The whole knot of the ignorance which has bewildered his human mind and has made his will recoil from his divinely appointed work, will have been cut entirely asunder. This is the wisdom of all wisdoms, the secret of all secrets, the king-knowledge, the king-secret. It is a pure and supreme light which one can verify by direct spiritual experience and see in oneself as the truth: it is the right and just knowledge, the very law of being. It is easy to practise when one gets hold of it, sees it, tries faithfully to live in it.

But faith is necessary; if faith is absent, if one trusts to the critical intelligence which goes by outward facts and jealously questions the revelatory knowledge because that does not square with the divisions and imperfections of the apparent nature and seems to exceed it and state something which carries us beyond the first practical facts of our present existence, its grief, its pain, evil, defect, undivine error and stumbling, *aśubham*, then there is no possibility of living out that greater knowledge. The soul that fails to get faith in the higher truth and law, must return into the path of ordinary mortal living subject to death and error and evil: it cannot grow into the Godhead which it denies. For this is a truth which has to be lived – and lived in the soul's growing light, not argued out in the mind's darkness. One has to grow into it, one has to become it; that is the only way to verify it. It is only by an exceeding of the lower self that one can become the real divine self and live the truth of our spiritual existence. All the apparent truths one can oppose to it are appearances of the lower Nature. The release from the evil and the defect of the lower Nature, *aśubham*, can only come by accepting a higher knowledge in which all this apparent evil becomes convinced of ultimate unreality, is shown to be a creation of our darkness. But to grow thus into the freedom of the divine Nature one must accept and believe in the Godhead secret within our present limited nature. For the reason why the practice of this Yoga becomes possible and easy is that in doing it we give up the whole working of all that we naturally are into the hands of that inner divine Purusha. The Godhead works out the divine birth in us progressively, simply, infallibly, by taking up our being into his and by filling it with his own knowledge and power, *jñānadīpena bhāsvatā*; he lays hands on our obscure ignorant nature and transforms it into his own light and wideness. What with entire faith and without egoism we believe in and impelled by him will to be, the God within will surely accomplish. But the egoistic mind and life we now and apparently are, must first surrender itself for transmutation into the hands of that inmost secret Divinity within us.

The Supreme Word of the Gita

We have now got to the inmost kernel of the Gita's Yoga, the whole living and breathing centre of its teaching. We can see now quite clearly that the ascent of the limited human soul when it withdraws from the ego and the lower nature into the immutable Self calm, silent and stable, was only a first step, an initial change. And now too we can see why the Gita from the first insisted on the Ishwara, the Godhead in the human form, who speaks always of himself, '*aham, mām*,' as of some great secret and omnipresent Being, lord of all the worlds and master of the human soul, one who is greater even than that immutable self-existence which is still and unmoved for ever and abides for ever untouched by the subjective and objective appearances of the natural universe.

All Yoga is a seeking after the Divine, a turn towards union with the Eternal. According to the adequacy of our perception of the Divine and the Eternal will be the way of the seeking, the depth and fullness of the union and the integrality of the realisation. Man, the mental being, approaches the Infinite through his finite mind and has to open some near gate of this finite upon that Infinite. He seeks for some conception on which his mind is able to seize, selects some power of his nature which by force of an absolute self-heightening can reach out and lay its touch on the infinite Truth that in itself is beyond his mental comprehension. Some face of that infinite Truth – for, because it is infinite, it has numberless faces, words of its meaning, self-suggestions – he attempts to see, so that by attaching himself to it he can arrive through direct experience to the immeasurable reality it figures. However narrow the gate may be, he is satisfied if it offers some prospect into the wideness which attracts him, if it sets him on the way to the fathomless profundity and unreachable heights of that which calls to his spirit. And as he approaches it, so it receives him, *ye yathā māṁ prapadyante*.

Philosophic mind attempts to attain to the Eternal by an abstractive knowledge. The business of knowledge is to comprehend and for the finite intellect that means to define and determine. But the only way to determine the indeterminable is by some kind of universal negation, *neti neti*. Therefore, the mind proceeds to exclude from the conception of the Eternal all that offers itself as limitable by the senses and the heart and the understanding. An entire opposition is made between the Self and the not-self, between an eternal, immutable, indefinable self-existence and all forms of existence – between Brahman and Maya, between the ineffable Reality and all that undertakes to express, but cannot express the Ineffable – between

Karma and Nirvana, between the ever continuous but ever impermanent action and conception of the universal Energy and some absolute ineffable supreme Negation of its action and conception which is empty of all life and mentality and dynamic significance. That strong drive of knowledge towards the Eternal leads away from everything that is transient. It negates life in order to return to its source, cuts away from us all that we seem to be in order to get from it to the nameless and impersonal reality of our being. The desires of the heart, the works of the will and the conceptions of the mind are rejected; even in the end knowledge itself is negated and abolished in the Identical and Unknowable. By the way of an increasing quietude ending in an absolute passivity the Maya-created soul or the bundle of associations we call ourselves enters into annihilation of its idea of personality, makes an end of the lie of living, disappears into Nirvana.

But this difficult abstractive method of self-negation, however it may draw to it some exceptional natures, cannot satisfy universally the embodied soul in man, because it does not give an outlet to all the straining of his complex nature towards the perfect Eternal. Not only his abstracting contemplative intellect but his yearning heart, his active will, his positive mind in search of some Truth to which his existence and the existence of the world is a manifold key, have their straining towards the Eternal and Infinite and seek to find in it their divine Source and the justification of their being and their nature. From this need arise the religions of love and works, whose strength is that they satisfy and lead Godwards the most active and developed powers of our humanity, for only by starting from these can knowledge be effective. Even Buddhism with its austere and uncompromising negation both of subjective self and objective things had still to found itself initially on a divine discipline of works and to admit as a substitute for bhakti the spiritualised emotionalism of a universal love and compassion, since so only could it become an effective way for mankind, a truly liberating religion. Even illusionist Mayavada with its ultralogical intolerance of action and the creations of mentality had to allow a provisional and practical reality to man and the universe and to God in the world in order to have a first foothold and a feasible starting-point; it had to affirm what it denied in order to give some reality to man's bondage and to his effort for liberation.

But the weakness of the kinetic and the emotional religions is that they are too much absorbed in some divine Personality and in the divine values of the finite. And, even when they have a conception of the infinite Godhead, they do not give us the full satisfaction of knowledge because they do not follow it out into its most ultimate and supernal tendencies. These religions fall short of a complete absorption in the Eternal and the perfect union by identity – and yet to that identity in some other way, if not in the abstractive, since there all oneness has its basis, the spirit that is in man must one day arrive. On the other hand, the weakness of a contemplative quietistic spirituality is that it arrives at this result by a too absolute abstraction and in the end, it turns into a nothing or a fiction the human soul whose aspiration was yet all the time the whole sense of this attempt at union; for without the soul and its aspiration liberation and union could have no meaning. The little that this way of thinking recognises of his other powers of existence, it relegates to an inferior preliminary action which never arrives at any full or satisfying realisation in the Eternal and Infinite. Yet these things too which it restricts unduly, the potent will, the strong yearning of love, the positive light and all-embracing intuition of the conscious mental being are from the Divine, represent essential powers of him and must have some justification in their Source and some dynamic way of self-fulfilment in him. No God-knowledge can be integral, perfect or universally satisfying which leaves unfulfilled their absolute claim, no wisdom utterly wise which in its intolerant asceticism of search negates or in the pride of pure knowledge belittles the spiritual reality behind these ways of the Godhead.

The idea of the Divine on which the Gita insists as the secret of the whole mystery of existence, the knowledge that leads to liberation, is one that bridges the opposition between the cosmic procession in Time and a supracosmic eternity without denying either of them or taking anything from the reality of either. It harmonises the pantheistic, the theistic and the highest transcendental terms of our spiritual conception and spiritual experience. The Divine is the unborn Eternal who has no origin; there is and can be nothing before him from which he proceeds, because he is one and timeless and absolute. 'Neither the gods nor the great Rishis know any birth of me. . . He who knows me as the unborn without origin...' are the opening utterances of this supreme word. And it gives the high promise that this knowledge, not limiting, not intellectual, but pure and spiritual, for the form and nature, if we can use such language, of this transcendental Being, his *svarūpa*, are necessarily unthinkable by the mind, *acintyarūpa*.

But there is another supreme reality of the Infinite that must also be recognised as an indispensable element of the liberating knowledge. This reality is that of the transcendent down look as well as the close immanent presence of the divine government of the universe. The Supreme who becomes all creation, yet infinitely transcends it, is not a will-less cause aloof from his creation. He is not an aloof and indifferent Witness who waits impassively for all to abolish itself or return to its unmoved original principle. He is the mighty lord of the worlds and peoples, *loka-maheśvara*, and governs all not only from within but from above, from his supreme transcendence. Unaffected by its oppositions, unbound by his creation, exceeding, yet intimately related to this Nature and closely one with her creatures, their Spirit, Self, highest Soul, Lord, Lover, Friend, Refuge, he is ever leading them from within them and from above through the mortal appearances of ignorance and suffering and sin and evil, ever leading each through his nature and all through universal Nature towards a supreme light and bliss and immortality and transcendence. This is the fullness of the liberating knowledge. It is a knowledge of the Divine within us and in the world as at the same time a transcendent Infinite.

This knowledge translated into the affective, emotional, temperamental plane becomes a calm love and intense adoration of the original and transcendental Godhead above us, the ever-present Master of all things here, God in man, God in Nature. It is at first a wisdom of the intelligence, the *buddhi*; but that is accompanied by a moved spiritualised state of the affective nature, *bhāva*. This change of the heart and mind is the beginning of a total change of all the nature. A new inner birth and becoming prepares us for oneness with the supreme object of our love and adoration, *madbhāvāya*. There is an intense delight of love in the greatness and beauty and perfection of this divine Being now seen everywhere in the world and above it, *prīti*. The whole consciousness becomes full of the Godhead and replete with his answering consciousness; the whole life flows into one sea of bliss-experience.

The Theory of the Vibhuti

The importance of this chapter of the Gita is very much greater than appears at first view or to an eye of prepossession which is looking into the text only for the creed of the last transcendence and the detached turning of the human soul away from the world to a distant Absolute. The message of the Gita is the gospel of the Divinity in man who by force of an increasing union unfolds himself out of the veil of the lower Nature, reveals to the human soul his cosmic spirit, reveals his absolute transcendences, reveals himself in man and in all beings. The potential outcome here of this union, this divine Yoga, man growing towards the Godhead, the Godhead manifest in the human soul and to the inner human vision, is our liberation from limited ego and our elevation to the higher nature of a divine humanity. For dwelling in this greater spiritual nature and not in the mortal weft, the tangled complexity of the three gunas, man, one with God by knowledge, love and will and the giving up of his whole being into the Godhead, is able indeed to rise to the absolute Transcendence, but also to act upon the world, no longer in ignorance, but in the right relation of the individual to the Supreme, in the truth of the Spirit, fulfilled in immortality, for God in the world and no longer for the ego. To call Arjuna to this action, to make him aware of the being and power that he is and of the Being and Power whose will acts through him, is the purpose of the embodied Godhead. To this end the divine Krishna is his charioteer; to this end there came upon him that great discouragement and deep dissatisfaction with the lesser human motives of his work; to substitute for them the larger spiritual motive this revelation is given to him in the supreme moment of the work to which he has been appointed. The vision of the World-Purusha and the divine command to action is the culminating point to which he was being led. That is already imminent; but without the knowledge now given to him through the Vibhuti-Yoga it would not bring with it its full meaning.

The mystery of the world-existence is in part revealed by the Gita. In part, for who shall exhaust its infinite depths or what creed or philosophy say that it has enlightened in a narrow space or shut up in a brief system all the significance of the cosmic miracle? But so far as is essential for the Gita's purpose, it is revealed to us. We have the way of the origination of the world from God, the immanence of the Divine in it and its immanence in the Divine, the essential unity of all existence, the relation of the human soul obscured in Nature to the Godhead, its awakening to self-knowledge, its birth into a greater consciousness, its ascension into its own spiritual heights. But when this new self-vision and consciousness have been acquired in place of the original ignorance, what will be the liberated man's view of the world around him, his attitude towards the cosmic manifestation of which he has now the central secret? He will have first the knowledge of the unity of existence and the regarding eye of that knowledge. He will see all around him as souls and forms and powers of the one divine Being. Henceforward, that vision will be the starting-point of all the inward and outward operations of his consciousness; it will be the fundamental seeing, the spiritual basis of all his actions. He will see all things and every creature living, moving and acting in the One, contained in the divine and eternal Existence. But he will also see that One as the Inhabitant in all, their Self, the essential Spirit within them without whose secret presence in their conscious nature they could not at all live, move or act and without whose will, power, sanction or sufferance not one of their movements at any moment would be in the least degree possible. Themselves too, their soul, mind, life and physical mould he will see only as a result of the power, will and force of this one Self and Spirit. All will be to him a becoming of this one universal Being. Their consciousness he will see to be derived entirely from its consciousness, their power and will to be drawn from and dependent on its power and will, their partial phenomenon of nature to be a resultant from its greater divine Nature, whether in the immediate actuality of things it strikes the mind as a manifestation or a disguise, a figure or a disfigurement of the Godhead. No untoward or bewildering appearance of things will in any smallest degree diminish or conflict with the completeness of this vision. It is the essential foundation of the greater consciousness into which he has arisen, it is the indispensable light that has opened around him and the one perfect way of seeing, the one Truth that makes all others possible.

But the world is only a partial manifestation of the Godhead, it is not itself that Divinity. The Godhead is infinitely greater than any natural manifestation can be. By his very infinity, by its absolute freedom he exists beyond all possibility of integral formulation in any scheme of worlds or extension of cosmic Nature, however wide, complex, endlessly varied this and every world may seem to us – *nāsti anto vistarasya me* – however to our finite view infinite. Therefore, beyond cosmos the eye of the liberated spirit will see the utter Divine. Cosmos he will see as a figure drawn from the Divinity who is beyond all figure, a constant minor term in the absolute existence. Every relative and finite he will see as a figure of the divine Absolute and Infinite, and both beyond all finites and through each finite he will arrive at that alone, see always that beyond each phenomenon and natural creature and relative action and every quality and every happening; looking at each of these things and beyond it, he will find in the Divinity its spiritual significance.

These things will not be to his mind intellectual concepts or this attitude to the world simply a way of thinking or a pragmatic dogma. For if his knowledge is conceptual only, it is a philosophy, an intellectual construction, not a spiritual knowledge and vision, not a spiritual state of consciousness. The spiritual seeing of God and world is not ideative only, not even mainly or primarily ideative. It is direct experience and as real, vivid, near, constant, effective, intimate as to the mind its sensuous seeing and feeling of images, objects and persons. It is only the physical mind that thinks of God and spirit as an abstract conception which it cannot visualise or represent to itself except by words and names and symbolic images and fictions. Spirit sees spirit, the divinised consciousness sees God as directly and more directly, as intimately and more intimately than bodily consciousness sees matter. It sees, feels, thinks, senses the Divine. For to the spiritual consciousness all manifest existence appears as a world of spirit and not a world of matter, not a world of life, not a world even of mind; these other things are to its view only God-thought, God-force, God-form. That is what the Gita means by living and acting in Vasudeva, *mayi vartate*. The spiritual consciousness is aware of the Godhead with that close knowledge by identity which is so much more tremendously real than any mental perception of the thinkable or any sensuous experience of the sensible. It is so aware even of the Absolute who is behind and beyond all world-existence and who originates and surpasses it and is for ever outside its vicissitudes. And of the immutable self of this Godhead that pervades and supports the world's mutations with his unchanging eternity, this consciousness is similarly aware, by identity, by the oneness of this self with our own timeless unchanging immortal spirit. It is aware again in the same manner of the divine Person who knows himself in all these things and persons and becomes all things and persons in his consciousness and shapes their thoughts and forms and governs their actions by his immanent will. It is intimately conscious of God absolute, God as self, God as spirit, soul and nature. Even this external Nature it knows by identity and self-experience, but an identity freely admitting variation, admitting relations, admitting greater and lesser degrees of the action of the one power of existence. For Nature is God's power of various self-becoming, *ātma-vibhūti*.

But this spiritual consciousness of world-existence will not see Nature in the world as the normal mind of man sees it in the ignorance or only as it is in the effects of the ignorance. All in this Nature that is of the ignorance, all that is imperfect or painful or perverse and repellent, does not exist as an absolute opposite of the nature of the Godhead, but goes back to something behind itself, goes back to a saving power of spirit in which it can find its own true being and redemption. There is an original and originating Supreme Prakriti, in which the divine power and will to be enjoys its own absolute quality and pure revelation. There is found the highest, there the perfect energy of all the energies we see in the universe. That is what presents itself to us as the ideal nature of the Godhead, a nature of absolute knowledge, absolute power and will, absolute love and delight. And all the infinite variations of its quality and energy, *ananta-guṇa, agaṇana-śakti*, are there wonderfully various, admirably and spontaneously harmonised free self-formulations of this absolute wisdom and will and power and delight and love. All is there a many-sided untrammelled unity of infinites. Each energy, each quality is in the ideal divine nature pure, perfect, self-possessed, harmonious in its action; nothing there strives for its own separate limited self-fulfilment, all act in an inexpressible oneness. There all dharmas, all laws of being – dharma, law of being, is only characteristic action of divine energy and quality, *guṇa-karma* – are one free and plastic dharma. The one divine Power of being[1] works with an immeasurable liberty and, tied to no single excluding law, not limited by any binding system, rejoices in her own play of infinity and never falters in her truth of self-expression perfect for ever.

But in the universe in which we live, there is a separating principle of selection and differentiation. There we see each energy, each quality which comes out for expression labouring as if for its own hand, trying to get as much self-expression as it can in whatever way it can, and accommodating somehow as best or as worst it may that effort with the concomitant or rival effort of other energies and qualities for their separate self-expression. The Spirit, the Divine dwells in this struggling world-nature and imposes on it a certain harmony by the inalienable law of the inner secret oneness on which the action of all these powers is based. But it is a relative harmony which seems to result from an original division, to emerge

[1] *tapas*, *cit-śakti*.

from and subsist by the shock of divisions and not from an original oneness. Or at least the oneness seems to be suppressed and latent, not to find itself, never to put off its baffling disguises. And in fact, it does not find itself till the individual being in this world-nature discovers in himself the higher divine Prakriti from whom this lesser movement is a derivation. Nevertheless, the qualities and energies at work in the world, operating variously in man, animal, plant, inanimate thing, are, whatever forms they may take, always divine qualities and energies. All energies and qualities are powers of the Godhead. Each comes from the divine Prakriti there, works for its self-expression in the lower Prakriti here, increases its potency of affirmation and actualised values under these hampering conditions, and as it reaches its heights of self-power, comes near to the visible expression of the Divinity and directs itself upward to its own absolute in the supreme, the ideal, the divine Nature. For each energy is being and power of the Godhead and the expansion and self-expression of energy is always the expansion and expression of the Godhead.

One might even say that at a certain point of intensity each force in us, force of knowledge, force of will, force of love, force of delight, can result in an explosion which breaks the shell of the lower formulation and liberates the energy from its separative action into union with the infinite freedom and power of the divine Being. A highest Godward tension liberates the mind through an absolute seeing of knowledge, liberates the heart through an absolute love and delight, liberates the whole existence through an absolute concentration of will towards a greater existence. But the percussion and the delivering shock come by the touch of the Divine on our actual nature which directs the energy away from its normal limited separative action and objects towards the Eternal, Universal and Transcendent, orientates it towards the infinite and absolute Godhead. This truth of the dynamic omnipresence of the divine Power of being is the foundation of the theory of the Vibhuti.

The infinite divine Shakti is present everywhere and secretly supports the lower formulation, *parā prakṛtir me yayā dhāryate jagat*, but it holds itself back, hidden in the heart of each natural existence, *sarvabhūtānāṁ hṛddeśe*, until the veil of Yogamaya is rent by the light of knowledge. The spiritual being of man, the Jiva, possesses the divine Nature. He is a manifestation of God in that Nature, *parā prakṛtir jīvā-bhūtā*, and he has latent in him all the divine energies and qualities, the light, the force, the power of being of the Godhead. But in this inferior Prakriti in which we live, the Jiva follows the principle of selection and finite determination, and there, whatever nexus of energy, whatever quality or spiritual principle he brings into birth with him or brings forward as the seed of his self-expression, becomes an operative portion of his swabhava, his law of self-becoming, and determines his swadharma, his law of action. And if that were all, there would be no perplexity or difficulty; the life of man would be a luminous unfolding of godhead. But this lower energy of our world is a nature of ignorance, of egoism, of the three gunas. Because this is a nature of egoism, the Jiva conceives of himself as the separative ego: he works out his self-expression egoistically as a separative will to be in conflict as well as in association with the same will to be in others. He attempts to possess the world by strife and not by unity and harmony; he stresses an ego-centric discord. Because this is a nature of ignorance, a blind seeing and an imperfect or partial self-expression, he does not know himself, does not know his law of being, but follows it instinctively under the ill-understood compulsion of the world-energy, with a struggle, with much inner conflict, with a very large possibility of deviation. Because this is a nature of the three gunas, this confused and striving self-expression takes various forms of incapacity, perversion or partial self-finding. Dominated by the guna of tamas, the mode of darkness and inertia, the power of being works in a weak confusion, a prevailing incapacity, an unaspiring subjection to the blind mechanism of the forces of the Ignorance. Dominated by the guna of rajas, the mode of action, desire and possession, there is a struggle, there is an effort, there is a growth of power and capacity, but it is stumbling, painful, vehement, misled by wrong notions, methods and ideals, impelled to a misuse, corruption and perversion of right notions, methods or ideals and prone, especially, to a great, often an enormous exaggeration of the ego. Dominated by the guna of sattwa, the mode of light and poise and peace, there is a more harmonious action, a right dealing with the nature, but right only within the limits of an individual light and a capacity unable to exceed the better forms of this lower mental will and knowledge.

To escape from this tangle, to rise beyond the ignorance, the ego and the gunas is the first real step towards divine perfection. By that transcendence the Jiva finds his own divine nature and his true existence.

The liberated eye of knowledge in the spiritual consciousness does not in its outlook on the world see this struggling lower Nature alone. If we perceive only the apparent outward fact of our nature and others' nature, we are looking with the eye of the ignorance and cannot know God equally in all, in the sattwic, the rajasic, the tamasic creature, in God and Titan, in saint and sinner, in the wise man and the ignorant, in the great and in the little, in man, animal, plant and inanimate existence. The liberated vision sees three things at once as the whole occult truth of the natural being. First and foremost, it sees the divine Prakriti in all, secret, present, waiting for evolution; it sees her as the real power in all things, that which gives its value to all this apparent action of diverse quality and force, and it reads the significance of these latter phenomena not in their own language of ego and ignorance, but in the light of the divine Nature. Therefore, it sees too, secondly, the differences of the apparent action in Deva and Rakshasa, man and beast and bird and reptile, good and wicked, ignorant and learned, but as action of divine quality and energy under these conditions, under these masks. It is not deluded by the mask, but detects behind every mask the Godhead. It observes the perversion or the imperfection, but it pierces to the truth of the spirit behind, it discovers it even in the perversion and imperfection self-blinded, struggling to find itself, groping through various forms of self-expression and experience towards complete self-knowledge, towards its own infinite and absolute. The liberated eye does not lay undue stress on the perversion and imperfection, but is able to see all with a complete love and charity in the heart, a complete understanding in the intelligence, a complete equality in the spirit. Finally, it sees the upward urge of the striving powers of the Will to be towards Godhead; it respects, welcomes, encourages all high manifestations of energy and quality, the flaming tongues of the Divinity, the mounting greatnesses of soul and mind and life in their intensities uplifted from the levels of the lower nature towards heights of luminous wisdom and knowledge, mighty power, strength, capacity, courage, heroism, benignant sweetness and ardour and grandeur of love and self-giving, preeminent virtue, noble action, captivating beauty and harmony, fine and godlike creation. The eye of the spirit sees and marks out the rising godhead of man in the great Vibhuti.

This is a recognition of the Godhead as Power, but power in its widest sense, power not only of might, but of knowledge, will, love, work, purity, sweetness, beauty. The Divine is being, consciousness and delight, and in the world, all throws itself out and finds itself again by energy of being, energy of consciousness and energy of delight; this is a world of the works of the divine Shakti. That Shakti shapes herself here in innumerable kinds of beings and each of them has its own characteristic powers of her force. Each power is the Divine himself in that form, in the lion as in the hind, in the Titan as in the God, in the inconscient sun that flames through ether as in man who thinks upon earth. The deformation given by the gunas is the minor, not really the major aspect; the essential thing is the divine power that is finding self-expression. It is the Godhead who manifests himself in the great thinker, the hero, the leader of men, the great teacher, sage, prophet, religious founder, saint, lover of man, the great poet, the great artist, the great scientist, the ascetic self-tamer, the tamer of things and events and forces. The work itself, the high poem, the perfect form of beauty, the deep love, the noble act, the divine achievement is a movement of godhead; it is the Divine in manifestation.

This is a truth which all ancient cultures recognised and respected, but one side of the modern mind has singular repugnances to the idea, sees in it a worship of mere strength and power, an ignorant or self-degrading hero-worship or a doctrine of the Asuric superman. Certainly, there is an ignorant way of taking this truth, as there is an ignorant way of taking all truths; but it has its proper place, its indispensable function in the divine economy of Nature. The Gita puts it in that right place and perspective. It must be based on the recognition of the divine self in all men and all creatures; it must be consistent with an equal heart to the great and the small, the eminent and the obscure manifestation. God must be seen and loved in the ignorant, the humble, the weak, the vile, the outcaste. In the Vibhuti himself it is not, except as a symbol, the outward individual that is to be thus recognised and set high, but the one Godhead who displays himself in the power. But this does not abrogate the fact that there is an ascending scale in manifestation and that Nature mounts upward in her degrees of self-expression from her groping, dark or suppressed symbols to the first visible expressions of the Godhead. Each great being, each great achievement is a sign of her power of self-exceeding and a promise of the final, the supreme exceeding. Man himself is a superior degree of natural manifestation to the beast and reptile, though in both there is the one equal Brahman. But man has not reached his own highest heights of self-exceeding and meanwhile every hint of a greater power of the Will to be in him must be recognised as a promise and an indication. Respect for the divinity in man, in all men, is not diminished, but heightened and given a richer significance by lifting our eyes to the trail of the great Pioneers who lead or point him by whatever step of attainment towards supermanhood.

Arjuna himself is a Vibhuti; he is a man high in the spiritual evolution, a figure marked out in the crowd of his contemporaries, a chosen instrument of the divine Narayana, the Godhead in humanity. In one place the Teacher speaking as the supreme and equal Self of all declares that there is none dear to him, none hated, but in others he says that Arjuna is dear to him and his bhakta and therefore guided and safe in his hands, chosen for the vision and the knowledge. There is here only an apparent inconsistency. The Power as the self of the cosmos is equal to all, therefore to each being he gives according to the workings of his nature; but there is also a personal relation of the Purushottama to the human being in which he is especially near to the man who has come near to him. All these heroes and men of might who have joined in battle on the plain of Kurukshetra are vessels of the divine Will and through each he works according to his nature but behind the veil of his ego. Arjuna has reached that point when the veil can be rent and the embodied Godhead can reveal the mystery of his workings to his Vibhuti. It is even essential that there should be the revelation. He is the instrument of a great work, a work terrible in appearance but necessary for a long step forward in the march of the race, a decisive movement in its struggle towards the kingdom of the Right and the Truth, *dharmarājya*. The history of the cycles of man is a progress towards the unveiling of the Godhead in the soul and life of humanity; each high event and stage of it is a divine manifestation. Arjuna, the chief instrument of the hidden Will, the great protagonist, must become the divine man capable of doing the work consciously as the action of the Divine. So only can that action become psychically alive and receive its spiritual import and its light and power of secret significance. He is called to self-knowledge; he must see God as the Master of the universe and the origin of the world's creatures and happenings, all as the Godhead's self-expression in Nature, God in all, God in himself as man and as Vibhuti, God in the lownesses of being and on its heights, God on the topmost summits, man too upon heights as the Vibhuti and climbing to the last summits in the supreme liberation and union. Time in its creation and destruction must be seen by him as the figure of the Godhead in its steps – steps that accomplish the cycles of the cosmos on whose spires of movement the divine spirit in the human body rises doing God's work in the world as his Vibhuti to the supreme transcendences. This knowledge has been given; the Time-figure of the Godhead is now to be revealed and from the million mouths of that figure will issue the command for the appointed action to the liberated Vibhuti.

PART II

THE SUPREME SECRET

Above the Gunas[1]

The distinctions between the Soul and Nature rapidly drawn in the verses of the thirteenth chapter by a few decisive epithets, a few brief but packed characterisations of their separate power and functioning, and especially the distinction between the embodied soul subjected to the action of Nature by its enjoyment of her gunas, qualities or modes and the Supreme Soul which dwells enjoying the gunas, but not subject because it is itself beyond them, are the basis on which the Gita rests its whole idea of the liberated being made one in the conscious law of its existence with the Divine.

To be immortal was never held in the ancient spiritual teaching to consist merely in a personal survival of the death of the body: all beings are immortal in that sense and it is only the forms that perish. The souls that do not arrive at liberation, live through the returning aeons; all exist involved or secret in the Brahman during the

[1] Gita, XIV.

dissolution of the manifest worlds and are born again in the appearance of a new cycle. Pralaya, the end of a cycle of aeons, is the temporary disintegration of a universal form of existence and of all the individual forms which move in its rounds, but that is only a momentary pause, a silent interval followed by an outburst of new creation, reintegration and reconstruction in which they reappear and recover the impetus of their progression. Our physical death is also a pralaya; the Gita will presently use the word in the sense of this death, *pralayaṁ yāti deha-bhṛt*, 'the soul bearing the body comes to a pralaya,' to a disintegration of that form of matter with which its ignorance identified its being and which now dissolves into the natural elements. But the soul itself persists and after an interval resumes in a new body formed from those elements its round of births in the cycle, just as after the interval of pause and cessation the universal Being resumes his endless round of the cyclic aeons. This immortality in the rounds of Time is common to all embodied spirits.

To be immortal in the deeper sense is something different from this survival of death and this constant recurrence. Immortality is that supreme status in which the Spirit knows itself to be superior to death and birth, not conditioned by the nature of its manifestation, infinite, imperishable, immutably eternal, immortal, because never being born it never dies. The divine Purushottama, who is the supreme Lord and supreme Brahman, possesses for ever this immortal eternity and is not affected by his taking up a body or by his continuous assumption of cosmic forms and powers because he exists always in this self-knowledge. But to arrive here at this greater spiritual immortality the embodied soul must cease to live according to the law of the lower nature; it must put on the law of the Divine's supreme way of existence which is in fact the real law of its own eternal essence. In the spiritual evolution of its becoming, no less than in its secret original being, it must grow into the likeness of the Divine.

But, again, the whole qualitative action of Nature, so infinitely intricate in its detail and variety, is figured as cast into the mould of three general modes of quality everywhere present, intertwined, almost inextricable, *sattva*, *rajas*, *tamas*. These modes are described in the Gita only by their psychological action in man, or incidentally in things such as food according as they produce a psychological or vital effect on human beings. If we look for a more general definition, we shall perhaps catch a glimpse of it in the symbolic idea of Indian religion which attributes each of these qualities respectively to one member of the cosmic Trinity, sattwa to the preserver Vishnu, rajas to the creator Brahma, tamas to the destroyer Rudra. Looking behind this idea for the rationale of the triple ascription, we might define the three modes or qualities in terms of the motion of the universal Energy as Nature's three concomitant and inseparable powers of equilibrium, kinesis and inertia. But that is only their appearance in terms of the external action of Force. It is otherwise if we regard consciousness and force as twin terms of the one Existence, always coexistent in the reality of being, however in the primal outward phenomenon of material Nature light of consciousness may seem to disappear in a vast action of nescient unillumined energy, while at an opposite pole of spiritual quiescence action of force may seem to disappear in the stillness of the observing or witness consciousness. On their psychological side the three qualities may be defined, tamas as Nature's power of nescience, rajas as her power of active seeking ignorance enlightened by desire and impulsion, sattwa as her power of possessing and harmonising knowledge.

The three qualitative modes of Nature are inextricably intertwined in all cosmic existence. Tamas, the principle of inertia, is a passive and inert nescience which suffers all shocks and contacts without any effort of mastering response and by itself would lead to a disintegration of the whole action of the energy and a radical dispersion of substance. But it is driven by the kinetic power of rajas and even in the nescience of Matter is met and embraced by an innate though unpossessed preserving principle of harmony and balance and knowledge. Material energy appears to be tamasic in its basic action, *jaḍa*, nescient, mechanic and in movement disintegrative. But it is dominated by a huge force and impulsion of mute rajasic kinesis which drives it, even in and even by its dispersion and disintegration, to build and create and again by a sattwic ideative element in its apparently inconscient force which is always imposing a harmony and preservative order on the two opposite tendencies. Rajas, the principle of creative endeavour and motion and impulsion in Prakriti, kinesis, *pravṛtti*, so seen in Matter, appears more evidently as a conscious or half-conscious passion of seeking and desire and action in the dominant character of Life, for that passion is the nature of all vital existence. And it would lead by itself in its own nature to a persistent but always mutable and unstable life and activity and creation without any settled result. But met on one side by the disintegrating power of tamas with death and decay and inertia, its ignorant action is on the other side of its functioning settled and harmonised and sustained by the power of sattwa, subconscient in the lower forms of life, more and more conscient in the emergence of mentality, most conscious in the effort of the evolved intelligence figuring as will and reason in the fully developed mental being. Sattwa, the principle of understanding knowledge and of according assimilation, measure and equilibrium, which by itself would lead only to some lasting concord of fixed and luminous harmonies, is in the motions of this world impelled to follow the mutable strife and action of the eternal kinesis and constantly overpowered or hedged in by the forces of inertia and nescience. This is the appearance of a world governed by the interlocked and mutually limited play of the three qualitative modes of Nature.

The Gita applies this generalised analysis of the universal Energy to the psychological nature of man in relation to his bondage to Prakriti and the realisation of spiritual freedom. Sattwa, it tells us, is by the purity of its quality a cause of light and illumination and by virtue of that purity it produces no disease or morbidity or suffering in the nature. When into all the doors in the body there comes a flooding of light, as if the doors and windows of a closed house were opened to sunshine, a light of understanding, perception and knowledge – when the intelligence is alert and illumined, the senses quickened, the whole mentality satisfied and full of brightness and the nervous being calmed and filled with an illumined ease and clarity, *prasāda*, one should understand that there has been a great increase and uprising of the sattwic guna in the nature. For knowledge and a harmonious ease and pleasure and happiness are the characteristic results of sattwa. The pleasure that is sattwic is not only that contentment which an inner clarity of satisfied will and intelligence brings with it, but all delight and content produced by the soul's possession of itself in light or by an accord or an adequate and truthful adjustment between the regarding soul and the surrounding Nature and her offered objects of desire and perception.

Rajas, again, the Gita tells us, has for its essence attraction of liking and longing. Rajas is a child of the attachment of the soul to the desire of objects; it is born from the nature's thirst for an unpossessed satisfaction. It is therefore full of unrest and fever and lust and greed and excitement, a thing of seeking impulsions, and all this mounts in us when the middle guna increases. It is the force of desire which motives all ordinary personal initiative of action and all that movement of stir and seeking and propulsion in our nature which is the impetus towards action and works, *pravṛtti*. Rajas, then, is evidently the kinetic force in the modes of Nature. Its fruit is the lust of action, but also grief, pain, all kinds of suffering; for it has no right possession of its object – desire in fact implies non-possession – and even its pleasure of acquired possession is troubled and unstable because it has not clear knowledge and does not know how to possess nor can it find the secret of accord and right enjoyment. All the ignorant and passionate seeking of life belongs to the rajasic mode of Nature.

Tamas, finally, is born of inertia and ignorance and its fruit too is inertia and ignorance. It is the darkness of tamas which obscures knowledge and causes all confusion and delusion. Therefore, it is the opposite of sattwa, for the essence of sattwa is enlightenment, *prakāśa*, and the essence of tamas is absence of light, nescience, *aprakāśa*. But tamas brings incapacity and negligence of action as well as the incapacity and negligence of error, inattention and misunderstanding or non-understanding; indolence, languor and sleep belong to this guna. Therefore, it is the opposite too of rajas; for the essence of rajas is movement and impulsion and kinesis, *pravṛtti*, but the essence of tamas is inertia, *apravṛtti*. Tamas is inertia of nescience and inertia of inaction, a double negative.

These three qualities of Nature are evidently present and active in all human beings and none can be said to be quite devoid of one and another or free from any one of the three; none is cast in the mould of one guna to the exclusion of the others. All men have in them in whatever degree the rajasic impulse of desire and activity and the sattwic boon of light and happiness, some balance, some adjustment of mind to itself and its surroundings and objects, and all have their share of tamasic incapacity and ignorance or nescience.

But these qualities are not constant in any man in the quantitative action of their force or in the combination of their elements; for they are variable and in a continual state of mutual impact, displacement and interaction. Now one leads, now another increases and predominates, and each subjects us to its characteristic action and consequences. Only by a general and ordinary predominance of one or other of the qualities can a man be said to be either sattwic or rajasic or tamasic in his nature; but this can only be a general and not an exclusive or absolute description. The three qualities are a triple power which by their interaction determine the character and disposition and through that and its various motions the actions of the natural man. But this triple power is at the same time a triple cord of bondage. 'The three gunas born of Prakriti' says the Gita 'bind in the body the imperishable dweller in the body.' In a certain sense we can see at once that there must be this bondage in following the action of the gunas; for they are all limited by their finite of quality and operation and cause limitation. Tamas is on both its sides an incapacity and therefore very obviously binds to limitation. Rajasic desire as an initiator of action is a more positive power, but still, we can see well enough that desire with its limiting and engrossing hold on man must always be a bondage. But how does sattwa, the power of knowledge and happiness, become a chain? It so becomes because it is a principle of mental nature, a principle of limited and limiting knowledge and of a happiness which depends upon right following or attainment of this or that object or else on particular states of the mentality, on a light of mind which can be only a more or less clear twilight. Its pleasure can only be a passing intensity or a qualified ease. Other is the infinite spiritual knowledge and the free self-existent delight of our spiritual being.

But then there is the question, how does our infinite and imperishable spirit, even involved in Nature, come thus to confine itself to the lower action of Prakriti and undergo this bondage and how is it not, like the supreme spirit of which it is a portion, free in its infinity even while enjoying the self-limitations of its active evolution? The reason, says the Gita, is our attachment to the gunas and to the result of their workings. Sattwa, it says, attaches to happiness, rajas attaches to action, tamas covers up the knowledge and attaches to negligence of error and inaction. Or again, 'sattwa binds by attachment to knowledge and attachment to happiness, rajas binds the embodied spirit by attachment to works, tamas binds by negligence and indolence and sleep.' In other words, the soul by attachment to the enjoyment of the gunas and their results concentrates its consciousness on the lower and outward action of life, mind and body in Nature, imprisons itself in the form of these things and becomes oblivious of its own greater consciousness behind in the spirit, unaware of the free power and scope of the liberating Purusha. Evidently, in order to be liberated and perfect, we must get back from these things, away from the gunas and above them and return to the power of that free spiritual consciousness above Nature.

But this would seem to imply a cessation of all doing, since all natural action is done by the gunas, by Nature through her modes. The soul cannot act by itself, it can only act through Nature and her modes. And yet the Gita, while it demands freedom from the modes, insists upon the necessity of action. Here comes in the importance of its insistence on the abandonment of the fruits; for it is the desire of the fruits which is the most potent cause of the soul's bondage and by abandoning it the soul can be free in action. Ignorance is the result of tamasic action, pain the consequence of rajasic works, pain of reaction, disappointment, dissatisfaction or transience, and therefore in attachment to the fruits of this kind of activity attended as they are with these undesirable accompaniments there is no profit. But of works rightly done the fruit is pure and sattwic, the inner result is knowledge and happiness. Yet attachment even to these pleasurable things must be entirely abandoned, first, because in the mind they are limited and limiting forms and, secondly, because, since sattwa is constantly entangled with and besieged by rajas and tamas which may at any moment overcome it, there is a perpetual insecurity in their tenure. But even if one is free from any clinging to the fruit, there may be an attachment to the work itself, either for its own sake, the essential rajasic bond, or owing to a lax subjection to the drive of Nature, the tamasic, or for the sake of the attracting rightness of the thing done, which is the sattwic attaching cause powerful on the virtuous man or the man of knowledge. And here evidently the resource is in that other injunction of the Gita, to give up the action itself to the Lord of works and be only a desireless and equal-minded instrument of his will. To see that the modes of Nature are the whole agency and cause of our works and to know and turn to that which is supreme above the gunas, is the way to rise above the lower nature. Only so can we attain to the movement and status of the Divine, *mad-bhāva*, by which free from subjection to birth and death and their concomitants, decay, old age and suffering, the liberated soul shall enjoy in the end immortality and all that is eternal.

But what, asks Arjuna, are the signs of such a man, what his action and how is he said even in action to be above the three gunas? The sign, says Krishna, is that equality of which I have so constantly spoken; the sign is that inwardly he regards happiness and suffering alike, gold and mud and stone as of equal value and that to him the pleasant and the unpleasant, praise and blame, honour and insult, the faction of his friends and the faction of his enemies are equal things. He is steadfast in a wise imperturbable and immutable inner calm and quietude. He initiates no action but leaves all works to be done by the gunas of Nature. Sattwa, rajas or tamas may rise or cease in his outer mentality and his physical movements with their results of enlightenment, of impulsion to works or of inaction and the clouding over of the mental and nervous being, but he does not rejoice when this comes or that ceases, nor on the other hand does he abhor or shrink from the operation or the cessation of these things. He has seated himself in the conscious light of another principle than the nature of the gunas and that greater consciousness remains steadfast in him, above these powers and unshaken by their motions like the sun above clouds to one who has risen into a higher atmosphere. He from that height sees that it is the gunas that are in process of action and that their storm and calm are not himself but only a movement of Prakriti; his self is immovable above and his spirit does not participate in that shifting mutability of things unstable. This is the impersonality of the Brahmic status; for that higher principle, that greater wide high-seated consciousness, *kūṭastha*, is the immutable Brahman.

But still there is evidently here a double status, there is a scission of the being between two opposites; a liberated spirit in the immutable Self or Brahman watches the action of an unliberated mutable Nature – Akshara and Kshara. Is there no greater status, no principle of more absolute perfection, or is this division the highest consciousness possible in the body, and is the end of Yoga to drop the mutable nature and the gunas born of the embodiment in Nature and disappear into the impersonality and everlasting peace of the Brahman? Is that *laya* or dissolution of the individual Purusha the greatest liberation? There is, it would seem, something else; for the Gita says at the close, always returning to this one final note, 'He also who loves and strives after Me with an undeviating love and adoration, passes beyond the three gunas and he too is prepared for becoming the Brahman.' This 'I' is the Purushottama who is the foundation of the silent Brahman and of immortality and imperishable spiritual existence and of the eternal dharma and of an utter bliss of happiness. There is a status then which is greater than the peace of the Akshara as it watches unmoved the strife of the gunas. There is a highest spiritual experience and foundation above the immutability of the Brahman, there is an eternal dharma greater than the rajasic impulsion to works, *pravṛtti*, there is an absolute delight which is untouched by rajasic suffering and beyond the sattwic happiness, and these things are found and possessed by dwelling in the being and power of the Purushottama. But since it is acquired by bhakti, its status must be that divine delight, Ananda, in which is experienced the union of utter love[2] and possessing oneness, the crown of bhakti. And to rise into that Ananda, into that imperishable oneness must be the completion of spiritual perfection and the fulfilment of the eternal immortalising dharma.

[2] *niratiśayapremāspadatvam ānandatattvam*

The Three Purushas[1]

The doctrine of the Gita from the beginning to the end converges on all its lines and through all the flexibility of its turns towards one central thought, and to that it is arriving in all its balancing and reconciliation of the disagreements of various philosophic systems and its careful synthetising of the truths of spiritual experience, lights often conflicting or at least divergent when taken separately and exclusively pursued along their outer arc and curve of radiation, but here brought together into one focus of grouping vision. This central thought is the idea of a triple consciousness, three and yet one, present in the whole scale of existence.

There is a spirit here at work in the world that is one in innumerable appearances. It is the developer of birth and action, the moving power of life, the inhabiting and associating consciousness in the myriad mutabilities of Nature; it is the constituting reality of all this stir in Time

[1] Gita, XV.

and Space; it is itself Time and Space and Circumstance. It is this multitude of souls in the worlds; it is the gods and men and creatures and things and forces and qualities and quantities and powers and presences. It is Nature, which is power of the Spirit, and objects, which are its phenomena of name and idea and form, and existences, who are portions and births and becomings of this single self-existent spiritual entity, the One, the Eternal. But what we see obviously at work before us is not this Eternal and his conscious Shakti, but a Nature which in the blind stress of her operations is ignorant of the spirit within her action. Her work is a confused, ignorant and limiting play of certain fundamental modes, qualities, principles of force in mechanical operation and the fixity or the flux of their consequences. And whatever soul comes to the surface in her action, is itself in appearance ignorant, suffering, bound to the incomplete and unsatisfying play of this inferior Nature. The inherent Power in her is yet other than what it thus seems to be; for, hidden in its truth, manifest in its appearances, it is the Kshara, the universal Soul, the spirit in the mutability of cosmic phenomenon and becoming, one with the Immutable and the Supreme. We have to arrive at the hidden truth behind its manifest appearances; we have to discover the Spirit behind these veils and to see all as the One, *vāsudevaḥ sarvam iti*, individual, universal, transcendent. But this is a thing impossible to achieve with any completeness of inner reality, so long as we live concentrated in the inferior Nature. For in this lesser movement Nature is an ignorance, a Maya;

she shelters the Divine within its folds and conceals him from herself and her creatures. The Godhead is hidden by the Maya of his own all-creating Yoga, the Eternal figured in transience, Being absorbed and covered up by its own manifesting phenomena. In the Kshara taken alone as a thing in itself, the mutable universal apart from the undivided Immutable and the Transcendent, there is no completeness of knowledge, no completeness of our being and therefore no liberation.

But then, there is another spirit of whom we become aware and who is none of these things, but self and self only. This Spirit is eternal, always the same, never changed or affected by manifestation, the one, the stable, a self-existence undivided and not even seemingly divided by the division of things and powers in Nature, inactive in her action, immobile in her motion. It is the Self of all and yet unmoved, indifferent, intangible, as if all these things which depend upon it were not-self, not its own results and powers and consequences, but a drama of action developed before the eye of an unmoved unparticipating spectator. For the mind that stages and shares in the drama is other than the Self which indifferently contains the action. This spirit is timeless, though we see it in Time; it is unextended in space, though we see it as if pervading space. We become aware of it in proportion as we draw back from out inward, or look behind the action and motion for something that is eternal and stable, or get away from time and its creation to the uncreated, away from phenomenon to being, from the personal to impersonality, from becoming to unalterable self-existence. This is the Akshara, the immutable in the mutable, the immobile in the mobile, the imperishable in things perishable. Or rather, since there is only an appearance of pervasion, it is the immutable, immobile and imperishable in which proceeds all the mobility of mutable and perishable things.

The Kshara spirit visible to us as all natural existence and the totality of all existences moves and acts pervadingly in the immobile and eternal Akshara. This mobile Power of Self acts in that fundamental stability of Self, as the second principle of material Nature, Vayu, with its contactual force of aggregation and separation, attraction and repulsion, supporting the formative force of the fiery (radiant, gaseous and electric) and other elemental movements, ranges pervadingly in the subtly massive stability of ether. This Akshara is the self higher than the buddhi – it exceeds even that highest subjective principle of Nature in our being, the liberating intelligence, through which man returning beyond his restless mobile mental to his calm eternal spiritual self is at last free from the persistence of birth and the long chain of action, of Karma. This self in its highest status, *paraṁ dhāma*, is an unmanifest beyond even the unmanifest principle of the original cosmic Prakriti, Avyakta, and, if the soul turns to this Immutable, the hold of cosmos and Nature falls away from it and it passes beyond birth to an unchanging eternal existence. These two then are the two spirits we see in the world; one emerges in front in its action, the other remains behind it steadfast in that perpetual silence from which the action comes and in which all actions cease and disappear into timeless being, Nirvana. *Dvāv imau puruṣ au loke kṣaraś cākṣara*.

The difficulty which baffles our intelligence is that these two seem to be irreconcilable opposites with no real nexus between them or any transition from the one to the other except by an intolerant movement of separation. The Kshara acts, or at least motives action, separately in the Akshara; the Akshara stands apart, self-centred, separate in its inactivity from the Kshara. At first sight it would almost seem better, more logical, more easy of comprehension, if we admitted with the Sankhyas an original and eternal duality of Purusha and Prakriti, if not even an eternal plurality of souls. Our experience of the Akshara would then be simply the withdrawal of each Purusha into himself, his turning away from Nature and therefore from all contact with other souls in the relations of existence; for each is self-sufficient and infinite and complete in his own essence. But after all the final experience is that of a unity of all beings which is not merely a community of experience, a common subjection to one force of Nature, but a oneness in the spirit, a vast identity of conscious being beyond all this endless variety of determination, behind all this apparent separativism of relative existence. The Gita takes its stand in that highest spiritual experience. It appears indeed to admit an eternal plurality of souls subject to and sustained by their eternal unity, for cosmos is for ever and manifestation goes on in unending cycles; nor does it affirm anywhere or use any expression that would indicate an absolute disappearance, *laya*, the annullation of the individual soul in the Infinite. But at the same time, it affirms with a strong insistence that the Akshara is the one self of all these many souls, and it is therefore evident that these two spirits are a dual status of one eternal and universal existence. That is a very ancient doctrine; it is the whole basis of the largest vision of the Upanishads – as when the Isha tells us that Brahman is both the mobile and the immobile, is the One and the Many, is the Self and all existences, *ātman*, *sarvabhūtāni*, is the Knowledge and the Ignorance, is the eternal unborn status and also the birth of existences, and that to dwell only on one of these things to the rejection of its eternal counterpart is a darkness of exclusive knowledge or a darkness of ignorance. It too insists like the Gita that man must know and must embrace both and learn of the Supreme in his entirety – *samagraṁ mām*, as the Gita puts it – in order to enjoy immortality and live in the Eternal. The teaching of the Gita and this side of the teaching of the Upanishads are so far at one; for they look at and admit both sides of the reality and still arrive at identity as the conclusion and the highest truth of existence.

But this greater knowledge and experience, however true and however powerful in its appeal to our highest seeing, has still to get rid of a very real and pressing difficulty, a practical as well as a logical contradiction which seems at first sight to persist up to the highest heights of spiritual experience. The Eternal is other than this mobile subjective and objective experience, there is a greater consciousness, *na idaṁ yad upaāsate*:[2] and yet at the same time all this is the Eternal, all this is the perennial self-seeing of the Self, *sarvaṁ khalu idaṁ brahma*,[3] *ayam ātmā brahma*.[4] The Eternal has become all existences, *ātmā abhūt sarvāṇi bhūtāni*;[5] as the Swetaswatara puts it, 'Thou art this boy and yonder girl and that old man walking supported on his staff,' – even as in the Gita the Divine says that he is Krishna and Arjuna and Vyasa and Ushanas, and the lion and the aswattha tree, and consciousness and intelligence and all qualities and the self of all creatures. But how are these two the same, when they seem not only so opposite in nature, but so difficult to unify in experience? For when we live in the mobility of the becoming, we may be aware of but hardly live in the immortality of timeless self-existence. And when we fix ourselves in timeless being, Time and Space and circumstance fall away from us and begin to appear as a troubled dream in the Infinite. The most persuasive conclusion would be, at first sight, that the mobility of the spirit in Nature is an illusion, a thing real only when we live in it, but not real in essence, and that is why, when we go back into self, it falls away from our incorruptible essence. That is the familiar cutting of the knot of the riddle, *brahma satyaṁ jagan mithyā*.

The Gita does not take refuge in this explanation which has enormous difficulties of its own, besides its

[2] *Kena Upanishad*.

[3] *Chhandogya Upanishad*: Verily all this that is is the Brahman.

[4] *Mandukya Upanishad*: The Self is the Brahman.

[5] *Isha Upanishad*.

failure to account for the illusion, for it only says that it is all a mysterious and incomprehensible Maya, and then we might just as well say that it is all a mysterious and incomprehensible double reality, spirit concealing itself from spirit. The Gita speaks of Maya, but only as a bewildering partial consciousness which loses hold of the complete reality, lives in the phenomenon of mobile Nature and has no sight of the Spirit of which she is the active Power, *me prakṛtiḥ*. When we transcend this Maya, the world does not disappear, it only changes its whole heart of meaning. In the spiritual vision we find not that all this does not really exist, but rather that all is, but with a sense quite other than its present mistaken significance: all is self and soul and nature of the God-head, all is Vasudeva. The world for the Gita is real, a creation of the Lord, a power of the Eternal, a manifestation from the Parabrahman, and even this lower nature of the triple Maya is a derivation from the supreme divine Nature. Nor can we take refuge altogether in this distinction that there is a double, an inferior active and temporal and a superior calm, still and eternal reality beyond action and that our liberation is to pass from this partiality to that greatness, from the action to the silence. For the Gita insists that we can and should, while we live, be conscious in the self and its silence and yet act with power in the world of Nature. And it gives the example of the Divine himself who is not bound by necessity of birth, but free, superior to the cosmos, and yet abides eternally in action, *varta eva ca karmaṇi* Therefore it is by putting on a likeness of the divine nature in its completeness that the unity of this double experience becomes entirely possible.

But what is the principle of that oneness? The Gita finds it in its supreme vision of the Purushottama; for that is the type, according to its doctrine, of the complete and the highest experience, it is the knowledge of the whole-knowers, *kṛtsnavidaḥ*. The Akshara is para, supreme in relation to the elements and action of cosmic Nature. It is the immutable Self of all, and the immutable Self of all is the Purushottama. The Akshara is he in the freedom of his self-existence unaffected by the action of his own power in Nature, not impinged on by the urge of his own becoming, undisturbed by the play of his own qualities. But this is only one aspect though a great aspect of the integral knowledge. The Purushottama is at the same time greater than the Akshara, because he is more than this immutability and he is not limited even by the highest eternal status of his being, *paraṁ dhāma*. Still, it is through whatever is immutable and eternal in us that we arrive at that highest status from which there is no returning to birth, and that was the liberation which was sought by the wise of old, the ancient sages. But when pursued through the Akshara alone, this attempt at liberation becomes the seeking of the Indefinable, a thing hard for our nature embodied as we are here in Matter. The Indefinable, to which the Akshara, the pure intangible self here in us rises in its separative urge, is some supreme Unmanifest, *paro avyaktaḥ*, and that highest unmanifest Akshara is still the Purushottama.

Thus, the Divine is manifest in a double soul of his mystery, a twofold power, *dvāv imau puruṣau*; he supports at once the spirit of mutable things that is all these existences, *kṣaraḥ sarvāṇi bhūtāni*, and the immutable spirit that stands above them in his imperturbable immobility of eternal silence and calm. And it is by the force of the Divine in them that the mind and heart and will of man are so powerfully drawn in different directions by these two spirits as if by opposing and incompatible attractions one insistent to annul the other. But the Divine is neither wholly the Kshara, nor wholly the Akshara. He is greater than the immutable Self and he is much greater than the Soul of mutable things. If he is capable of being both at once, it is because he is other than they, *anyaḥ*, the Purushottama above all cosmos and yet extended in the world and extended in the Veda, in self-knowledge and in cosmic experience. And whoever thus knows and sees him as the Purushottama, is no longer bewildered whether by the world-appearance or by the separate attraction of these two apparent contraries. These at first confront each other here in him as a positive of the cosmic action and as its negative in the Self who has no part in an action that belongs or seems to belong entirely to the ignorance of Nature. Or again they challenge his consciousness as a positive of pure, indeterminable, stable, eternal self-existence and as its negative of a world of elusive determinations and relations, ideas and forms, perpetual unstable becoming and the creating and uncreating tangle of action and evolution, birth and death, appearance and disappearance. He embraces and escapes them, overcomes their opposition and becomes all-knowing, *sarvavid*, a whole-knower. He sees the entire sense both of the self and of things; he restores the integral reality of the Divine; he unites the Kshara and the Akshara in the Purushottama. He loves, worships, cleaves to and adores the supreme Self of his and all existence, the one Lord of his and all energies, the close and far-off Eternal in and beyond the world. And he does this too with no single side or portion of himself, exclusive spiritualised mind, blinding light of the heart intense but divorced from largeness, or sole aspiration of the will in works, but in all the perfectly illumined ways of his being and his becoming, his soul and his nature. Divine in the equality of his imperturbable self-existence, one in it with all objects and creatures, he brings that boundless equality, that deep oneness down into his mind and heart and life and body and founds on it in an indivisible integrality the trinity of divine love, divine works and divine knowledge. This is the Gita's way of salvation.

And is that not too after all the real Adwaita which makes no least scission in the one eternal Existence? This utmost undividing Monism sees the one as the one even in the multiplicities of Nature, in all aspects, as much in the reality of self and of cosmos as in that greatest reality of the supracosmic which is the source of self and the truth of the cosmos and is not bound either by any affirmation of universal becoming or by any universal or absolute negation. That at least is the Adwaita of the Gita. This is the most secret Shastra, says the Teacher to Arjuna; this is the supreme teaching and science which leads us into the heart of the highest mystery of existence. Absolutely to know it, to seize it in knowledge and feeling and force and experience is to be perfected in the transformed understanding, divinely satisfied in heart and successful in the supreme sense and objective of all will and action and works. It is the way to be immortal, to rise towards the highest divine nature and to assume the eternal Dharma.

Deva and Asura[1]

The practical difficulty of the change from the ignorant and shackled normal nature of man to the dynamic freedom of a divine and spiritual being will be apparent if we ask ourselves, more narrowly, how the transition can be effected from the fettered embarrassed functioning of the three qualities to the infinite action of the liberated man who is no longer subject to the gunas. The transition is indispensable; for it is clearly laid down that he must be above or else without the three gunas, *triguṇātītā, nistraiguṇya*. On the other hand, it is no less clearly, no less emphatically laid down that in every natural existence here on earth the three gunas are there in their inextricable working and it is even said that all action of man or creature or force is merely the action of these three modes upon each other, a functioning in which one or other predominates and the rest modify its operation and results, *guṇā guṇeṣu vartante*. How then can there be another dynamic and

[1] Gita, XVI.

kinetic nature or any other kind of works? To act is to be subject to the three qualities of Nature; to be beyond these conditions of her working is to be silent in the Spirit. The Ishwara, the Supreme who is master of all her works and functions and guides and determines them by his divine will, is indeed above this mechanism of quality, not touched or limited by her modes, but still it would seem that he acts always through them, always shapes by the power of the swabhava and through the psychological machinery of the gunas. These three are fundamental properties of Prakriti, necessary operations of the executive Nature-force which takes shape here in us, and the Jiva himself is only a portion of the Divine in this Prakriti. If then the liberated man still does works, still moves in the kinetic movement, it must be so that he moves and acts, in Nature and by the limitation of her qualities, subject to their reactions, not, in so far as the natural part of him persists, in the freedom of the Divine. But the Gita has said exactly the opposite, that the liberated Yogin is delivered from the guna reactions and whatever he does; however he lives, moves and acts in God, in the power of his freedom and immortality, in the law of the supreme eternal Infinite, *sarvathā vartamāno'pi sa yogī mayi vartate*. There seems here to be a contradiction, an impasse.

But this is only when we knot ourselves up in the rigid logical oppositions of the analytic mind, not when we look freely and subtly at the nature of spirit and at the spirit in Nature. What moves the world is not really the modes of Prakriti – these are only the lower aspect, the mechanism of our normal nature. The real motive power is a divine spiritual Will which uses at present these inferior conditions, but is itself not limited, not dominated, not mechanised, as is the human will, by the gunas. No doubt, since these modes are so universal in their action, they must proceed from something inherent in the power of the Spirit; there must be powers in the divine Will-force from which these aspects of Prakriti have their origin. For everything in the lower normal nature is derived from the higher spiritual power of being of the Purushottama, *mattaḥ pravartate*; it does not come into being *de novo* and without a spiritual cause. Something in the essential power of the spirit there must be from which the sattwic light and satisfaction, the rajasic kinesis, the tamasic inertia of our nature are derivations and of which they are the imperfect or degraded forms. But once we get back to these sources in their purity above this imperfection and degradation of them in which we live, we shall find that these motions put on a quite different aspect as soon as we begin to live in the spirit. Being and action and the modes of being and action become altogether different things, far above their present limited appearance.

For what is behind this troubled kinesis of the cosmos with all its clash and struggle? What is it that when it touches the mind, when it puts on mental values, creates the reactions of desire, striving, straining, error of will, sorrow, sin, pain? It is a will of the spirit in movement, it is a large divine will in action which is not touched by these things;

it is a power[2] of the free and infinite conscious Godhead which has no desire because it exercises a universal possession and a spontaneous Ananda of its movements. Wearied by no striving and straining, it enjoys a free mastery of its means and its objects; misled by no error of the will, it holds a knowledge of self and things which is the source of its mastery and its Ananda; overcome by no sorrow, sin or pain, it has the joy and purity of its being and the joy and purity of its power. The soul that lives in God acts by this spiritual will and not by the normal will of the unliberated mind: its kinesis takes place by this spiritual force and not by the rajasic mode of Nature, precisely because it no longer lives in the lower movement to which that deformation belongs, but has got back in the divine nature to the pure and perfect sense of the kinesis.

And again what is behind the inertia of Nature, behind this Tamas which, when complete, makes her action like the blind driving of a machine, a mechanical impetus unobservant of anything except the groove in which it is set to spin and not conscious even of the law of that motion – this Tamas that turns cessation of the accustomed action into death and disintegration and becomes in the mind a power for inaction and ignorance? This tamas is an obscurity which mistranslates, we may say, into inaction of power and inaction of knowledge the Spirit's eternal principle of calm and repose – the repose which the Divine

[2] *tapas, cit-śakti.*

never loses even while he acts, the eternal repose which supports his integral action of knowledge and the force of his creative will both there in its own infinities and here in an apparent limitation of its working and self-awareness. The peace of the Godhead is not a disintegration of energy or a vacant inertia; it would keep all that Infinity has known and done gathered up and concentratedly conscious in an omnipotent silence even if the Power everywhere ceased for a time actively to know and create. The Eternal does not need to sleep or rest; he does not get tired and flag; he has no need of a pause to refresh and recreate his exhausted energies; for his energy is inexhaustibly the same, indefatigable and infinite. The Godhead is calm and at rest in the midst of his action, and on the other hand, his very cessation of action would retain in it the full power and all the potentialities of his kinesis. The liberated soul enters into this calm and participates in the eternal repose of the spirit. This is known to everyone who has had any taste at all of the joy of liberation, that it contains an eternal power of calm. And that profound tranquillity can remain in the very heart of action, can persevere in the most violent motion of forces. There may be an impetuous flood of thought, doing, will, movement, an overflowing rush of love, the emotion of the self-existent spiritual ecstasy at its strongest intensity, and that may extend itself to a fiery and forceful spiritual enjoyment of things and beings in the world and in the ways of Nature, and yet this tranquillity and repose would be behind the surge and in it, always conscious of its depths, always the same. The calm of the liberated man is not an indolence, incapacity, insensibility, inertia; it is full of immortal power, capable of all action, attuned to deepest delight, open to profoundest love and compassion and to every manner of intensest Ananda.

And so too beyond the inferior light and happiness of that purest quality of Nature, Sattwa, the power that makes for assimilation and equivalence, right knowledge and right dealing, fine harmony, firm balance, right law of action, right possession and brings so full a satisfaction to the mind, beyond this highest thing in the normal nature, admirable in itself so far as it goes and while it can be maintained, but precarious, secured by limitation, dependent on rule and condition, there is at its high and distant source a greater light and bliss free in the free spirit. That is not limited nor dependent on limitation or rule or condition but self-existent and unalterable, not the result of this or that harmony amid the discords of our nature but the fount of harmony and able to create whatever harmony it will. That is a luminous spiritual and in its native action a direct supramental force of knowledge, *jyotiḥ*, not our modified and derivative mental light, *prakāśa*. That is the light and bliss of widest self-existence, spontaneous self-knowledge, intimate universal identity, deepest self-interchange, not of acquisition, assimilation, adjustment and laboured equivalence. That light is full of a luminous spiritual will and there is no gulf or disparateness between its knowledge and its action. That delight is not our paler mental happiness, *sukham*, but a profound concentrated intense self-existent bliss extended to all that our being does, envisages, creates, a fixed divine rapture, Ananda. The liberated soul participates more and more profoundly in this light and bliss and grows the more perfectly into it, the more integrally it unites itself with the Divine. And while among the gunas of the lower Nature there is a necessary disequilibrium, a shifting inconstancy of measures and a perpetual struggle for domination, the greater light and bliss, calm, will of kinesis of the Spirit do not exclude each other, are not at war, are not even merely in equilibrium, but each an aspect of the two others and in their fullness, all are inseparable and one. Our mind when it approaches the Divine may seem to enter into one to the exclusion of another, may appear for instance to achieve calm to the exclusion of kinesis of action, but that is because we approach him first through the selecting spirit in the mind. Afterwards when we are able to rise above even the spiritual mind, we can see that each divine power contains all the rest and can get rid of this initial error.[3]

We see then that action is possible without the subjection of the soul to the normal degraded functioning of the modes of Nature. That functioning depends on the mental,

[3] The account given here of the supreme spiritual and supramental forms of highest Nature action corresponding to the gunas is not derived from the Gita, but introduced from spiritual experience. The Gita does not describe in any detail the action of the highest Nature, *rahasyam uttamam*; it leaves that for the seeker to discover by his own spiritual experience. It only points out the nature of the high sattwic temperament and action through which this supreme mystery has to be reached and insists at the same time on the overpassing of Sattwa and transcendence of the three gunas.

vital and physical limitation into which we are cast; it is a deformation, an incapacity, a wrong or depressed value imposed on us by the mind and life in matter. When we grow into the spirit, this dharma or inferior law of Nature is replaced by the immortal dharma of the spirit; there is the experience of a free immortal action, a divine illimitable knowledge, a transcendent power, an unfathomable repose. But still there remains the question of the transition; for there must be a transition, a proceeding by steps, since nothing in God's workings in this world is done by an abrupt action without procedure or basis. We have the thing we seek in us, but we have in practice to evolve it out of the inferior forms of our nature.[4] Therefore, in the action of the modes itself there must be some means, some leverage, some *point d'appui*, by which we can effect this transformation. The Gita finds it in the full development of the sattwic guna till that in its potent expansion reaches a point at which it can go beyond itself and disappear into its source. The reason is evident, because sattwa is a power of light and happiness, a force that makes for calm and knowledge, and at its highest point it can arrive at a certain reflection, almost a mental identity with the spiritual light and bliss from which it derives. The other two gunas cannot get this

[4] This is from the point of view of our nature ascending upwards by self-conquest, effort and discipline. There must also intervene more and more a descent of the divine Light, Presence and Power into the being to transform it; otherwise the change at the point of culmination and beyond it cannot take place. That is why there comes in as the last movement the necessity of an absolute self-surrender.

transformation, rajas into the divine kinetic will or tamas into the divine repose and calm, without the intervention of the sattwic power in Nature. The principle of inertia will always remain an inert inaction of power or an incapacity of knowledge until its ignorance disappears in illumination and its torpid incapacity is lost in the light and force of the omnipotent divine will of repose. Then only can we have the supreme calm. Therefore, tamas must be dominated by sattwa. The principle of rajas for the same reason must remain always a restless, troubled, feverish or unhappy working because it has not right knowledge; its native movement is a wrong and perverse action, perverse through ignorance. Our will must purify itself by knowledge; it must get more and more to a right and luminously informed action before it can be converted into the divine kinetic will. That again means the necessity of the intervention of sattwa. The sattwic quality is a first mediator between the higher and the lower nature. It must indeed at a certain point transform or escape from itself and break up and dissolve into its source; its conditioned derivative seeking light and carefully constructed action must change into the free direct dynamics and spontaneous light of the spirit. But meanwhile a high increase of sattwic power delivers us largely from the tamasic and the rajasic disqualification; and its own disqualification, once we are not pulled too much downward by rajas and tamas, can be surmounted with a greater ease. To develop sattwa till it becomes full of spiritual light and calm and happiness is the first condition of this preparatory discipline of the nature.

That, we shall find, is the whole intention of the remaining chapters of the Gita. But first it prefaces the consideration of this enlightening movement by a distinction between two kinds of being, the Deva and the Asura; for the Deva is capable of a high self-transforming sattwic action, the Asura incapable.

The distinction between the Deva and the Asura is not comprehensive of all humanity, not rigidly applicable to all its individuals, neither is it sharp and definite in all stages of the moral or spiritual history of the race or in all phases of the individual evolution. The tamasic man who makes so large a part of the whole, falls into neither category as it is here described, though he may have both elements in him in a low degree and for the most part serves tepidly the lower qualities. The normal man is ordinarily a mixture; but one or the other tendency is more pronounced, tends to make him predominantly rajaso-tamasic or sattwo-rajasic and can be said to be preparing him for either culmination, for the divine clarity or the titanic turbulence.

On one side there can be a sublimation of the sattwic quality, the culmination or manifestation of the unborn Deva, on the other a sublimation of the rajasic turn of the soul in nature, the entire birth of the Asura. The one leads towards that movement of liberation on which the Gita is about to lay stress; it makes possible a high self-exceeding of the sattwa quality and a transformation into the likeness of the divine being, *vimokṣāya*. The other leads away from that universal potentiality and precipitates towards an exaggeration of our bondage to the ego. The Deva nature is distinguished by an acme of the sattwic habits and qualities; self-control, sacrifice, the religious habit, cleanness and purity, candour and straightforwardness, truth, calm and self-denial, compassion to all beings, modesty, gentleness, forgivingness, patience, steadfastness, a deep sweet and serious freedom from all restlessness, levity and inconstancy are its native attributes. The Asuric qualities, wrath, greed, cunning, treachery, wilful doing of injury to others, pride and arrogance and excessive self-esteem have no place in its composition. But its gentleness and self-denial and self-control are free too from all weakness: it has energy and soul force, strong resolution, the fearlessness of the soul that lives in the right and according to the truth as well as its harmlessness, *tejaḥ*, *abhayam*, *dhṛtiḥ*, *ahimsā*, *satyam*. This is the wealth, the plenitude of the man born into the Deva nature.

The Asuric nature has too its wealth, its plenitude of force, but it is of a very different, a powerful and evil kind. Asuric men have no true knowledge of the way of action or the way of abstention, the fulfilling or the holding in of the nature. Truth is not in them, nor clean doing, nor faithful observance. They see naturally in the world nothing but a huge play of the satisfaction of self; theirs is a world with Desire for its cause and seed and governing force and law, a world of Chance, a world devoid of just relation and linked Karma, a world without God, not true, not founded in Truth. Whatever better intellectual or higher religious dogma they may possess, this alone is the true creed of their mind and will in action; they follow always the cult of Desire and Ego. On that way of seeing life they lean in reality and by its falsehood they ruin their souls and their reason. The Asuric man becomes the centre or instrument of a fierce, Titanic, violent action, a power of destruction in the world, a fount of injury and evil. Arrogant, full of self-esteem and the drunkenness of their pride, these misguided souls delude themselves, persist in false and obstinate aims and pursue the fixed impure resolution of their longings. They imagine that desire and enjoyment are all the aim of life and in their inordinate and insatiable pursuit of it they are the prey of a devouring, a measurelessly unceasing care and thought and endeavour and anxiety till the moment of their death. They sacrifice and give, but from a self-regarding ostentation, from vanity and with a stiff and foolish pride. In the egoism of their strength and power, in the violence of their wrath and arrogance they hate, despise and belittle the God hidden in themselves and the God in man. And because they have this proud hatred and contempt of good and of God, because they are cruel and evil, the Divine casts them down continually into more and more Asuric births.

The Gunas, Faith and Works[1]

The Gita has made a distinction between action according to the licence of personal desire and action done according to the Shastra. We must understand by the latter the recognised science and art of life which is the outcome of mankind's collective living, its culture, religion, science, its progressive discovery of the best rule of life – but mankind still walking in the ignorance and proceeding in a half-light towards knowledge. The action of personal desire belongs to the unregenerated state of our nature and is dictated by ignorance or false knowledge and an unregulated or ill-regulated kinetic or rajasic egoism. The action controlled by Shastra is an outcome of intellectual, ethical, aesthetic, social and religious culture; it embodies an attempt at a certain right living, harmony and right order and is evidently an effort, more or less advanced according to circumstances, of the sattwic element in man

[1] Gita, XVII

to overtop, regulate and control or guide, where it must be admitted, his rajasic and tamasic egoism.

This is a general rule which humanity has always recognised wherever it has arrived at any kind of established and developed society; it has an idea of an order, a law, a standard of its perfection, something other than the guidance of its desires or the crude direction of its raw impulses. This greater rule the individual finds usually outside himself in some more or less fixed outcome of the experience and wisdom of the race, which he accepts, to which his mind and the leading parts of his being give their assent or sanction and which he tries to make his own by living it in his mind, will and action. And this assent of the being, its conscious acceptance and will to believe and realise, may be called by the name which the Gita gives to it, his faith, *śraddhā*.

But we see also that there is a freer tendency in man other than the leading of his desires and other than his will to accept the Law, the fixed idea, the safe governing rule of the Shastra. The individual frequently enough, the community at any moment of its life, is seen to turn away from the Shastra, becomes impatient of it, loses that form of its will and faith and goes in search of another law which it is now more disposed to accept as the right rule of living and regard as a more vital or higher truth of existence. This may happen when the established Shastra ceases to be a living thing and degenerates or stiffens into a mass of customs and conventions. Or it may come because it is found that the Shastra is imperfect or no longer useful for the progress demanded; a new truth, a more perfect law of living has become imperative.

But this practically means that there is an ideal, an eternal Dharma which religion, philosophy, ethics and all other powers in man that strive after truth and perfection are constantly endeavouring to embody in new statements of the science and art of the inner and outer life, a new Shastra. The Mosaic law of religious, ethical and social righteousness is convicted of narrowness and imperfection and is now besides a convention; the law of Christ comes to replace it and claims at once to abrogate and to fulfil, to abrogate the imperfect form and fulfil in a deeper and broader light and power the spirit of the thing which it aimed at, the divine rule of living. And the human search does not stop there, but leaves these formulations too, goes back to some past truth it had rejected or breaks forward to some new truth and power, but is always in search of the same thing, the law of its perfection, its rule of right living, its complete, highest and essential self and nature.

This movement begins with the individual, who is no longer satisfied with the law because he finds that it no longer corresponds to his idea and largest or intensest experience of himself and existence and therefore he can no longer bring to it the will to believe and practise. The Shastra is something impersonal to the individual, and that gives it its authority over the narrow personal law of his members; but at the same time, it is personal to the collectivity and is the outcome of its experience, its culture or its nature.

The leading in him that departs from the Shastra may not indeed be always a higher movement; it may take the form of a revolt of the egoistic or rajasic nature seeking freedom from the yoke of something which it feels to be cramping to its liberty of self-fulfilment and self-finding. But even then, it is often justified by some narrowness or imperfection of the Shastra or by the degradation of the current rule of living into a merely restricting or lifeless convention.

The rajasic is always stronger, always more forcefully inspired and has more possibilities in it than the tamasic nature. But also, this leading may be sattwic at its heart; it may be a turn to a larger and greater ideal which will carry us nearer to a more complete and ample truth of our self and universal existence than has yet been seen and nearer therefore to that highest law which is one with the divine freedom. And in effect this movement is usually an attempt to lay hold on some forgotten truth or to move on to a yet undiscovered or unlived truth of our being.

But what then shall be the secure base of an action which departs both from the guidance of desire and from the normal law? For the rule of desire has an authority of its own, no longer safe or satisfactory to us as it is to the animal or as it might have been to a primitive humanity, but still, so far as it goes, founded on a very living part of our nature and fortified by its strong indications; and the law, the Shastra has behind it all the authority of long established rule, old successful sanctions and a secure past experience. But this new movement is of the nature of a powerful adventure into the unknown or partly known, a daring development and a new conquest, and what then is the clue to be followed, the guiding light on which it can depend or its strong basis in our being? The answer is that the clue and support is to be found in man's *śraddhā*, his faith, his will to believe, to live what he sees or thinks to be the truth of himself and of existence. In other words, this movement is man's appeal to himself or to something potent and compelling in himself or in universal existence for the discovery of his truth, his law of living, his way to fullness and perfection. And everything depends on the nature of his faith, the thing in himself or in the universal soul – of which he is a portion or manifestation – to which he directs it and on how near he gets by it to his real self and the Self or true being of the universe. If he is tamasic, obscure, clouded, if he has an ignorant faith, an inept will, he will reach nothing true and will fall away to his lower nature. If he is lured by false rajasic lights, he can be carried away by self-will into bypaths that may lead to morass or precipice. In either case his only chance of salvation lies in a return of sattwa upon him to impose a new enlightened order and rule upon his members which will liberate him from the violent error of his self-will or the dull error of his clouded ignorance. If on the other hand he has the sattwic nature and a sattwic faith and direction for his steps, he will arrive in sight of a higher yet unachieved ideal rule which may lead him even in rare instances beyond the sattwic light some way at least towards a highest divine illumination and divine way of being and living.

Now we have to see how the Gita deals with this question on its own line of spiritual teaching and self-discipline. Arjuna puts immediately a suggestive query from which the problem or one aspect of it arises. When men, he says, sacrifice to God or the gods with faith, *śraddhā*, but abandon the rule of the Shastra, what is that concentrated will of devotion in them, *niṣṭhā*, which gives them this faith and moves them to this kind of action? Is it sattwa, rajas or tamas? to which strand of our nature does it belong? The answer of the Gita first states the principle that the faith in us is of a triple kind like all things in Nature and varies according to the dominating quality of our nature. The faith of each man takes the shape, hue, quality given to it by his stuff of being, his constituting temperament, his innate power of existence, *sattvānurūpā sarvasya śraddhā*. And then there comes a remarkable line in which the Gita tells us that this Purusha, this soul in man, is, as it were, made of *śraddhā*, a faith, a will to be, a belief in itself and existence, and whatever is that will, faith or constituting belief in him, he is that and that is he. *Śraddhāmayo 'yaṁ puruṣo yo yac-chraddhaḥ sa eva saḥ*. If we look into this pregnant saying a little closely, we shall find that this single line contains implied in its few forceful words almost the whole theory of the modern gospel of pragmatism. For if a man or the soul in a man consists of the faith which is in him, taken in this deeper sense, then it follows that the truth which he sees and wills to live is for him the truth of his being, the truth of himself that he has created or is creating and there can be for him no other real truth. This truth is a thing of his inner and outer action, a thing of his becoming, of the soul's dynamics, not of that in him which never changes. He is what he is today by some past will of his nature sustained and continued by a present will to know, to believe and to be in his intelligence and vital force, and whatever new turn is taken by this will and faith active in his very substance, that he will tend to become in the future. We create our own truth of existence in our own action of mind and life, which is another way of saying that we create our own selves, are our own makers.

But very obviously this is only one aspect of the truth, and all one-aspected statements are suspect to the thinker. Truth is not merely whatever our own personality is or creates; that is only the truth of our becoming, one point or line of emphasis in a movement of widest volume. Beyond our personality there is, first, a universal being as well as a universal becoming of which ours is a little movement; and beyond that too there is the eternal Being out of which all becoming derives and to which it owes its potentialities, elements, original and final motives. We may say indeed that all becoming is only an act of universal consciousness, is Maya, is a creation of the will to become, and the only other reality, if there is any, is a pure eternal existence beyond consciousness, featureless, unexpressed and inexpressible. That is practically the standpoint taken by the Mayavadin's Adwaita and the sense of the distinction he makes between pragmatic truth which to his mind is illusory or at least only temporarily and partly real – while modern pragmatism takes it to be the true truth or at least the only recognisable reality because the only reality that we can act and know – between that pragmatic illusion and on the other side of creative Maya the lonely Absolute featureless and inexpressible. But for the Gita absolute Brahman is also supreme Purusha, and Purusha is always conscious Soul, though its highest consciousness, its superconsciousness, if we will – as, one may add, its lowest which we call the Inconscient – is something very different from our mind consciousness to which alone we are accustomed to give the name. There is in that highest superconscience a highest truth and dharma of immortality, a greatest divine way of being, a way of the eternal and infinite. That eternal way of existence and divine manner of being exists already in the eternity of the Purushottama, but we are now attempting to create it here too in our becoming by Yoga; our endeavour is to become the Divine, to be as He, *madbhāva*. That also depends on *śraddhā*. It is by an act of our conscious substance and a belief in its truth, an inmost will to live it or be it that we come by it; but this does not mean that it does not already exist beyond us. Though it may not exist for our outward mind until we see and create ourselves anew into it, it is still there in the Eternal and we may say even that it is already there in our own secret self; for in us also, in our depths the Purushottama always is. Our growing into that, our creation of it is his and its manifestation in us. All creation indeed since it proceeds from the conscious substance of the Eternal, is a manifestation of him and proceeds by a faith, acceptance, will to be in the originating consciousness, Chit-Shakti.

We are concerned at present, however, not with the metaphysical issue, but with the relation of this will or faith in our being to our possibility of growth into the perfection of the divine nature. This power, this *śraddhā* is in any case our basis. When we live, when we are and do according to our desires, that is a persistent act of *śraddhā* belonging mostly to our vital and physical, our tamasic and rajasic nature. And when we try to be, to live and to do according to the Shastra, we proceed by a persistent act of *śraddhā* which belongs, supposing it to be not a routine faith, to a sattwic tendency that is constantly labouring to impose itself on our rajasic and tamasic parts. When we leave both these things and try to be, to live and to do according to some ideal or novel conception of truth of our own finding or our own individual acceptance, that too is a persistent act of *śraddhā* which may be dominated by any one of these three qualities that constantly govern our every thought, will, feeling and act. And again, when we try to be, to live and to do according to the divine nature, then too we must proceed by a persistent act of *śraddhā*, which must be according to the Gita the faith of the sattwic nature when it culminates and is preparing to exceed its own clear-cut limits. But all and any of these things implies some kinesis or displacement of nature, all suppose an inner or outer or ordinarily both an inner and an outer action. And what then will be the character of this action? The Gita states three main elements of the work we have to do, *kartavyaṁ karma*, and these three are sacrifice, giving and askesis. For when questioned by Arjuna on the difference between the outer and inner renunciation, *sannyāsa* and *tyāga*, Krishna insists that these three things ought not to be renounced at all but ought altogether to be done, for they are the work before us, *kartavyaṁ karma*, and they purify the wise. In other words, these acts constitute the means of our perfection. But at the same time, they may be done unwisely or less wisely by the unwise. All dynamic action may be reduced in its essential parts to these three elements. For all dynamic action, all kinesis of the nature involves a voluntary or an involuntary tapasya or askesis, an energism and concentration of our forces or capacities or of some capacity which helps us to achieve, to acquire or to become something, *tapas*. All action involves a giving of what we are or have, an expenditure which is the price of that achievement, acquisition or becoming, *dāna*. All action involves too a sacrifice to elemental or to universal powers or to the supreme Master of our works. The question is whether we do these things inconsciently, passively, or at best with an unintelligent ignorant half-conscient will, or with an unwisely or perversely conscient energism, or with a wisely conscient will rooted in knowledge, in other words, whether our sacrifice, giving and askesis are tamasic, rajasic or sattwic in nature.

For everything here, including physical things, partakes of this triple character. Our food, for example, the Gita tells us, is either sattwic, rajasic or tamasic according to its character and effect on the body. The sattwic temperament in the mental and physical body turns naturally to the things that increase the life, increase the inner and outer strength, nourish at once the mental, vital and physical force and increase the pleasure and satisfaction and happy condition of mind and life and body, all that is succulent and soft and firm and satisfying. The rajasic temperament prefers naturally food that is violently sour, pungent, hot, acrid, rough and strong and burning, the aliments that increase ill-health and the distempers of the mind and body. The tamasic temperament takes a perverse pleasure in cold, impure, stale, rotten or tasteless food or even accepts like the animals the remnants half-eaten by others. All-pervading is the principle of the three gunas. The gunas apply at the other end in the same way to the things of the mind and spirit, to sacrifice, giving and askesis, and the Gita distinguishes under each of these three heads between the three kinds in the customary terms of these things as they were formulated by the symbolism of the old Indian culture. But, remembering the very wide sense which the Gita itself gives to the idea of sacrifice, we may well enlarge the surface meaning of these hints and open them to a freer significance. And it will be convenient to take them in the reverse order, from tamas to sattwa, since we are considering how we go upward out of our lower nature through a certain sattwic culmination and self-exceeding to a divine nature and action beyond the three gunas.

The tamasic sacrifice is work which is done without faith, without, that is to say, any full conscious idea and acceptance and will towards the thing Nature yet compels us to execute. It is done mechanically, because the act of living demands it, because it comes in our way, because others do it, to avoid some other greater difficulty which may arise from not doing it, or from any other tamasic motive. And it is apt to be done, if we have in the full this kind of temperament, carelessly, perfunctorily, in the wrong way. It will not be performed by the *vidhi* or right rule of the Shastra, will not be led in its steps according to the right method laid down by the art and science of life and the true science of the thing to be done. There will be no giving of food in the sacrifice – and that act in the Indian ritual is symbolic of the element of helpful giving inherent in every action that is real sacrifice, the indispensable giving to others, the fruitful help to others, to the world, without which our action becomes a wholly self-regarding thing and a violation of the true universal law of solidarity and interchange. The work will be done without the dakshina, the much-needed giving or self-giving to the leaders of the sacrificial action, whether to the outward guide and helper of our work or to the veiled or manifest godhead within us. It will be done without the mantra, without the dedicating thought which is the sacred body of our will and knowledge lifted upwards to the godheads we serve by our sacrifice. The tamasic man does not offer his sacrifice to the gods, but to inferior elemental powers or to those grosser spirits behind the veil who feed upon his works and dominate his life with their darkness.

The rajasic man offers his sacrifice to lower godheads or to perverse powers, the Yakshas, the keepers of wealth, or to the Asuric and the Rakshasic forces. His sacrifice may be performed outwardly according to the Shastra, but its motive is ostentation, pride or a strong lust after the fruit of his action, a vehement demand for the reward of his works. All work therefore that proceeds from violent or egoistic personal desire or from an arrogant will intent to impose itself on the world for personal objects is of the rajasic nature, even if it mask itself with the insignia of the light, even if it be done outwardly as a sacrifice. Although it is ostensibly given to God or to the gods, it remains essentially an Asuric action. It is the inner state, motive and direction which give their value to our works, and not merely the apparent outer direction, the divine names we may call to sanction them or even the sincere intellectual belief which seems to justify us in the performance. Wherever there is a dominating egoism in our acts, there our work becomes a rajasic sacrifice. The true sattwic sacrifice on the other hand is distinguished by three signs that are the quiet seal of its character. First, it is dictated by the effective truth, executed according to the *vidhi*, the right principle, the exact method and rule, the just rhythm and law of our works, their true functioning, their dharma; that means that the reason and enlightened will are the guides and determinants of their steps and their purpose. Secondly, it is executed with a mind concentrated and fixed on the idea of the thing to be done as a true sacrifice imposed on us by the divine law that governs our life and therefore performed out of a high inner obligation or imperative truth and without desire for the personal fruit – the more impersonal the motive of the action and the temperament of the force put out in it, the more sattwic is its nature. And finally, it is offered to the gods without any reservation; it is acceptable to the divine powers by whom – for they are his masks and personalities – the Master of existence governs the universe.

This sattwic sacrifice comes then very near to the ideal and leads directly towards the kind of action demanded by the Gita; but it is not the last and highest ideal, it is not yet the action of the perfected man who lives in the divine nature. For it is carried out as a fixed dharma, and it is offered as a sacrifice or service to the gods, to some partial power or aspect of the Divine manifested in ourselves or in the universe. Work done with a disinterested religious faith or selflessly for humanity or impersonally from devotion to the Right or the Truth is of this nature, and action of that kind is necessary for our perfection; for it purifies our thought and will and our natural substance. The culmination of the sattwic action at which we have to arrive is of a still larger and freer kind; it is the high last sacrifice offered by us to the supreme Divine in his integral being and with a seeking for the Purushottama or with the vision of Vasudeva in all that is, the action done impersonally, universally, for the good of the world, for the fulfilment of the divine will in the universe. That culmination leads to its own transcending, to the immortal Dharma. For then comes a freedom in which there is no personal action at all, no sattwic rule of dharma, no limitation of Shastra; the inferior reason and will are themselves overpassed and it is not they but a higher wisdom that dictates and guides the work and commands its objective. There is no question of personal fruit; for the will that works is not our own but a supreme Will of which the soul is the instrument. There is no self-regarding and no selflessness; for the Jiva, the eternal portion of the Divine, is united with the highest Self of his existence and he and all are one in that Self and Spirit. There is no personal action, for all actions are given up to the Master of our works and it is he that does the action through the divinised Prakriti. There is no sacrifice – unless we can say that the Master of sacrifice is offering the works of his energy in the Jiva to himself in his own cosmic form. This is the supreme self-surpassing state arrived at by the action that is sacrifice, this the perfection of the soul that has come to its full consciousness in the divine nature.

Tamasic tapasya is that which is pursued under a clouded and deluded idea hard and obstinate in its delusion, maintained by an ignorant faith in some cherished falsehood, performed with effort and suffering imposed on oneself in pursuit of some narrow and vulgar egoistic object empty of relation to any true or great aim or else with a concentration of the energy in a will to do hurt to others. That which makes this kind of energism tamasic is not any principle of inertia, for inertia is foreign to tapasya, but a darkness in the mind and nature, a vulgar narrowness and ugliness in the doing or a brutish instinct or desire in the aim or in the motive feeling. Rajasic energisms of askesis are those which are undertaken to get honour and worship from men, for the sake of personal distinction and outward glory and greatness or from some other of the many motives of egoistic will and pride. This kind of askesis is devoted to fleeting particular objects which add nothing to the heavenward growth and perfection of the soul; it is a thing without fixed and helpful principle, an energy bound up with changeful and passing occasion and itself of that nature. Or even if there is ostensibly a more inward and noble object and the faith and will are of a higher kind, yet if any kind of arrogance or pride or any great strength of violent self-will or desire enters into the askesis or if it drives some violent, lawless or terrible action contrary to the Shastra, opposed to the right rule of life and works and afflicting to oneself and to others, or if it is of the nature of self-torture and hurts the mental, vital and physical elements or violates the God within us who is seated in the inner subtle body, then too it is an unwise, an Asuric, a rajasic or rajaso-tamasic tapasya.

Sattwic tapasya is that which is done with a highest enlightened faith, as a duty deeply accepted or for some ethical or spiritual or other higher reason and with no desire for any external or narrowly personal fruit in the action. It is of the character of self-discipline and asks for self-control and a harmonising of one's nature. The Gita describes three kinds of sattwic askesis. First comes the physical, the askesis of the outward act; under this head are especially mentioned worship and reverence of those deserving reverence, cleanness of the person, the action and the life, candid dealing, sexual purity and avoidance of killing and injury to others. Next is askesis of speech, and that consists in the study of Scripture, kind, true and beneficent speech and a careful avoidance of words that may cause fear, sorrow and trouble to others. Finally, there is the askesis of mental and moral perfection, and that means the purifying of the whole temperament, gentleness and a clear and calm gladness of mind, self-control and silence. Here comes in all that quiets or disciplines the rajasic and egoistic nature and all that replaces it by the happy and tranquil principle of good and virtue. This is the askesis of the sattwic dharma so highly prized in the system of the ancient Indian culture. Its greater culmination will be a high purity of the reason and will, an equal soul, a deep peace and calm, a wide sympathy and preparation of oneness, a reflection of the inner soul's divine gladness in the mind, life and body. There at that lofty point the ethical is already passing away into the spiritual type and character. And this culmination too can be made to transcend itself, can be raised into a higher and freer light, can pass away into the settled godlike energy of the supreme nature. And what will remain then will be the spirit's immaculate Tapas, a highest will and luminous force in all the members acting in a wide and solid calm and a deep and pure spiritual delight, Ananda. There will then be no farther need of askesis, no tapasya, because all is naturally and easily divine, all is that Tapas. There will be no separate labour of the lower energism, because the energy of Prakriti will have found its true source and base in the transcendent will of the

Purushottama. Then, because of this high initiation, the acts of this energy on the lower planes also will proceed naturally and spontaneously from an innate perfect will and by an inherent perfect guidance. There will be no limitation by any of the present dharmas; for there will be a free action far above the rajasic and tamasic nature, but also far beyond the too careful and narrow limits of the sattwic rule of action.

As with tapasya, all giving also is of an ignorant tamasic, an ostentatious rajasic or a disinterested and enlightened sattwic character. The tamasic gift is offered ignorantly with no consideration of the right conditions of time, place and object; it is a foolish, inconsiderate and in reality a self-regarding movement, an ungenerous and ignoble generosity, the gift offered without sympathy or true liberality, without regard for the feelings of the recipient and despised by him even in the acceptance. The rajasic kind of giving is that which is done with regret, unwillingness or violence to oneself or with a personal and egoistic object or in the hope of a return of some kind from whatever quarter or a corresponding or greater benefit to oneself from the receiver. The sattwic way of giving is to bestow with right reason and goodwill and sympathy in the right conditions of time and place and on the right recipient who is worthy or to whom the gift can be really helpful. Its act is performed for the sake of the giving and the beneficence, without any view to a benefit already done or yet to be done to oneself by the receiver of the benefit and without any personal object in the action.

The culmination of the sattwic way of *dāna* will bring into the action an increasing element of that wide self-giving to others and to the world and to God, *ātma-dāna*, *ātma-samarpaṇa*, which is the high consecration of the sacrifice of works enjoined by the Gita. And the transcendence in the divine nature will be a greatest completeness of self-offering founded on the largest meaning of existence. All this manifold universe comes into birth and is constantly maintained by God's giving of himself and his powers and the lavish outflow of his self and spirit into all these existences; universal being, says the Veda, is the sacrifice of the Purusha. All the action of the perfected soul will be even such a constant divine giving of itself and its powers, an outflowing of the knowledge, light, strength, love, joy, helpful shakti which it possesses in the Divine and by his influence and effluence on all around it according to their capacity of reception or on all this world and its creatures. That will be the complete result of the complete self-giving of the soul to the Master of our existence.

The Gita closes this chapter with what seems at first sight a recondite utterance. The formula OM, Tat, Sat, is, it says, the triple definition of the Brahman, by whom the Brahmanas, the Vedas and sacrifices were created of old and in it resides all their significance. Tat, That, indicates the Absolute. Sat indicates the supreme and universal existence in its principle. OM is the symbol of the triple Brahman, the outward-looking, the inward or subtle and the superconscient causal Purusha. Each letter A, U, M indicates one of these three in ascending order and the syllable as a whole brings out the fourth state, Turiya, which rises to the Absolute. OM is the initiating syllable pronounced at the outset as a benedictory prelude and sanction to all act of sacrifice, all act of giving and all act of askesis; it is a reminder that our work should be made an expression of the triple Divine in our inner being and turned towards him in the idea and motive. The seekers of liberation indeed do these actions without desire of fruit and only with the idea, feeling, Ananda of the absolute Divine behind their nature. It is that which they seek by this purity and impersonality in their works, this high desirelessness, this vast emptiness of ego and plenitude of Spirit. Sat means good and it means existence. Both these things, the principle of good and the principle of reality, must be there behind all the three kinds of action. All good works are Sat, for they prepare the soul for the higher reality of our being; all firm abiding in sacrifice, giving and askesis and all works done with that central view, as sacrifice, as giving, as askesis, are Sat, for they build the basis for the highest truth of our spirit. And because *śraddhā* is the central principle of our existence, any of these things done without *śraddhā* is a falsity and has no true meaning or true substance on earth or beyond, no reality, no power to endure or create in life here or after the mortal life in greater regions of our conscious spirit. The soul's faith, not a mere intellectual belief, but its concordant will to know, to see, to believe and to do and be according to its vision and knowledge, is that which determines by its power the measure of our possibilities of becoming, and it is this faith and will turned in all our inner and outer self, nature and action towards all that is highest, most divine, most real and eternal that will enable us to reach the supreme perfection.

The Gunas, Mind and Works[1]

This part of the subject is introduced by a last question of Arjuna regarding the principle of Sannyasa and the principle of Tyaga and their difference. The frequent harping, the reiterated emphasis of the Gita on this crucial distinction has been amply justified by the subsequent history of the later Indian mind, its constant confusion of these two very different things and its strong bent towards belittling any activity of the kind taught by the Gita as at best only a preliminary to the supreme inaction of Sannyasa. As a matter of fact, when people talk of Tyaga, of renunciation, it is always the physical renunciation of the world which they understand by the word or at least on which they lay emphasis, while the Gita takes absolutely the opposite view that the real Tyaga has action and living in the world as its basis and not a flight to the monastery, the cave or the hill-top. The real Tyaga is action with a renunciation of desire and that too is the real Sannyasa.

[1] Gita, XVIII. 1–39.

The liberating activity of the sattwic self-discipline must no doubt be pervaded by a spirit of renunciation – that is an essential element: but what renunciation and in what manner of the spirit? Not the renunciation of work in the world, not any outward asceticism or any ostentation of a visible giving up of enjoyment, but a renunciation, a leaving, *tyāga*, of vital desire and ego, a total laying aside, *sannyāsa*, of the separate personal life of the desire soul and ego-governed mind and rajasic vital nature. That is the true condition for entering into the heights of Yoga whether through the impersonal self and Brahmic oneness or through universal Vasudeva or inwardly into the supreme Purushottama. More conventionally taken, Sannyasa in the standing terminology of the sages means the physical depositing or laying aside of desirable actions: Tyaga – this is the Gita's distinction – is the name given by the wise to a mental and spiritual renunciation, an entire abandonment of all attached clinging to the fruit of our works, to the action itself or to its personal initiation or rajasic impulse. In that sense Tyaga, not Sannyasa, is the better way. It is not the desirable actions that must be laid aside, but the desire which gives them that character has to be put away from us. The fruit of the action may come in the dispensation of the Master of works, but there is to be no egoistic demand for that as a reward and condition of doing works. Or the fruit may not at all come and still the work has to be performed as the thing to be done, *kartavyaṁ karma*, the thing which the Master within demands of us. The success, the failure are in his hands and he will regulate them according to his omniscient will and inscrutable purpose. Action, all action has indeed to be given up in the end, not physically by abstention, by immobility, by inertia, but spiritually to the Master of our being by whose power alone can any action be accomplished. There has to be a renunciation of the false idea of ourselves as the doer; for in reality, it is the universal Shakti that works through our personality and our ego. The spiritual transference of all our works to the Master and his Shakti is the real Sannyasa in the teaching of the Gita.

The question still arises, what works are to be done? Those even who stand for a final physical renunciation are not at one in this difficult matter. Some would have it that all works must be excised from our life, as if that were possible. But it is not possible so long as we are in the body and alive; nor can salvation consist in reducing our active selves by trance to the lifeless immobility of the clod and the pebble. The silence of Samadhi does not abrogate the difficulty, for as soon as the breath comes again into the body, we are once more in action and have toppled down from the heights of this salvation by spiritual slumber. But the true salvation, the release by an inner renunciation of the ego and union with the Purushottama remains steady in whatever state, persists in this world or out of it or in whatever world or out of all world, is self-existent, *sarvathā vartamā no'pi*, and does not depend upon inaction or action. What then are the actions to be done? The thoroughgoing ascetic answer, not noted by the Gita – it was perhaps not altogether current at the time – might be that solely begging, eating and meditation are to be permitted among voluntary activities and otherwise only the necessary actions of the body. But the more liberal and comprehensive solution was evidently to continue the three most sattwic activities, sacrifice, giving and askesis. And these certainly are to be done, says the Gita, for they purify the wise. But more generally, and understanding these three things in their widest sense, it is the rightly regulated action, *niyataṁ karma*, that has to be done, action regulated by the Shastra, the science and art of right knowledge, right works, right living, or regulated by the essential nature, *svabhāva-niyataṁ karma*, or, finally and best of all, regulated by the will of the Divine within and above us. The last is the true and only action of the liberated man, *muktasya karma*. To renounce these works is not a right movement – the Gita lays that down plainly and trenchantly in the end, *niyatasya tu sannyāsaḥ karmaṇ onopapadyate*. To renounce them from an ignorant confidence in the sufficiency of that withdrawal for the true liberation is a tamasic renunciation. The gunas follow us, we see, into the renunciation of works as well as into works. A renunciation with attachment to inaction, *saṅgo akarmaṇi*, would be equally a tamasic withdrawal. And to give them up because they bring sorrow or are a trouble to the flesh and a weariness to the mind or in the feeling that all is vanity and vexation of spirit, is a rajasic renunciation and does not bring the high spiritual fruit; that too is not the true Tyaga. It is a result of intellectual pessimism or vital weariness, it has its roots in ego. No freedom can come from a renunciation governed by this self-regarding principle.

The sattwic principle of renunciation is to withdraw not from action, but from the personal demand, the ego factor behind it. It is to do works not dictated by desire but by the law of right living or by the essential nature, its knowledge, its ideal, its faith in itself and the Truth it sees, its *śraddhā*. Or else, on a higher spiritual plane, they are dictated by the will of the Master and done with the mind in Yoga, without any personal attachment either to the action or to the fruit of the action. There must be a complete renunciation of all desire and of all self-regarding egoistic choice and impulse and finally of that much subtler egoism of the will which either says, 'The work is mine, I am the doer', or even 'The work is God's, but I am the doer.' There must be no attachment to pleasant, desirable, lucrative or successful work and no doing of it because it has that nature; but that kind of work too has to be done – done totally, selflessly, with the assent of the spirit – when it is the action demanded from above and from within us, *kartavyaṁ karma*. There must be no aversion to unpleasant, undesirable or ungratifying action or work that brings or is likely to bring with it suffering, danger, harsh conditions, inauspicious consequences; for that too has to be accepted, totally, selflessly, with a deep understanding of its need and meaning, when it is the work that should be done, *kartavyaṁ karma*. The wise man puts away the shrinkings and hesitations of the desire-soul and the doubts of the ordinary human intelligence, that measure by little personal, conventional or otherwise limited standards. He follows in the light of the full sattwic mind and with the power of an inner renunciation lifting the soul to impersonality, towards God, towards the universal and eternal the highest ideal law of his nature or the will of the Master of works in his secret spirit. He will not do action for the sake of any personal result or for any reward in this life or with any attachment to success, profit or consequence: neither will his works be undertaken for the sake of a fruit in the invisible hereafter or ask for a reward in other births or in worlds beyond us, the prizes for which the half-baked religious mind hungers. The three kinds of result, pleasant, unpleasant and mixed, in this or other worlds, in this or another life are for the slaves of desire and ego; these things do not cling to the free spirit. The liberated worker who has given up his works by the inner sannyasa to a greater Power is free from Karma. Action he will do, for some kind of action, less or more, small or great, is inevitable, natural, right for the embodied soul – action is part of the divine law of living, it is the high dynamics of the spirit. The essence of renunciation, the true Tyaga, the true Sannyasa is not any rule of thumb of inaction but a disinterested soul, a selfless mind, the transition from ego to the free impersonal and spiritual nature. The spirit of this inner renunciation is the first mental condition of the highest culminating sattwic discipline.

The Gita then speaks of the five causes or indispensable requisites for the accomplishment of works as laid down by the Sankhya. These five are, first, the frame of body, life and mind which are the basis or standing-ground of the soul in Nature, *adhiṣṭhāna*, next, the doer, *kartā*, third, the various instrumentation of Nature, *karaṇa*, fourth, the many kinds of effort which make up the force of action, *ceṣṭāḥ*, and last, Fate, *daivam*, that is to say, the influence of the Power or powers other than the human factors, other than the visible mechanism of Nature, that stand behind these and modify the work and dispose its fruits in the steps of act and consequence. These five elements make up among them all the efficient causes, *kāraṇa*, that determine the shaping and outcome of whatever work man undertakes with mind and speech and body.

The doer is ordinarily supposed to be our surface personal ego, but that is the false idea of the understanding that has not arrived at knowledge. The ego is the ostensible doer, but the ego and its will are creations and instruments of Nature with which the ignorant understanding wrongly identifies our self and they are not the only determinants even of human action, much less of its turn and consequence. When we are liberated from ego, our real self behind comes forward, impersonal and universal, and it sees in its self-vision of unity with the universal Spirit universal Nature as the doer of the work and the Divine Will behind as the master of universal Nature. Only so long as we have not this knowledge, are we bound by the character of the ego and its will as the doer and do good and evil and have the satisfaction of our tamasic, rajasic or sattwic nature. But once we live in this greater knowledge, the character and consequences of the work can make no difference to the freedom of the spirit. The work may be outwardly a terrible action like this great battle and slaughter of Kurukshetra; but although the liberated man takes his part in the struggle and though he slay all these peoples, he slays no man and he is not bound by his work, because the work is that of the Master of the Worlds and it is he who has already slain in his hidden omnipotent will all these armies. This work of destruction was needed that humanity might move forward to another creation and a new purpose, might get rid as in a fire of its past karma of unrighteousness and oppression and injustice and move towards a kingdom of the Dharma. The liberated man does all his appointed work as the living instrument one in spirit with the universal Spirit. And knowing that all this must be and looking beyond the outward appearance he acts not for self but for God and man and the human and cosmic order,[2] not in fact himself acting, but conscious of the presence and power of the divine Force in his deeds and their issue. He knows that the supreme Shakti is doing in his mental, vital and physical body, *adhiṣṭhāna*, as the sole doer the thing appointed by a Fate which is in truth not Fate, not a mechanical dispensation, but the wise and all-seeing Will that is at work behind human Karma. This 'terrible work' on which the whole teaching of the Gita turns, is an extreme example of action inauspicious in appearance, *akuśalam*, though a great good lies beyond the appearance. Impersonally has it to be done by the divinely appointed man for the holding together of the world purpose, *loka-saṅgrahārtham*, without personal aim or desire, because it is the appointed service.

[2] The cosmic order comes into question, because the triumph of the Asura in humanity means to that extent the triumph of the Asura in the balance of the world-forces.

Swabhava and Swadharma[1]

It is then by a liberating development of the soul out of this lower nature of the triple gunas into the supreme divine nature beyond the three gunas that we can best arrive at spiritual perfection and freedom. And this again can best be brought about by an anterior development of the predominance of the highest sattwic quality to a point at which sattwa also is overpassed, mounts beyond its own limitations and breaks up into a supreme freedom, absolute light, serene power of the conscious spirit in which there is no determination by conflicting gunas. A highest sattwic faith and aim new-shaping what we are according to the highest mental conception of our inner possibilities that we can form in the free intelligence, is changed by this transition into a vision of our own real being, a spiritual self-knowledge. A loftiest ideality or standard of dharma, a pursuit of the right law of our natural existence, is transformed into a free assured self-existent perfection in which all dependence

[1] Gita, XVIII. 40–48.

on standards is transcended and the spontaneous law of the immortal self and spirit displaces the lower rule of the instruments and members. The sattwic mind and will change into that spiritual knowledge and dynamic power of identical existence in which the whole nature puts off its disguise and becomes a free self-expression of the godhead within it. The sattwic doer becomes the Jiva in contact with his source, united with the Purushottama; he is no longer the personal doer of the act, but a spiritual channel of the works of the transcendent and universal Spirit. His natural being transformed and illumined remains to be the instrument of a universal and impersonal action, the bow of the divine Archer. What was sattwic action becomes the free activity of the perfected nature in which there is no longer any personal limitation, any tethering to this or that quality, any bondage of sin and virtue, self and others or any but a supreme spiritual self-determination. That is the culmination of works uplifted to the sole Divine Worker by a God-seeking and spiritual knowledge.

But there is still an incidental question of great importance in the old Indian system of culture and, even apart from that antique view, of considerable general importance, on which we have had some passing pronouncements already by the Gita and which now falls into its proper place. All action on the normal level is determined by the gunas; the action which is to be done, *kartavyaṁ karma*, takes the triple form of giving, askesis and sacrifice, and any or all of these three may assume the character of any of the gunas. Therefore, we have to proceed by the raising of these things to the highest sattwic height of which they are capable and go yet farther beyond to a largeness in which all works become a free self-giving, an energy of the divine Tapas, a perpetual sacrament of the spiritual existence. But this is a general law and all these considerations have been the enunciation of quite general principles and refer indiscriminately to all actions and to all men alike. All can eventually arrive by spiritual evolution to this strong discipline, this large perfection, this highest spiritual state. But while the general rule of mind and action is the same for all men, we see too that there is a constant law of variation and each individual acts not only according to the common laws of the human spirit, mind, will, life, but according to his own nature; each man fulfils different functions or follows a different bent according to the rule of his own circumstances, capacities, turn, character, powers. What place is to be assigned to this variation, this individual rule of nature in the spiritual discipline?

The Gita has laid some stress on this point and even assigned to it a great preliminary importance. At the very start it has spoken of the nature, rule and function of the Kshatriya as Arjuna's own law of action, *svadharma*;[2] it has proceeded to lay it down with a striking emphasis that one's own nature, rule, function should be observed and followed – even if defective, it is better than the well-performed rule of another's nature. Death in one's own law of nature is better for a man than victory in an alien movement.

[2] II. 31. *svadharmam api cāvekṣya*.

To follow the law of another's nature is dangerous to the soul,[3] contradictory, as we may say, to the natural way of his evolution, a thing mechanically imposed and therefore imported, artificial and sterilising to one's growth towards the true stature of the spirit. What comes out of the being is the right and healthful thing, the authentic movement, not what is imposed on it from outside or laid on it by life's compulsions or the mind's error. This swadharma is of four general kinds formulated outwardly in the action of the four orders of the old Indian social culture, *cāturvarṇya*. That system corresponds, says the Gita, to a divine law, it 'was created by me according to the divisions of the gunas and works,' – created from the beginning by the Master of existence. In other words, there are four distinct orders of the active nature, or four fundamental types of the soul in nature, *svabhāva*, and the work and proper function of each human being corresponds to his type of nature. This is now finally explained in preciser detail. The works of Brahmins, Kshatriyas, Vaishyas and Shudras, says the Gita, are divided according to the qualities (*guṇas*) born of their own inner nature, spiritual temperament, essential character (*svabhāva*). Calm, self-control, askesis, purity, long-suffering, candour, knowledge, acceptance of spiritual truth are the work of the Brahmin, born of his swabhava. Heroism, high spirit, resolution, ability, not fleeing in the battle, giving, lordship (*īśvara-bhāva*, the temperament of the ruler and leader) are the natural work of the Kshatriya.

[3] III. 35.

Agriculture, cattle-keeping, trade inclusive of the labour of the craftsman and the artisan are the natural work of the Vaishya. All work of the character of service falls within the natural function of the Shudra. A man, it goes on to say, who devotes himself to his own natural work in life acquires spiritual perfection, not indeed by the mere act itself, but if he does it with right knowledge and the right motive, if he can make it a worship of the Spirit of this creation and dedicate it sincerely to the Master of the universe from whom is all impulse to action. All labour, all action and function, whatever it be, can be consecrated by this dedication of works, can convert the life into a self-offering to the Godhead within and without us and is itself converted into a means of spiritual perfection. But a work not naturally one's own, even though it may be well performed, even though it may look better from the outside when judged by an external and mechanical standard or may lead to more success in life, is still inferior as a means of subjective growth precisely because it has an external motive and a mechanical impulsion. One's own natural work is better, even if it looks from some other point of view defective. One does not incur sin or stain when one acts in the true spirit of the work and in agreement with the law of one's own nature. All action in the three gunas is imperfect, all human work is subject to fault, defect or limitation; but that should not make us abandon our own proper work and natural function. Action should be rightly regulated action, *niyataṁ karma*, but intrinsically one's own, evolved from within, in harmony with the truth of one's being, regulated by the Swabhava, *svabhāva-niyataṁ karma*.

What precisely is the intention of the Gita? Let us take it first in its more outward meaning and consider the tinge given to the principle it enounces by the ideas of the race and the time – the hue of the cultural environment, the ancient significance. These verses and the earlier pronouncements of the Gita on the same subject have been seized upon in current controversies on the caste question and interpreted by some as a sanction of the present system, used by others as a denial of the hereditary basis of caste. In point of fact the verses in the Gita have no bearing on the existing caste system, because that is a very different thing from the ancient social ideal of *cāturvarṇya*, the four clear-cut orders of the Aryan community, and in no way corresponds with the description of the Gita. Agriculture, cattle-keeping and trade of every kind are said here to be the work of the Vaishya; but in the later system the majority of those concerned in trade and in cattle-keeping, artisans, small craftsmen and others are actually classed as Shudras – where they are not put altogether outside the pale – and, with some exceptions, the merchant class is alone and that too not everywhere ranked as Vaishya. Agriculture, government and service are the professions of all classes from the Brahmin down to the Shudra. And if the economical divisions of function have been confounded beyond any possibility of rectification, the law of the guna or quality is still less a part of the later system. There all is rigid custom, *ācāra*, with no reference to the need of the individual nature. If again we take the religious side of the contention advanced by the advocates of the caste system, we can certainly fasten no such absurd idea on the words of the Gita as that it is a law of a man's nature that he shall follow without regard to his personal bent and capacities the profession of his parents or his immediate or distant ancestors, the son of a milkman be a milkman, the son of a doctor a doctor, the descendants of shoemakers remain shoemakers to the end of measurable time, still less that by doing so, by this unintelligent and mechanical repetition of the law of another's nature without regard to his own individual call and qualities a man automatically farthers his own perfection and arrives at spiritual freedom. The Gita's words refer to the ancient system of *cāturvarṇya*, as it existed or was supposed to exist in its ideal purity – there is some controversy whether it was ever anything more than an ideal or general norm more or less loosely followed in practice – and it should be considered in that connection alone. Here too there is considerable difficulty as to the exact outward significance.

The ancient system of the four orders had a triple aspect; it took a social and economic, a cultural and a spiritual appearance. On the economic side it recognised four functions of the social man in the community, the religious and intellectual, the political, the economic and the servile functions. There are thus four kinds of work, the work of religious ministration, letters, learning and knowledge, the work of government, politics, administration and war, the work of production, wealth-making and exchange, the work of hired labour and service. An endeavour was made to found and stabilise the whole arrangement of society on the partition of these four functions among four clearly marked classes. This system was not peculiar to India, but was with certain differences the dominating feature of a stage of social evolution in other ancient or mediaeval societies. The four functions are still inherent in the life of all normal communities, but the clear divisions no longer exist anywhere. The old system everywhere broke down and gave place to a more fluid order or, as in India, to a confused and complex social rigidity and economic immobility degenerating towards a chaos of castes. Along with this economic division there existed the association of a cultural idea which gave to each class its religious custom, its law of honour, ethical rule, suitable education and training, type of character, family ideal and discipline. The facts of life did not always correspond to the idea – there is always a certain gulf found between the mental ideal and the vital and physical practice – but there was a constant and strenuous endeavour to keep up as much as possible a real correspondence. The importance of this attempt and of the cultural ideal and atmosphere it created in the past training of the social man, can hardly be put too high; but at the present day it has little more than a historical, a past and evolutionary significance. Finally, wherever this system existed, it was given more or less a religious sanction (more in the East, very little in Europe) and in India a profounder spiritual use and significance.

This spiritual significance is the real kernel of the teaching of the Gita.

The Gita found this system in existence and its ideal in possession of the Indian mind and it recognised and accepted both the ideal and system and its religious sanction. 'The fourfold order was created by me,' says Krishna, 'according to the divisions of quality and active function.' On the mere strength of this phrase it cannot altogether be concluded that the Gita regarded this system as an eternal and universal social order. Other ancient authorities did not so regard it; rather they distinctly state that it did not exist in the beginning and will collapse in a later age of the cycle. Still we may understand from the phrase that the fourfold function of social man was considered as normally inherent in the psychological and economic needs of every community and therefore a dispensation of the Spirit that expresses itself in the human corporate and individual existence. The Gita's line is in fact an intellectual rendering of the well-known symbol in the Vedic Purusha-Sukta. But what then should be the natural basis and form of practice of these functions? The practical basis in ancient times came to be the hereditary principle. A man's social function and position were no doubt determined originally, as they are still in freer, less closely ordered communities by environment, occasion, birth and capacity; but as there set in a more fixed stratification, his rank came practically to be regulated by birth mainly or alone and in the later system of caste birth came to be the sole rule of status. The son of a Brahmin is always a Brahmin in status, though he may have nothing of the typical Brahmin qualities or character, no intellectual training or spiritual experience or religious worth or knowledge, no connection whatever with the right function of his class, no Brahminhood in his work and no Brahminhood in his nature.

Towards the Supreme Secret[1]

The teacher has completed all else that he needed to say, he has worked out all the central principles and the supporting suggestions and implications of his message and elucidated the principal doubts and questions that might rise around it, and now all that rests for him to do is to put into decisive phrase and penetrating formula the one last word, the heart itself of the message, the very core of his gospel. And we find that this decisive, last and crowning word is not merely the essence of what has been already said on the matter, not merely a concentrated description of the needed self-discipline, the Sadhana, and of that greater spiritual consciousness which is to be the result of all its effort and askesis; it sweeps out, as it were, yet farther, breaks down every limit and rule, canon and formula and opens into a wide and illimitable spiritual truth with an infinite potentiality of significance. And that is a sign of the profundity, the wide reach, the

[1] Gita, XVIII. 49–56.

greatness of spirit of the Gita's teaching. An ordinary religious teaching or philosophical doctrine is well enough satisfied to seize on certain great and vital aspects of truth and turn them into utilisable dogma and instruction, method and practice for the guidance of man in his inner life and the law and form of his action; it does not go farther, it does not open doors out of the circle of its own system, does not lead us out into some widest freedom and unimprisoned largeness. This limitation is useful and indeed for a time indispensable. Man bounded by his mind and will has need of a law and rule, a fixed system, a definite practice selective of his thought and action; he asks for the single unmistakable hewn path hedged, fixed and secure to the tread, for the limited horizons, for the enclosed resting-places. It is only the strong and few who can move through freedom to freedom. And yet in the end the free soul ought to have an issue out of the forms and systems in which the mind finds its account and takes its limited pleasure. To exceed our ladder of ascent, not to stop short even on the topmost stair but move untrammelled and at large in the wideness of the spirit is a release important for our perfection; the spirit's absolute liberty is our perfect status. And this is how the Gita leads us: it lays down a firm and sure but very large way of ascent, a great Dharma, and then it takes us out beyond all that is laid down, beyond all dharmas, into infinitely open spaces, divulges to us the hope, lets us into the secret of an absolute perfection founded in an absolute spiritual liberty, and that secret, *guhyatamam*, is the substance of what it calls its supreme word, that the hidden thing, the inmost knowledge.

And first the Gita restates the body of its message. It summarises the whole outline and essence in the short space of fifteen verses, lines of a brief and concentrated expression and significance that miss nothing of the kernel of the matter, couched in phrases of the most lucid precision and clearness. And they must therefore be scanned with care, must be read deeply in the light of all that has gone before, because here it is evidently intended to extract what the Gita itself considers to be the central sense of its own teaching. The statement sets out from the original starting-point of the thought in the book, the enigma of human action, the apparently insuperable difficulty of living in the highest self and spirit while yet we continue to do the works of the world. The easiest way is to give up the problem as insoluble, life and action as an illusion or an inferior movement of existence to be abandoned as soon as we can rise out of the snare of the world into the truth of spiritual being. That is the ascetic solution, if it can be called a solution; at any rate it is a decisive and effective way out of the enigma, a way to which ancient Indian thought of the highest and most meditative kind, as soon as it commenced to turn at a sharp incline from its first large and free synthesis, had moved with an always increasing preponderance. The Gita, like the Tantra and on certain sides the later religions attempts to preserve the ancient balance: it maintains the substance and foundation of the original synthesis, but the form has been changed and renovated in the light of a developing spiritual experience. This teaching does not evade the difficult problem of reconciling the full active life of man with the inner life in the highest self and spirit; it advances what it holds to be the real solution. It does not at all deny the efficacy of the ascetic renunciation of life for its own purpose, but it sees that that cuts instead of loosening the knot of the riddle and therefore it accounts it an inferior method and holds its own for the better way. The two paths both lead us out of the lower ignorant normal nature of man to the pure spiritual consciousness and so far both must be held to be valid and even one in essence: but where one stops short and turns back, the other advances with a firm subtlety and high courage, opens a gate on unexplored vistas, completes man in God and unites and reconciles in the spirit soul and Nature.

And therefore in the first five of these verses the Gita so phrases its statement that it shall be applicable to both the way of the inner and the way of the outer renunciation and yet in such a manner that one has only to assign to some of their common expressions a deeper and more inward meaning in order to get the sense and thought of the method favoured by the Gita. The difficulty of human action is that the soul and nature of man seem fatally subjected to many kinds of bondage, the prison of the ignorance, the meshes of the ego, the chain of the passions, the hammering insistence of the life of the moment, an obscure and limited circle without an issue. The soul shut up in this circle of action has no freedom, no leisure or light of self-knowledge to make the discovery of its self and the true value of life and meaning of existence. It has indeed such hints of its being as it can get from its active personality and dynamic nature, but the standards of perfection it can erect there are much too temporal, restricted and relative to be a satisfactory key to its own riddle. How, while absorbed and continually forced outward by the engrossing call of its active nature, is it to get back to its real self and spiritual existence? The ascetic renunciation and the way of the Gita are both agreed that it must first of all renounce this absorption, must cast from it the external solicitation of outward things and separate silent self from active nature; it must identify itself with the immobile Spirit and live in the silence. It must arrive at an inner inactivity, *naiṣkarmya*. It is therefore this saving inner passivity that the Gita puts here as the first object of its Yoga, the first necessary perfection in it or Siddhi. 'An understanding without attachment in all things, a soul self-conquered and empty of desire, man attains by renunciation a supreme perfection of *naiṣkarmya*.'

This ideal of renunciation, of a self-conquered stillness, spiritual passivity and freedom from desire is common to all the ancient wisdom. The Gita gives us its psychological foundation with an unsurpassed completeness and clearness. It rests on the common experience of all seekers of self-knowledge that there are two different natures and as it were two selves in us. There is the lower self of the obscure mental, vital and physical nature subject to ignorance and inertia in the very stuff of its consciousness and especially in its basis of material substance, kinetic and vital indeed by the power of life but without inherent self-possession and self-knowledge in its action, attaining in the mind to some knowledge and harmony, but only with difficult effort and by a constant struggle with its own disabilities. And there is the higher nature and self of our spiritual being, self-possessed and self-luminous but in our ordinary mentality inaccessible to our experience. At times we get glimpses of this greater thing within us, but we are not consciously within it, we do not live in its light and calm and illimitable splendour. The first of these two very different things is the Gita's nature of the three gunas. Its seeing of itself is centred in the ego idea, its principle of action is desire born of ego, and the knot of ego is attachment to the objects of the mind and sense and the life's desire. The inevitable constant result of all these things is bondage, settled subjection to a lower control, absence of self-mastery, absence of self-knowledge. The other greater power and presence is discovered to be nature and being of the pure spirit unconditioned by ego, that which is called in Indian philosophy self and impersonal Brahman. Its principle is an infinite and an impersonal existence one and the same in all: and, since this impersonal existence is without ego, without conditioning quality, without desire, need or stimulus, it is immobile and immutable; eternally the same, it regards and supports but does not share or initiate the action of the universe. The soul when it throws itself out into active Nature is the Gita's Kshara, its mobile or mutable Purusha; the same soul gathered back into pure silent self and essential spirit is the Gita's Akshara, immobile or immutable Purusha.

Then evidently the straight and simplest way to get out of the close bondage of the active nature and back to spiritual freedom is to cast away entirely all that belongs to the dynamics of the ignorance and to convert the soul into a pure spiritual existence. That is what is called becoming Brahman, *brahmabhūya*. It is to put off the lower mental, vital, physical existence and to put on the pure spiritual being. This can best be done by the intelligence and will, *buddhi*, our present topmost principle. It has to turn away from the things of the lower existence and first and foremost from its effective knot of desire, from our attachment to the objects pursued by the mind and the senses. One must become an understanding unattached in all things, *asakta-buddhiḥ sarvatra*. Then all desire passes away from the soul in its silence; it is free from all longings, *vigata-spṛhaḥ*. That brings with it or it makes possible the subjection of our lower and the possession of our higher self, a possession dependent on complete self-mastery, secured by a radical victory and conquest over our mobile nature, *jitātmā*. And all this amounts to an absolute inner renunciation of the desire of things, *sannyāsa*. Renunciation is the way to this perfection and the man who has thus inwardly renounced all is described by the Gita as the true Sannyasin. But because the word usually signifies as well an outward renunciation or sometimes even that alone, the Teacher uses another word, *tyāga*, to distinguish the inward from the outward withdrawal and says that Tyaga is better than Sannyasa. The ascetic way goes much farther in its recoil from the dynamic Nature. It is enamoured of renunciation for its own sake and insists on an outward giving up of life and action, a complete quietism of soul and nature. That, the Gita replies, is not possible entirely so long as we live in the body. As far as it is possible, it may be done, but such a rigorous diminution of works is not indispensable: it is not even really or at least ordinarily advisable. The one thing needed is a complete inner quietism and that is all the Gita's sense of *naiṣkarmya*.

If we ask why this reservation, why this indulgence to the dynamic principle when our object is to become the pure self and the pure self is described as inactive, *akartā*, the answer is that that inactivity and divorce of self from Nature are not the whole truth of our spiritual release. Self and Nature are in the end one thing; a total and perfect spirituality makes us one with all the Divine in self and in nature. In fact this becoming Brahman, this assumption into the self of eternal silence, *brahma-bhūya*, is not all our objective, but only the necessary immense base for a still greater and more marvellous divine becoming, *madbhāva*. And to get to that greatest spiritual perfection we have indeed to be immobile in the self, silent in all our members, but also to act in the power, Shakti, Prakriti, the true and high force of the Spirit. And if we ask how a simultaneity of what seem to be two opposites is possible, the answer is that that is the very nature of a complete spiritual being; always it has this double poise of the Infinite. The impersonal self is silent; we too must be inwardly silent, impersonal, withdrawn into the spirit. The impersonal self looks on all action as done not by it but by Prakriti; it regards with a pure equality all the working of her qualities, modes and forces: the soul impersonalised in the self must similarly regard all our actions as done not by itself but by the qualities of Prakriti; it must be equal in all things, *sarvatra*. And at the same time in order that we may not stop here, in order that we may eventually go forward and find a spiritual rule and direction in our works and not only a law of inner immobility and silence, we are asked to impose on the intelligence and will the attitude of sacrifice, all our action inwardly changed and turned into an offering to the Lord of Nature, to the Being of whom she is the self-power, *svā prakṛtiḥ*, the supreme Spirit. Even we have eventually to renounce all into his hands, to abandon all personal initiation of action, *sarvārambhāḥ*, to keep our natural selves only as an instrument of his works and his purpose. These things have been already explained fully and the Gita does not here insist, but uses simply without farther qualification the common terms, *sannyāsa* and *naiṣkarmya*.

To be one with all and with the Divine and his will in the cosmos we must become at first impersonal and free from our ego and its claims and from the ego's way of seeing ourselves and the world and others. And we cannot do this if there is not something in our being other than the personality, other than the ego, an impersonal self one with all existences. To lose ego and be this impersonal self, to become this impersonal Brahman in our consciousness is therefore the first movement of this Yoga.

How then is this to be done? First, says the Gita, through a union of our purified intelligence with the pure spiritual substance in us by the yoga of the buddhi, *buddhyā viśuddhayā yuktaḥ*. This spiritual turning of the buddhi from the outward and downward to the inward and upward look is the essence of the Yoga of knowledge. The purified understanding has to control the whole being, *ātmānaṁ niyamya*; it must draw us away from attachment to the outward-going desires of the lower nature by a firm and a steady will, *dhṛtyā*, which in its concentration faces entirely towards the impersonality of the pure spirit. The senses must abandon their objects, the mind must cast away the liking and disliking which these objects excite in it – for the impersonal self has no desires and repulsions; these are vital reactions of our personality to the touches of things and the corresponding response of the mind and senses to the touches is their support and their basis. An entire control has to be acquired over the mind, speech and body, over even the vital and physical reactions, hunger and cold and heat and physical pleasure and pain; the whole of our being must become indifferent, unaffected by these things, equal to all outward touches and to their inward reactions and responses. This is the most direct and powerful method, the straight and sharp way of Yoga. There has to be a complete cessation of desire and attachment, *vairāgya*; a strong resort to impersonal solitude, a constant union with the inmost self by meditation is demanded of the seeker. One must put away utterly first the rajasic kind of egoism, egoistic strength and violence, arrogance, desire, wrath, the sense and instinct of possession, the urge of the passions, the strong lusts of life. But afterwards must be discarded egoism of all kinds, even of the most sattwic type; for the aim is to make soul and mind and life free in the end from all imprisoning I-ness and my-ness, *nirmama*.

For the pure impersonal self which, unshaken, supports the universe has no egoism and makes no demand on thing or person; it is calm and luminously impassive and silently regards all things and persons with an equal and impartial eye of self-knowledge and world-knowledge. Then clearly it is by living inwardly in a similar or identical impersonality that the soul within, released from the siege of things, can best become capable of oneness with this immutable Brahman which regards and knows but is not affected by the forms and mutations of the universe.

And it then becomes evident how action continual and unceasing and of all kinds without diminution or abandonment of any part of the activities of life can be not only quite consistent with a supreme spiritual experience, but as forceful a means of reaching this highest spiritual condition as bhakti or knowledge. Nothing can be more positive than the Gita's statement in this matter. 'And by doing also all actions always lodged in Me he attains by my grace the eternal and imperishable status.'

All that we do is done for the sake of the Lord seated in the heart of all, for the Godhead in the individual and for the fulfilment of his will in us, for the sake of the Divine in the world, for the good of all beings, for the fulfilment of the world action and the world purpose, or in one word for the sake of the Purushottama and done really by him through his universal Shakti.

Disengaged from these mixed and limited dharmas we escape into the immortal Dharma which comes upon us when we make ourselves one in all our consciousness and action with the Purushottama. That oneness here brings with it the power to rise there into the immortality beyond Time. There we shall exist in his eternal transcendence.

The Supreme Secret[1]

The essence of the teaching and the Yoga has thus been given to the disciple on the field of his work and battle and the divine Teacher now proceeds to apply it to his action, but in a way that makes it applicable to all action. Attached to a crucial example, spoken to the protagonist of Kurukshetra, the words bear a much wider significance and are a universal rule for all who are ready to ascend above the ordinary mentality and to live and act in the highest spiritual consciousness. To break out of ego and personal mind and see everything in the wideness of the self and spirit, to know God and adore him in his integral truth and in all his aspects, to surrender all oneself to the transcendent Soul of nature and existence, to possess and be possessed by the divine consciousness, to be one with the One in universality of love and delight and will and knowledge, one in him with all beings, to do works as an adoration and a sacrifice on the divine foundation of a world in which all is

[1] Gita, XVIII. 57–66, 73.

God and in the divine status of a liberated spirit, is the sense of the Gita's Yoga. It is a transition from the apparent to the supreme spiritual and real truth of our being, and one enters into it by putting off the many limitations of the separative consciousness and the mind's attachment to the passion and unrest and ignorance, the lesser light and knowledge, the sin and virtue, the dual law and standard of the lower nature. Therefore, says the Teacher, 'devoting all thyself to me, giving up in thy conscious mind all thy actions into Me, resorting to Yoga of the will and intelligence be always one in heart and consciousness with Me. If thou art that at all times, then by my grace thou shalt pass safe through all difficult and perilous passages; but if from egoism thou hear not, thou shalt fall into perdition. Vain is this thy resolve, that in thy egoism thou thinkest, saying "I will not fight"; thy nature shall appoint thee to thy work. What from delusion thou desirest not to do, that helplessly thou shalt do bound by thy own work born of thy swabhava. The Lord is stationed in the heart of all existences, O Arjuna, and turns them all round and round mounted on a machine by his Maya. In him take refuge in every way of thy being and by his grace thou shalt come to the supreme peace and the eternal status.'

These are lines that carry in them the innermost heart of this Yoga and lead to its crowning experience and we must understand them in their innermost spirit and the whole vastness of that high summit of experience. The words express the most complete, intimate and living relation possible between God and man; they are instinct with the concentrated force of religious feeling that springs from the human being's absolute adoration, his upward surrender of his whole existence, his unreserved and perfect self-giving to the transcendent and universal Divinity from whom he comes and in whom he lives. This stress of feeling is in entire consonance with the high and enduring place that the Gita assigns to bhakti, to the love of God, to the adoration of the Highest, as the inmost spirit and motive of the supreme action and the crown and core of the supreme knowledge. The phrases used and the spiritual emotion with which they vibrate seem to give the most intense prominence possible and an utmost importance to the personal truth and presence of the Godhead. It is no abstract Absolute of the philosopher, no indifferent impersonal Presence or ineffable Silence intolerant of all relations to whom this complete surrender of all our works can be made and this closeness and intimacy of oneness with him in all the parts of our conscious existence imposed as the condition and law of our perfection or of whom this divine intervention and protection and deliverance are the promise. It is a Master of our works, a Friend and Lover of our soul, an intimate Spirit of our life, an indwelling and over-dwelling Lord of all our personal and impersonal self and nature who alone can utter to us this near and moving message. And yet this is not the common relation established by the religions between man living in his sattwic or other ego-mind and some personal form and aspect of the Deity, *iṣṭa-deva*, constructed by that mind or offered to it to satisfy its limited ideal, aspiration or desire. That is the ordinary sense and actual character of the normal mental being's religious devotion; but here there is something wider that passes beyond the mind and its limits and its dharmas. It is something deeper than the mind that offers and something greater than the Ishta-deva that receives the surrender.

That which surrenders here is the Jiva, the essential soul, the original central and spiritual being of man, the individual Purusha. It is the Jiva delivered from the limiting and ignorant ego-sense who knows himself not as a separate personality but as an eternal portion and power and soul-becoming of the Divine, *aṁśa sanātana*, the Jiva released and uplifted by the passing away of ignorance and established in the light and freedom of his own true and supreme nature which is one with that of the Eternal. It is this central spiritual being in us who thus enters into a perfect and closely real relation of delight and union with the origin and continent and governing Self and Power of our existence. And he who receives our surrender is no limited Deity but the Purushottama, the one eternal Godhead, the one supreme Soul of all that is and of all Nature, the original transcendent Spirit of existence. An immutable impersonal self-existence is his first obvious spiritual self-presentation to the experience of our liberated knowledge, the first sign of his presence, the first touch and impression of his substance. A universal and transcendent infinite Person or Purusha is the mysterious hidden secret of his very being, unthinkable in form of mind, *acintya-rūpa*, but very near and present to the powers of our consciousness, emotion, will and knowledge when they are lifted out of themselves, out of their blind and petty forms into a luminous spiritual, an immeasurable supramental Ananda and power and gnosis. It is He, ineffable Absolute but also Friend and Lord and Enlightener and Lover, who is the object of this most complete devotion and approach and this most intimate inner becoming and surrender. This union, this relation is a thing lifted beyond the forms and laws of the limiting mind, too high for all these inferior dharmas it is a truth of our self and spirit. And yet or rather therefore, because it is the truth of our self and spirit, the truth of its oneness with that Spirit from which all comes and by it and as its derivations and suggestions all exists and travails, it is not a negation but a fulfilment of all that mind and life point to and bear in them as their secret and unaccomplished significance. Thus, it is not by a nirvana, an exclusion and negating extinction of all that we are here, but by a nirvana, an exclusion and negating extinction of ignorance and ego and a consequent ineffable fulfilment of our knowledge and will and heart's aspiration, an uplifted and limitless living of them in the Divine, in the Eternal, *nivasiṣyasi mayyeva*, a transfigurement and transference of all our consciousness to a greater inner status that there comes this supreme perfection and release in the spirit.

The crux of the spiritual problem, the character of this transition of which it is so difficult for the normal mind of man to get a true apprehension, turns altogether upon the capital distinction between the ignorant life of the ego in the lower nature and the large and luminous existence of the liberated Jiva in his own true spiritual nature. The renunciation of the first must be complete, the transition to the second absolute. This is the distinction on which the Gita dwells here with all possible emphasis. On the one side is this poor, trepidant, braggart egoistic condition of consciousness, *ahaṅkṛta bhāva*, the crippling narrowness of this little helpless separative personality according to whose view-point we ordinarily think and act, feel and respond to the touches of existence. On the other are the vast spiritual reaches of immortal fullness, bliss and knowledge into which we are admitted through union with the divine Being, of whom we are then a manifestation and expression in the eternal light and no longer a disguise in the darkness of the ego-nature. It is the completeness of this union which is indicated by the Gita's *satataṁ mac-cittaḥ.* The life of the ego is founded on a construction of the apparent mental, vital and physical truth of existence, on a nexus of pragmatic relations between the individual soul and Nature, on an intellectual, emotional and sensational interpretation of things used by the little limited I in us to maintain and satisfy the ideas and desires of its bounded separate personality amid the vast action of the universe. All our dharmas, all the ordinary standards by which we determine our view of things and our knowledge and our action, proceed upon this narrow and limiting basis, and to follow them even in the widest wheelings round our ego centre does not carry us out of this petty circle. It is a circle in which the soul is a contented or struggling prisoner, for ever subject to the mixed compulsions of Nature.

For Purusha veils himself in this round, veils his divine and immortal being in ignorance and is subject to the law of an insistent limiting Prakriti. That law is the compelling rule of the three gunas. It is a triple stair that stumbles upward towards the divine light but cannot reach it. At its base is the law or dharma of inertia: the tamasic man inertly obeys in a customary mechanical action the suggestions and impulses, the round of will of his material and his half-intellectualised vital and sensational nature. In the middle intervenes the kinetic law or dharma; the rajasic man, vital, dynamic, active, attempts to impose himself on his world and environment, but only increases the wounding weight and tyrant yoke of his turbulent passions, desires and egoisms, the burden of his restless self-will, the yoke of his rajasic nature. At the top presses down upon life the harmonic regulative law or dharma; the sattwic man attempts to erect and follow his limited personal standards of reasoning knowledge, enlightened utility or mechanised virtue, his religions and philosophies and ethical formulas, mental systems and constructions, fixed channels of idea and conduct which do not agree with the totality of the meaning of life and are constantly being broken in the movement of the wider universal purpose. The dharma of the sattwic man is the highest in the circle of the gunas; but that too is a limited view and a dwarfed standard. Its imperfect indications lead to a petty and relative perfection; temporarily satisfying to the enlightened personal ego, it is not founded either on the whole truth of the self or on the whole truth of Nature.

And in fact, the actual life of man is not at any time one of these things alone, neither a mechanical routine execution of the first crude law of Nature, nor the struggle of a kinetic soul of action, nor a victorious emergence of conscious light and reason and good and knowledge. There is a mixture of all these dharmas out of which our will and intelligence make a more or less arbitrary construction to be realised as best it can, but never in fact realised except by compromise with other compelling things in the universal Prakriti. The sattwic ideals of our enlightened will and reason are either themselves compromises, at best progressive compromises, subject to a constant imperfection and flux of change, or if absolute in their character, they can be followed only as a counsel of perfection ignored for the most part in practice or successful only as a partial influence. And if sometimes we imagine we have completely realised them, it is because we ignore in ourselves the subconscious or half-conscious mixture of other powers and motives that are usually as much or more than our ideals the real force in our action. That self-ignorance constitutes the whole vanity of human reason and self-righteousness; it is the dark secret lining behind the spotless white outsides of human sainthood and alone makes possible the specious egoisms of knowledge and virtue. The best human knowledge is a half knowledge and the highest human virtue a thing of mixed quality and, even when most sincerely absolute in standard, sufficiently relative in practice. As a general law of living the absolute sattwic ideals cannot prevail in conduct; indispensable as a power for the betterment and raising of personal aspiration and conduct, their insistence modifies life but cannot wholly change it, and their perfect fulfilment images itself only in a dream of the future or a world of heavenly nature free from the mixed strain of our terrestrial existence. It cannot be otherwise because neither the nature of this world nor the nature of man is or can be one single piece made of the pure stuff of sattwa.

For then, when we enter into that inmost self of our existence, we come to know that in us and in all is the one Spirit and Godhead whom all Nature serves and manifests and we ourselves are soul of this Soul, spirit of this Spirit, our body his delegated image, our life a movement of the rhythm of his life, our mind a sheath of his consciousness, our senses his instruments, our emotions and sensations the seekings of his delight of being, our actions a means of his purpose, our freedom only a shadow, suggestion or glimpse while we are ignorant, but when we know him and ourselves a prolongation and effective channel of his immortal freedom.

It is the Lord seated in the heart of every creature who has been turning us in all our inner and outer action during the ignorance as if mounted on a machine on the wheel of this Maya of the lower Nature. And whether obscure in the Ignorance or luminous in the Knowledge, it is for him in us and him in the world that we have our existence. To live consciously and integrally in this knowledge and this truth is to escape from ego and break out of Maya. All other highest dharmas are only a preparation for this Dharma, and all Yoga is only a means by which we can come first to some kind of union and finally, if we have the full light, to an integral union with the Master and supreme Soul and Self of our existence.

For after giving out all the laws, the dharmas, and the deepest essence of its Yoga, after saying that beyond all the first secrets revealed to the mind of man by the transforming light of spiritual knowledge, *guhyāt*, this is a still deeper more secret truth, *guhyataram*, the Gita suddenly declares that there is yet a supreme word that it has to speak, *paramaṁ vacaḥ*, and a most secret truth of all, *sarva-guhyatamam*. This secret of secrets the Teacher will tell to Arjuna as his highest good because he is the chosen and beloved soul, *iṣṭa*. For evidently, as had already been declared by the Upanishad, it is only the rare soul chosen by the Spirit for the revelation of his very body, *tanuṁ svām*, who can be admitted to this mystery, because he alone is near enough in heart and mind and life to the Godhead to respond truly to it in all his being and to make it a living practice. The last, the closing supreme word of the Gita expressing the highest mystery is spoken in two brief, direct and simple slokas as and these are left without farther comment or enlargement to sink into the mind and reveal their own fullness of meaning in the soul's experience.

Thus runs this secret of secrets, the highest most direct message of the Ishwara. 'Become my-minded, my lover and adorer, a sacrificer to me, bow thyself to me, to me thou shalt come, this is my pledge and promise to thee, for dear art thou to me. Abandon all dharmas and take refuge in me alone. I will deliver thee from all sin and evil, do not grieve.'

The secret thing, *guhyam*, that all deep spiritual knowledge reveals to us, mirrored in various teachings and justified in the soul's experience, is for the Gita the secret of the spiritual self hidden within us of which mind and external Nature are only manifestations or figures. It is the secret of the constant relations between soul and Nature, Purusha and Prakriti, the secret of an indwelling Godhead who is the lord of all existence and veiled from us in its forms and movements. These are the truths taught in many ways by Vedanta and Sankhya and Yoga and synthetised in the earlier chapters of the Gita. And amidst all their apparent distinctions they are one truth and all the different ways of Yoga are various means of spiritual self-discipline by which our unquiet mind and blinded life are stilled and turned towards this many-aspected One and the secret truth of self and God made so real to us and intimate that we can either consciously live and dwell in it or lose our separate selves in the Eternal and no longer be compelled at all by the mental Ignorance.

The more secret thing, *guhyataram*, developed by the Gita is the profound reconciling truth of the divine Purushottama, at once self and Purusha, supreme Brahman and a sole, intimate, mysterious, ineffable Godhead. That gives to the thought a larger and more deeply understanding foundation for an ultimate knowledge and to the spiritual experience a greater and more fully comprehending and comprehensive Yoga. This deeper mystery is founded on the secret of the supreme spiritual Prakriti and of the Jiva, an eternal portion of the Divine in that eternal and this manifested Nature and of one spirit and essence with him in his immutable self-existence. This profounder knowledge escapes from the elementary distinction of spiritual experience between the Beyond and what is here. For the Transcendent beyond the worlds is at the same time Vasudeva who is all things in all worlds; he is the Lord standing in the heart of every creature and the self of all existences and the origin and supernal meaning of everything that he has put forth in his Prakriti. He is manifested in his Vibhutis and he is the Spirit in Time who compels the action of the world and the Sun of all knowledge and the Lover and Beloved of the soul and the Master of all works and sacrifice. The result of an inmost opening to this deeper, truer, more secret mystery is the Gita's Yoga of integral knowledge, integral works and integral bhakti. It is the simultaneous experience of spiritual universality and a free and perfected spiritual individuality, of an entire union with God and an entire dwelling in him as at once the frame of the soul's immortality and the support and power of our liberated action in the world and the body.

And now there comes the supreme word and most secret thing of all, *guhyatamam*, that the Spirit and Godhead is an Infinite free from all dharmas and though he conducts the world according to fixed laws and leads man through his dharmas of ignorance and knowledge, sin and virtue, right and wrong, liking and disliking and indifference, pleasure and pain, joy and sorrow and the rejection of these opposites, through his physical and vital, intellectual, emotional, ethical and spiritual forms and rules and standards, yet the Spirit and Godhead transcends all these things, and if we too can cast away all dependence on dharmas, surrender ourselves to this free and eternal Spirit and, taking care only to keep ourselves absolutely and exclusively open to him, trust to the light and power and delight of the Divine in us and, unafraid and ungrieving, accept only his guidance, then that is the truest, the greatest release and that brings the absolute and inevitable perfection of our self and nature. This is the way offered to the chosen of the Spirit – to those only in whom he takes the greatest delight because they are nearest to him and most capable of oneness and of being even as he, freely consenting and concordant with Nature in her highest power and movement, universal in soul consciousness, transcendent in the spirit.

For a time comes in spiritual development when we become aware that all our effort and action are only our mental and vital reactions to the silent and secret insistence of a greater Presence in and around us. It is borne in upon us that all our Yoga, our aspiration and our endeavour are imperfect or narrow forms, because disfigured or at least limited by the mind's associations, demands, prejudgments, predilections, mistranslations or half translations of a vaster truth. Our ideas and experiences and efforts are mental images only of greatest things which would be done more perfectly, directly, freely, largely, more in harmony with the universal and eternal will by that Power itself in us if we could only put ourselves passively as instruments in the hands of a supreme and absolute strength and wisdom. That Power is not separate from us; it is our own self one with the self of all others and at the same time a transcendent Being and an immanent Person. Our existence, our action taken up into this greatest Existence would be no longer, as it seems to us now, individually our own in a mental separation. It would be the vast movement of an Infinity and an intimate ineffable Presence; it would be the constant spontaneity of formation and expression in us of this deep universal self and this transcendent Spirit. The Gita indicates that in order that that may wholly be, the surrender must be without reservations; our Yoga, our life, our state of inner being must be determined freely by this living Infinite, not predetermined by our mind's insistence on this or that dharma or any dharma. The divine Master of the Yoga, *yogeśvaraḥ kṛṣṇaḥ*, will then himself take up our Yoga and raise us to our utmost possible perfection, not the perfection of any external or mental standard or limiting rule, but vast and comprehensive, to the mind incalculable. It will be a perfection developed by an all-seeing Wisdom according to the whole truth, first indeed of our human swabhava, but afterwards of a greater thing into which it will open, a spirit and power illimitable, immortal, free and all-transmuting, the light and splendour of a divine and infinite nature.

All must be given as material of that transmutation. An omniscient consciousness will take up our knowledge and our ignorance, our truth and our error, cast away their forms of insufficiency, *sarva-dharmān parityajya*, and transform all into its infinite light. An almighty Power will take up our virtue and sin, our right and wrong, our strength and our weakness, cast away their tangled figures, *sarva-dharmān parityajya*, and transform all into its transcendent purity and universal good and infallible force. An ineffable Ananda will take up our petty joy and sorrow, our struggling pleasure and pain, cast away their discordances and imperfect rhythms, *sarva-dharmān parityajya*, and transform all into its transcendent and universal unimaginable delight. All that all the Yogas can do will be done and more; but it will be done in a greater seeing way, with a greater wisdom and truth than any human teacher, saint or sage can give us. The inner spiritual state to which this supreme Yoga will take us, will be above all that is here and yet comprehensive of all things in this and other worlds, but with a spiritual transformation of all, without limitation, without bondage, *sarva-dharmān parityajya*. The infinite existence, consciousness and delight of the Godhead in its calm silence and bright boundless activity will be there, will be its essential, fundamental, universal stuff, mould and character. And in that mould of infinity the Divine made manifest will overtly dwell, no longer concealed by his Yogamaya, and whenever and as he wills build in us whatever shapes of the Infinite, translucent forms of knowledge, thought, love, spiritual joy, power and action according to his self-fulfilling will and immortal pleasure. And there will be no binding effect on the free soul and the unaffected nature, no unescapable crystallising into this or that inferior formula. For all the action will be executed by the power of the Spirit in a divine freedom, *sarva-dharmān parityajya*. An unfallen abiding in the transcendent Spirit, *paraṁ dhāma*, will be the foundation and the assurance of this spiritual state. An intimate understanding oneness with universal being and all creatures, released from the evil and suffering of the separative mind but wisely regardful of true distinctions, will be the conditioning power. A constant delight, oneness and harmony of the eternal individual here with the Divine and all that he is will be the effect of this integral liberation. The baffling problems of our human existence of which Arjuna's difficulty stands as an acute example, are created by our separative personality in the Ignorance. This Yoga because it puts the soul of man into its right relation with God and world-existence and makes our action God's, the knowledge and will shaping and moving it his and our life the harmony of a divine self-expression, is the way to their total disappearance.

The whole Yoga is revealed, the great word of the teaching is given, and Arjuna the chosen human soul is once more turned, no longer in his egoistic mind but in this greatest self-knowledge, to the divine action. The Vibhuti is ready for the divine life in the human, his conscious spirit for the works of the liberated soul, *muktasya karma*. Destroyed is the illusion of the mind; the soul's memory of its self and its truth concealed so long by the misleading shows and forms of our life has returned to it and become its normal consciousness: all doubt and perplexity gone, it can turn to the execution of the command and do faithfully whatever work for God and the world may be appointed and apportioned to it by the Master of our being, the Spirit and Godhead self-fulfilled in Time and universe.

The Core of the Gita's Meaning

What then is the message of the Gita and what its working value, its spiritual utility to the human mind of the present day after the long ages that have elapsed since it was written and the great subsequent transformations of thought and experience? The human mind moves always forward, alters its viewpoint and enlarges its thought substance, and the effect of these changes is to render past systems of thinking obsolete or, when they are preserved, to extend, to modify and subtly or visibly to alter their value. The vitality of an ancient doctrine consists in the extent to which it naturally lends itself to such a treatment; for that means that whatever may have been the limitations or the obsolescences of the form of its thought, the truth of substance, the truth of living vision and experience on which its system was built is still sound and retains a permanent validity and significance. The Gita is a book that has worn extraordinarily well and it is almost as fresh and still in its real substance quite as new, because always renewable in experience, as when it first appeared in or was written into the frame of the Mahabharata. It is still received in India as one of the great bodies of doctrine that most authoritatively govern religious thinking and its teaching acknowledged as of the highest value if not wholly accepted by almost all shades of religious belief and opinion. Its influence is not merely philosophic or academic but immediate and living, an influence both for thought and action, and its ideas are actually at work as a powerful shaping factor in the revival and renewal of a nation and a culture. It has even been said recently by a great voice that all we need of spiritual truth for the spiritual life is to be found in the Gita. It would be to encourage the superstition of the book to take too literally that utterance. The truth of the spirit is infinite and cannot be circumscribed in that manner. Still it may be said that most of the main clues are there and that after all the later developments of spiritual experience and discovery we can still return to it for a large inspiration and guidance. Outside India too it is universally acknowledged as one of the world's great scriptures, although in Europe its thought is better understood than its secret of spiritual practice. What is it then that gives this vitality to the thought and the truth of the Gita? The central interest of the Gita's philosophy and Yoga is its attempt, the idea with which it sets out, continues and closes, to reconcile and even effect a kind of unity between the inner spiritual truth in its most absolute and integral realisation and the outer actualities of man's life and action. A compromise between the two is common enough, but that can never be a final and satisfactory solution. An ethical rendering of spirituality is also common and has its value as a law of conduct; but that is a mental solution which does not amount to a complete practical reconciliation of the whole truth of spirit with the whole truth of life and it raises as many problems as it solves. One of these is indeed the starting-point of the Gita; it sets out with an ethical problem raised by a conflict in which we have on one side the dharma of the man of action, a prince and warrior and leader of men, the protagonist of a great crisis, of a struggle on the physical plane, the plane of actual life, between the powers of right and justice and the powers of wrong and injustice, the demand of the destiny of the race upon him that he shall resist and give battle and establish even though through a terrible physical struggle and a giant slaughter a new era and reign of truth and right and justice, and on the other side the ethical sense which condemns the means and the action as a sin, recoils from the price of individual suffering and social strife, unsettling and disturbance and regards abstention from violence and battle as the only way and the one right moral attitude. A spiritualised ethics insists on Ahinsa, on non-injuring and non-killing as the highest law of spiritual conduct. The battle, if it is to be fought out at all, must be fought on the spiritual plane and by some kind of non-resistance or refusal of participation or only by soul resistance, and if this does not succeed on the external plane, if the force of injustice conquers, the individual will still have preserved his virtue and vindicated by his example the highest ideal. On the other hand a more insistent extreme of the inner spiritual direction, passing beyond this struggle between social duty and an absolutist ethical ideal, is apt to take the ascetic turn and to point away from life and all its aims and standards of action towards another and celestial or supracosmic state in which alone beyond the perplexed vanity and illusion of man's birth and life and death there can be a pure spiritual existence. The Gita rejects none of these things in their place, – for it insists on the performance of the social duty, the following of the dharma for the man who has to take his share in the common action, accepts Ahinsa as part of the highest spiritual-ethical ideal and recognises the ascetic renunciation as a way of spiritual salvation. And yet it goes boldly beyond all these conflicting positions; greatly daring, it justifies all life to the spirit as a significant manifestation of the one Divine Being and asserts the compatibility of a complete human action and a complete spiritual life lived in union with the Infinite, consonant with the highest Self, expressive of the perfect Godhead.

All the problems of human life arise from the complexity of our existence, the obscurity of its essential principle and the secrecy of the inmost power that makes out its determinations and governs its purpose and its processes. If our existence were of one piece, solely material-vital or solely mental or solely spiritual, or even if the others were entirely or mainly involved in one of these or were quite latent in our subconscient or our superconscient parts, there would be nothing to perplex us; the material and vital law would be imperative or the mental would be clear to its own pure and unobstructed principle or the spiritual self-existent and self-sufficient to spirit. The animals are aware of no problems; a mental god in a world of pure mentality would admit none or would solve them all by the purity of a mental rule or the satisfaction of a rational harmony; a pure spirit would be above them and self-content in the infinite. But the existence of man is a triple web, a thing mysteriously physical, vital, mental and spiritual at once, and he knows not what are the true relations of these things, which the real reality of his life and his nature, whither the attraction of his destiny and where the sphere of his perfection.

Matter and life are his actual basis, the thing from which he starts and on which he stands and whose requirement and law he has to satisfy if he would exist at all on earth and in the body. The material and vital law is a rule of survival, of struggle, of desire and possession, of self-assertion and the satisfaction of the body, the life and the ego. All the intellectual reasoning in the world, all the ethical idealism and spiritual absolutism of which the higher faculties of man are capable cannot abolish the reality and claim of our vital and material base or prevent the race from following under the imperative compulsion of Nature its aims and the satisfaction of its necessities or from making its important problems a great and legitimate part of human destiny and human interest and endeavour. And the intelligence of man even, failing to find any sustenance in spiritual or ideal solutions that solve everything else but the pressing problems of our actual human life, often turns away from them to an exclusive acceptance of the vital and material existence and the reasoned or instinctive pursuit of its utmost possible efficiency, well-being and organised satisfaction. A gospel of the will to live or the will to power or of a rationalised vital and material perfection becomes the recognised dharma of the human race and all else is considered either a pretentious falsity or a quite subsidiary thing, a side issue of a minor and dependent consequence.

The Message of the Gita

'The secret of action,' so we might summarise the message of the Gita, the word of its divine Teacher, 'is one with the secret of all life and existence. Existence is not merely a machinery of Nature, a wheel of law in which the soul is entangled for a moment or for ages; it is a constant manifestation of the Spirit. Life is not for the sake of life alone, but for God, and the living soul of man is an eternal portion of the Godhead. Action is for self-finding, for self-fulfilment, for self-realisation and not only for its own external and apparent fruits of the moment or the future. There is an inner law and meaning of all things dependent on the supreme as well as the manifested nature of the self; the true truth of works lies there and can be represented only incidentally, imperfectly and disguised by ignorance in the outer appearances of the mind and its action. The supreme, the faultless largest law of action is therefore to find out the truth of your own highest and inmost existence and live in it and not to follow any outer standard and dharma. All life and action must be till then an imperfection, a difficulty, a struggle and a problem. It is only by discovering your true self and living according to its true truth, its real reality that the problem can be finally solved, the difficulty and struggle overpassed and your doings perfected in the security of the discovered self and spirit turn into a divinely authentic action. Know then yourself; know your true self to be God and one with the self of all others; know your soul to be a portion of God. Live in what you know; live in the self, live in your supreme spiritual nature, be united with God and Godlike. Offer, first, all your actions as a sacrifice to the Highest and the One in you and to the Highest and the One in the world; deliver last all you are and do into his hands for the supreme and universal spirit to do through you his own will and works in the world. This is the solution that I present to you and in the end you will find that there is no other.'

Here it is necessary to state the Gita's view of the fundamental opposition on which like all Indian teaching it takes its position. This finding of the true self, this knowledge of the Godhead within us and all is not an easy thing; nor is it an easy thing either to turn this knowledge, even though seen by the mind, into the stuff of our consciousness and the whole condition of our action. All action is determined by the effective state of our being, and the effective state of our being is determined by the state of our constant self-seeing will and active consciousness and by its basis of kinetic movement. It is what we see and believe with our whole active nature ourselves to be and our relations with the world to mean, it is our faith, our *śraddhā*, that makes us what we are. But the consciousness of man is of a double kind and corresponds to a double truth of existence; for there is a truth of the inner reality and a truth of the outer appearance. According as he lives in one or the other, he will be a mind dwelling in human ignorance or a soul founded in divine knowledge.

In its outer appearance the truth of existence is solely what we call Nature or Prakriti, a Force that operates as the whole law and mechanism of being, creates the world which is the object of our mind and senses and creates too the mind and senses as a means of relation between the creature and the objective world in which he lives. In this outer appearance man in his soul, his mind, his life, his body seems to be a creature of Nature differentiated from others by a separation of his body, life and mind and especially by his ego-sense – that subtle mechanism constructed for him that he may confirm and centralise his consciousness of all this strong separateness and difference. All in him, his soul of mind and its action as well as the functioning of his life and body, is very evidently determined by the law of his nature, cannot get outside of it, cannot operate otherwise. He attributes indeed a certain freedom to his personal will, the will of his ego; but that in reality amounts to nothing, since his ego is only a sense which makes him identify himself with the creation that Nature has made of him, with the varying mind and life and body she has constructed. His ego is itself a product of her workings, and as is the nature of his ego, so will be the nature of its will and according to that he must act and he can no other.

This then is man's ordinary consciousness of himself, this his faith in his own being, that he is a creature of Nature, a separate ego establishing whatever relations with others and with the world, making whatever development of himself, satisfying whatever will, desire, idea of his mind may be permissible in her circle and consonant with her intention or law in his existence. There is, however, something in man's consciousness which does not fall in with the rigidity of this formula; he has a faith, which grows greater as his soul develops, in another and an inner reality of existence. In this inner reality the truth of existence is no longer Nature but Soul and Spirit, Purusha rather than Prakriti. Nature herself is only a power of Spirit, Prakriti the force of the Purusha. A Spirit, a Self, a Being one in all is the master of this world which is only his partial manifestation. That Spirit is the upholder of Nature and her action and the giver of the sanction by which alone her law becomes imperative and her force and its ways operative. That Spirit within her is the Knower who illuminates her and makes her conscient in us; his is the immanent and superconscient Will that inspires and motives her workings. The soul in man, a portion of this Divinity, shares his nature. Our nature is our soul's manifestation, operates by its sanction and embodies its secret self-knowledge and self-consciousness and its will of being in her motions and forms and changes.

The real soul and self of us is hidden from our intelligence by its ignorance of inner things, by a false identification, by an absorption in our outward mechanism of mind, life and body. But if the active soul of man can once draw back from this identification with its natural instruments, if it can see and live in the entire faith of its inner reality, then all is changed to it, life and existence take on another appearance, action a different meaning and character. Our being then becomes no longer this little egoistic creation of Nature, but the largeness of a divine, immortal and spiritual Power. Our consciousness becomes no longer that of this limited and struggling mental and vital creature, but an infinite, divine and spiritual consciousness. And our will and action too are no longer that of this bounded personality and its ego, but a divine and spiritual will and action, the will and power of the Universal, the Supreme, the All-Self and Spirit acting freely through the human figure.

'This is the great change and transfiguration,' runs the message of the Godhead in man, the Avatar, the divine Teacher, 'to which I call the elect, and the elect are all who can turn their will away from the ignorance of the natural instruments to the soul's deepest experience, its knowledge of the inner self and spirit, its contact with the Godhead, its power to enter into the Divine. The elect are all who can accept this faith and this greater law. It is difficult indeed to accept for the human intellect attached always to its own cloud-forms and half lights of ignorance and to the yet obscurer habits of man's mental, nervous and physical parts; but once received it is a great and sure and saving way, because it is identical with the true truth of man's being and it is the authentic movement of his inmost and supreme nature.

'But the change is a very great one, an enormous transformation, and it cannot be done without an entire turning and conversion of your whole being and nature. There will be needed a complete consecration of yourself and your nature and your life to the Highest and to nothing else but the Highest; for all must be held only for the sake of the Highest, nothing accepted except as it is in God and a form of God and for the sake of the Divine. There will be needed an admission of new truth, an entire turn and giving of your mind to a new knowledge of self and others and world and God and soul and Nature, a knowledge of oneness, a knowledge of universal Divinity, which will be at first an acceptance by the understanding but must become in the end a vision, a consciousness, a permanent state of the soul and the frame of its movements.

'There will be needed a will that shall make this new knowledge, vision, consciousness a motive of action and the sole motive. And it must be the motive not of an action grudging, limited, confined to a few necessary operations of Nature or to the few things that seem helpful to a formal perfection, apposite to a religious turn or to an individual salvation, but rather all action of human life taken up by the equal spirit and done for the sake of God and the good of all creatures. There will be needed an uplifting of the heart in a single aspiration to the Highest, a single love of the Divine Being, a single God-adoration. And there must be a widening too of the calmed and enlightened heart to embrace God in all beings. There will be needed a change of the habitual and normal nature of man as he is now to a supreme and divine spiritual nature. There will be needed in a word a Yoga which shall be at once a Yoga of integral knowledge, a Yoga of the integral will and its works, a Yoga of integral love, adoration and devotion and a Yoga of an integral spiritual perfection of the whole being and of all its parts and states and powers and motions.

'What then is this knowledge that will have to be admitted by the understanding, supported by the soul's faith and made real and living to the mind, heart and life? It is the knowledge of the supreme Soul and Spirit in its oneness and its wholeness. It is the knowledge of One who is for ever, beyond Time and Space and name and form and world, high beyond his own personal and impersonal levels and yet from whom all this proceeds, One whom all manifests in manifold Nature and her multitude of figures. It is the knowledge of him as an impersonal eternal immutable Spirit, the calm and limitless thing we call Self, infinite, equal and always the same, unaffected and unmodified and unchanged amid all this constant changing and all this multitude of individual personalities and soul powers and Nature powers and the forms and forces and eventualities of this transitory and apparent existence. It is the knowledge of him at the same time as the Spirit and Power who seems ever mutable in Nature, the Inhabitant who shapes himself to every form and modifies himself to every grade and degree and activity of his power, the Spirit who, becoming all that is even while he is for ever infinitely more than all that is, dwells in man and animal and thing, subject and object, soul and mind and life and matter, every existence and every force and every creature.

'It is not by insisting on this or that side only of the truth that you can practise this Yoga. The Divine whom you have to seek, the Self whom you have to discover, the supreme Soul of whom your soul is an eternal portion, is simultaneously all these things; you have to know them simultaneously in a supreme oneness, enter into all of them at once and in all states and all things see Him alone. If he were solely the Spirit mutable in Nature, there would be only an eternal and universal becoming. If you limit your faith and knowledge to that one aspect, you will never go beyond your personality and its constant changeful figures; on such a foundation you would be bound altogether in the revolutions of Nature. But you are not merely a succession of soul moments in Time. There is an impersonal self in you which supports the stream of your personality and is one with God's vast and impersonal spirit. And incalculable beyond this impersonality and personality, dominating these two constant poles of what you are here, you are eternal and transcendent in the Eternal Transcendence.

'If, again, there were only the truth of an eternal impersonal self that neither acts nor creates, then the world and your soul would be illusions without any real basis. If you limit your faith and knowledge to this one lonely aspect, the renunciation of life and action is your only resource. But God in the world and you in the world are realities; the world and you are true and actual powers and manifestations of the Supreme. Therefore, accept life and action and do not reject them. One with God in your impersonal self and essence, an eternal portion of the Godhead turned to him by the love and adoration of your spiritual personality for its own Infinite, make of your natural being what it is intended to be, an instrument of works, a channel, a power of the Divine. That it always is in its truth, but now unconsciously and imperfectly, through the lower nature, doomed to a disfigurement of the Godhead by your ego. Make it consciously and perfectly and without any distortion by ego a power of the Divine in his supreme spiritual nature and a vehicle of his will and his works. In this way you will live in the integral truth of your own being and you will possess the integral God-union, the whole and flawless Yoga.

'The Supreme is the Purushottama, eternal beyond all manifestation, infinite beyond all limitation by Time or Space or Causality or any of his numberless qualities and features. But this does not mean that in his supreme eternity he is unconnected with all that happens here, cut off from world and Nature, aloof from all these beings. He is the supreme ineffable Brahman, he is impersonal self, he is all personal existences. Spirit here and life and matter, soul and Nature and the works of Nature are aspects and movements of his infinite and eternal existence. He is the supreme transcendent Spirit and all comes into manifestation from him and are his forms and his self-powers. As the one self he is here all-pervasive and equal and impersonal in man and animal and thing and object and every force of Nature. He is the supreme Soul and all souls are tireless flames of this one Soul. All living beings are in their spiritual personality deathless portions of the one Person or Purusha. He is the eternal Master of all manifested existence, Lord of the worlds and their creatures. He is the omnipotent originator of all actions, not bound by his works, and to him go all action and effort and sacrifice. He is in all and all are in him; he has become all and yet too he is above all and not limited by his creations. He is the transcendent Divine; he descends as the Avatar; he is manifest by his power in the Vibhuti; he is the Godhead secret in every human being. All the gods whom men worship are only personalities and forms and names and mental bodies of the one Divine Existence.

'The Supreme has manifested the world from his spiritual essence and in his own infinite existence and manifested himself too variously in the world. All things are his powers and figures and to the powers and figures of him there is no end, because he himself is infinite. As a pervading and containing impersonal self-existence he informs and sustains equally and without any partiality, preference or attachment to any person or thing or happening or feature all this infinite manifestation in Time and the universe. This pure and equal Self does not act, but supports impartially all the action of things. And yet it is the Supreme, but as the cosmic Spirit and the Time Spirit, who wills and conducts and determines the action of the world through his multitudinous power-to-be, that power of the Spirit which we call Nature. He creates, sustains and destroys his creations. He is seated too in the heart of every living creature and from there as a secret Power in the individual, no less than from his universal presence in the Cosmos, he originates by force of Nature, manifests some line of his mystery in quality of nature and in executive energy of nature, shapes each thing and being separately according to its kind and initiates and upholds all action. It is this transcendent first origination from the Supreme and this constant universal and individual manifestation of Him in things and beings which makes the complex character of the cosmos.

'There are always these three eternal states of the Divine Being. There is always and for ever this one eternal immutable self-existence which is the basis and support of existent things. There is always and for ever this Spirit mutable in Nature manifested by her as all these existences. There is always and for ever this transcendent Divine who can be both of these others at once, can be a pure and silent Spirit and at the same time the active soul and life of the cycles of the universe, because he is something other and more than these two whether taken separately or together. In us is the Jiva, a spirit of this Spirit, a conscious power of the Supreme. He is one who carries in his deepest self the whole of the immanent Divine and in Nature lives in the universal Divine – no temporary creation but an eternal soul acting and moving in the eternal Self, in the eternal Infinite.

'This conscient soul in us can adopt either of these three states of the Spirit. Man can live here in the mutability of Nature and in that alone. Ignorant of his real self, ignorant of the Godhead within him, he knows only Nature: he sees her as a mechanical executive and creative Force and sees himself and others as her creations – egos, separated existences in her universe. It is thus, superficially, that he now lives and, while it is so and until he exceeds this outer consciousness and knows what is within him, all his thought and science can only be a shadow of light thrown upon screens and surfaces. This ignorance is possible, is even imposed, because the Godhead within is hidden by the veil of his own power. His greater reality is lost to our view by the completeness with which he has identified himself in a partial appearance with his creations and images and absorbed the created mind in the deceptive workings of his own Nature. And it is possible also because the real, the eternal, the spiritual Nature which is the secret of things in themselves is not manifest in their outward phenomena. The Nature which we see when we look outwards, the Nature which acts in our mind and body and senses is a lower Force, a derivation, a Magician who creates figures of the Spirit but hides the Spirit in its figures, conceals the truth and makes men look upon masks, a Force which is only capable of a sum of secondary and depressed values, not of the full power and glory and ecstasy and sweetness of the manifestation of the Divine. This Nature in us is a Maya of the ego, a tangle of the dualities, a web of ignorance and the three gunas. And so long as the soul of man lives in the surface fact of mind and life and body and not in his self and spirit, he cannot see God and himself and the world as they really are, cannot overcome this Maya, but must do what he can with its terms and figures.

'It is possible by drawing back from the lower turn of his nature in which man now lives, to awake from this light that is darkness and live in the luminous truth of the eternal and immutable self-existence. Man, then, is no longer bound up in his narrow prison of personality, no longer sees himself as this little I that thinks and acts and feels and struggles and labours for a little. He is merged in the vast and free impersonality of the pure spirit; he becomes the Brahman; he knows himself as one with the oneself in all things. He is no longer aware of ego, no longer troubled by the dualities, no longer feels anguish of grief or disturbance of joy, is no longer shaken by desire, is no longer troubled by sin or limited by virtue. Or if the shadows of these things remain, he sees and knows them only as Nature working in her own qualities and does not feel them to be the truth of himself in which he lives. Nature alone acts and works out her mechanical figures: but the pure spirit is silent, inactive and free. Calm, untouched by her workings, it regards them with a perfect equality and knows itself to be other than these things. This spiritual state brings with it a still peace and freedom but not the dynamic divinity, not the integral perfection; it is a great step, but it is not the integral God-knowledge and self-knowledge.

'A perfect perfection comes only by living in the supreme and the whole Divine. Then the soul of man is united with the Godhead of which it is a portion; then it is one with all beings in the self and spirit, one with them both in God and in Nature; then it is not only free but complete, plunged in the supreme felicity, ready for its ultimate perfection. He still sees the self as an eternal and changeless Spirit silently supporting all things; but he sees also Nature no longer as a mere mechanical force that works out things according to the mechanism of the gunas, but as a power of the Spirit and the force of God in manifestation. He sees that the lower Nature is not the inmost truth of the spirit's action; he becomes aware of a highest spiritual nature of the Divine in which is contained the source and the yet to be realised greater truth of all that is imperfectly figured now in mind, life and body. Arisen from the lower mental to this supreme spiritual nature, he is delivered there from all ego. He knows himself as a spiritual being, in his essence one with all existences and in his active nature a power of the one Godhead and an eternal soul of the transcendent Infinite. He sees all in God and God in all; he sees all things as Vasudeva. He is delivered from the dualities of joy and grief, from the pleasant and the unpleasant, from desire and disappointment, from sin and virtue. All henceforth is to his conscious sight and sense the will and working of the Divine. He lives and acts as a soul and portion of the universal consciousness and power; he is filled with the transcendent divine delight, a spiritual Ananda. His action becomes the divine action and his status the highest spiritual status.

***

'This is the solution, this the salvation, this the perfection that I offer to all those who can listen to a divine voice within them and are capable of this faith and knowledge. But to climb to this pre-eminent condition the first necessity, the original radical step is to turn away from all that belongs to your lower Nature and fix yourself by concentration of the will and intelligence on that which is higher than either will or intelligence, higher than mind and heart and sense and body. And first of all you must turn to your own eternal and immutable self, impersonal and the same in all creatures. So long as you live in ego and mental personality, you will always spin endlessly in the same rounds and there can be no real issue. Turn your will inward beyond the heart and its desires and the sense and its attractions; lift it upward beyond the mind and its associations and attachments and its bounded wish and thought and impulse. Arrive at something within you that is eternal, ever unchanged, calm, unperturbed, equal, impartial to all things and persons and happenings, not affected by any action, not altered by the figures of Nature. Be that, be the eternal self, be the Brahman. If you can become that by a permanent spiritual experience, you will have an assured basis on which you can stand delivered from the limitations of your mind-created personality, secure against any fall from peace and knowledge, free from ego.

'Thus, to impersonalise your being is not possible so long as you nurse and cherish and cling to your ego or anything that belongs to it. Desire and the passions that arise from desire are the principal sign and knot of ego.

It is desire that makes you go on saying I and mine and subjects you through a persistent egoism to satisfaction and dissatisfaction, liking and disliking, hope and despair, joy and grief, to your petty loves and hatreds, to wrath and passion, to your attachment to success and things pleasant and to the sorrow and suffering of failure and of things unpleasant. Desire brings always confusion of mind and limitation of the will, an egoistic and distorted view of things, a failure and clouding of knowledge. Desire and its preferences and violences are the first strong root of sin and error. There can be while you cherish desire no assured stainless tranquillity, no settled light, no calm pure knowledge. There can be no right being – for desire is a perversion of the spirit – and no firm foundation for right thought, action and feeling. Desire, if permitted to remain under whatever colour, is a perpetual menace even to the wisest and can at any moment subtly or violently cast down the mind from even its firmest and most surely acquired foundation. Desire is the chief enemy of spiritual perfection.

'Slay then desire; put away attachment to the possession and enjoyment of the outwardness of things. Separate yourself from all that comes to you as outward touches and solicitations, as objects of the mind and senses. Learn to bear and reject all the rush of the passions and to remain securely seated in your inner self even while they rage in your members, until at last, they cease to affect any part of your nature. Bear and put away similarly the forceful attacks and even the slightest insinuating touches of joy and sorrow. Cast away liking and disliking, destroy preference and hatred, root out shrinking and repugnance. Let there be a calm indifference to these things and to all the objects of desire in all your nature. Look on them with the silent and tranquil regard of an impersonal spirit.

'The result will be an absolute equality and the power of unshakable calm that the universal spirit maintains in front of its creations, facing ever the manifold action of Nature. Look with equal eyes; receive with an equal heart and mind all that comes to you, success and failure, honour and dishonour, the esteem and love of men and their scorn and persecution and hatred, every happening that would be to others a cause of joy and every happening that would be to others a cause of sorrow. Look with equal eyes on all persons, on the good and the wicked, on the wise and the foolish, on the Brahmin and the outcaste, on man at his highest and every pettiest creature. Meet equally all men whatever their relations to you, friend and ally, neutral and indifferent, opponent and enemy, lover and hater. These things touch the ego and you are called to be free from ego. These are personal relations and you have to observe all with the deep regard of the impersonal spirit. These are temporal and personal differences which you have to see but not be influenced by them; for you must fix not on these differences but on that which is the same in all, on the oneself which all are, on the Divine in every creature and on the one working of Nature which is the equal will of God in men and things and energies and happenings and in all endeavour and result and whatever outcome of the world's labour.

'Action will still be done in you because Nature is always at work; but you must learn and feel that your self is not the doer of the action. Observe simply, observe unmoved the working of Nature and the play of her qualities and the magic of the gunas. Observe unmoved this action in yourself; look on all that is being done around you and see that it is the same working in others. Observe that the result of your works and theirs is constantly other than you or they desired or intended, not theirs, not yours, but omnipotently fixed by a greater Power that wills and acts here in universal Nature. Observe too that even the will in your works is not yours but Nature's. It is the will of the ego sense in you and is determined by the predominant quality in your composition which she has developed in the past or else brings forward at the moment. It depends on the play of your natural personality and that formation of Nature is not your true person. Draw back from this external formation to your inner silent self; you will see that you the Purusha are inactive, but Nature continues to do always her works according to her gunas. Fix yourself in this inner inactivity and stillness: no longer regard yourself as the doer. Remain seated in yourself above the play, free from the perturbed action of the gunas. Live secure in the purity of an impersonal spirit, live untroubled by the mortal waves that persist in your members.

'If you can do this, then you will find yourself uplifted into a great release, a wide freedom and a deep peace.

Then you will be aware of God and immortal, possessed of your dateless self-existence, independent of mind and life and body, sure of your spiritual being, untouched by the reactions of Nature, unstained by passion and sin and pain and sorrow. Then you will depend for your joy and desire on no mortal or outward or worldly thing, but will possess inalienably the self-sufficient delight of a calm and eternal spirit. Then you will have ceased to be a mental creature and will have become spirit illimitable, the Brahman. And into this eternity of the silent self, rejecting from your mind all seed of thought and all root of desire, rejecting the figure of birth in the body, you can pass at your end by concentration in the pure Eternal and a mighty transference of your consciousness to the Infinite, the Absolute.

* * *

'This however is not all the truth of the Yoga and this end and way of departure, though a great end and a great way, is not the thing I propose to you. For I am the eternal Worker within you and I ask of you works. I demand of you not a passive consent to a mechanical movement of Nature from which in yourself you are wholly separated, indifferent and aloof, but action complete and divine, done as the willing and understanding instrument of the Divine, done for God in you and others and for the good of the world. This action I propose to you, first no doubt as a means of perfection in the supreme spiritual Nature, but as a part too of that perfection. Action is a part of the integral knowledge of

God, of his greater mysterious truth and of an entire living in the Divine; action can and should be continued even after perfection and freedom are won. I ask of you the action of the Jivanmukta, the works of the Siddha. Something has to be added to the Yoga already described, for that was only a first Yoga of knowledge. There is also a Yoga of action in the illumination of God-experience; works can be made one spirit with knowledge. For works done in a total self-vision and God-vision, a vision of God in the world and of the world in God are themselves a movement of knowledge, a movement of light, an indispensable means and an intimate part of spiritual perfection.

'Therefore now to the experience of a high impersonality add too this knowledge that the Supreme whom one meets as the pure silent Self can be met also as a vast dynamic Spirit who originates all works and is Lord of the worlds and the Master of man's action and endeavour and sacrifice. This apparently self-acting mechanism of Nature conceals an immanent divine Will that compels and guides it and shapes its purposes. But you cannot feel or know that Will while you are shut up in your narrow cell of personality, blinded and chained to your viewpoint of the ego and its desires. For you can wholly respond to it only when you are impersonalised by knowledge and widened to see all things in the self and in God and the self and God in all things. All becomes here by the power of the Spirit; all do their works by the immanence of God in things and his presence in the heart of every creature. The Creator of the worlds is not limited by his creations; the Lord of works is not bound by his works; the divine Will is not attached to its labour and the results of its labour, for it is omnipotent, all-possessing and all-blissful. But still the Lord looks down on his creations from his transcendence; he descends as the Avatar; he is here in you; he rules from within all things in the steps of their nature. And you too must do works in him, after the way and in the steps of the divine nature, untouched by limitation, attachment or bondage. Act for the best good of all, act for the maintenance of the march of the world, for the support or the leading of its peoples. The action asked of you is the action of the liberated Yogin; it is the spontaneous output of a free and God-held energy, it is an equal-minded movement, it is a selfless and desireless labour.

'The first step on this free, this equal, this divine way of action is to put from you attachment to fruit and recompense and to labour only for the sake of the work itself that has to be done. For you must deeply feel that the fruits belong not to you but to the Master of the world. Consecrate your labour and leave its returns to the Spirit who manifests and fulfils himself in the universal movement. The outcome of your action is determined by his will alone and whatever it be, good or evil fortune, success or failure, it is turned by him to the accomplishment of his world purpose. An entirely desireless and disinterested working of the personal will and the whole instrumental nature is the first rule of Karmayoga. Demand no fruit, accept whatever result is given to you; accept it with equality and a calm gladness: successful or foiled, prosperous or afflicted, continue unafraid, untroubled and unwavering on the steep path of the divine action.

'This is no more than the first step on the path. For you must be not only unattached to results, but unattached also to your labour. Cease to regard your works as your own; as you have abandoned the fruits of your work, so you must surrender the work also to the Lord of action and sacrifice. Recognise that your nature determines your action; your nature rules the immediate motion of your Swabhava and decides the expressive turn and development of your spirit in the paths of the executive force of Prakriti. Bring in no longer any self-will to confuse the steps of your mind in following the Godward way. Accept the action proper to your nature. Make of all you do from the greatest and most unusual effort to the smallest daily act, make of each act of your mind, each act of your heart, each act of your body, of every inner and outer turn, of every thought and will and feeling, of every step and pause and movement, a sacrifice to the Master of all sacrifice and Tapasya.

'Next know that you are an eternal portion of the Eternal and the powers of your nature are nothing without him, nothing if not his partial self-expression. It is the Divine Infinite that is being progressively fulfilled in your nature. It is the supreme power-to-be, it is the Shakti of the Lord that shapes and takes shape in your swabhava. Give up then all sense that you are the doer; see the Eternal alone as the doer of the action. Let your natural being be an occasion, an instrument, a channel of power, a means of manifestation. Offer up your will to him and make it one with his eternal will: surrender all your actions in the silence of yourself and spirit to the transcendent Master of your nature. This cannot be really done or done perfectly so long as there is any ego sense in you or any mental claim or vital clamour. Action done in the least degree for the sake of the ego or tinged with the desire and will of the ego is not a perfect sacrifice. Nor can this great thing be well and truly done so long as there is inequality anywhere or any stamp of ignorant shrinking and preference. But when there is a perfect equality to all works, results, things and persons, a surrender to the Highest and not to desire or ego, then the divine Will determines without stumbling or deflection and the divine Power executes freely without any nether interference or perverting reaction all works in the purity and safety of your transmuted nature. To allow your every act to be shaped through you by the divine Will in its immaculate sovereignty is the highest degree of the perfection that comes by doing works in Yoga. That done, your nature will follow its cosmic walk in a complete and constant union with the Supreme, express the highest Self, obey the Ishwara.

'This way of divine works is a far better release and a more perfect way and solution than the physical renunciation of life and works. A physical abstention is not entirely possible and is not in the measure of its possibility indispensable to the spirit's freedom; it is besides a dangerous example, for it exerts a misleading influence on ordinary men. The best, the greatest set the standard which the rest of humanity strive to follow. Then since action is the nature of the embodied spirit, since works are the will of the eternal Worker, the great spirits, the master minds should set this example. World-workers should they be, doing all works of the world without reservation, God-workers free, glad and desireless, liberated souls and natures.

* * *

'The mind of knowledge and the will of action are not all; there is within you a heart whose demand is for delight. Here too in the heart's power and illumination, in its demand for delight, for the soul's satisfaction your nature must be turned, transformed and lifted to one conscious ecstasy with the Divine. The knowledge of the impersonal self brings its own Ananda; there is a joy of impersonality, a singleness of joy of the pure spirit. But an integral knowledge brings a greater triple delight. It opens the gates of the Transcendent's bliss; it releases into the limitless delight of a universal impersonality; it discovers the rapture of all this multitudinous manifestation: for there is a joy of the Eternal in Nature. This Ananda in the Jiva, a portion here of the Divine, takes the form of an ecstasy founded in the Godhead who is his source, in his supreme self, in the Master of his existence. An entire God-love and adoration extends to a love of the world and all its forms and powers and creatures; in all the Divine is seen, is found, is adored, is served or is felt in oneness. Add to knowledge and works this crown of the eternal triune delight; admit this love, learn this worship; make it one spirit with works and knowledge. That is the apex of the perfect perfection.

'This Yoga of love will give you a highest potential force for spiritual largeness and unity and freedom. But it must be a love which is one with God-knowledge. There is a devotion which seeks God in suffering for consolation and succour and deliverance; there is a devotion which seeks him for his gifts, for divine aid and protection and as a fountain of the satisfaction of desire; there is a devotion that, still ignorant, turns to him for light and knowledge. And so long as one is limited to these forms, there may persist even in their highest and noblest Godward turn a working of the three gunas. But when the God-lover is also the God-knower, the lover becomes one self with the Beloved; for he is the chosen of the Most High and the elect of the Spirit. Develop in yourself this God-engrossed love; the heart spiritualised and lifted beyond the limitations of its lower nature will reveal to you most intimately the secrets of God's immeasurable being, bring into you the whole touch and influx and glory of his divine Power and open to you the mysteries of an eternal rapture. It is perfect love that is the key to a perfect knowledge.

'This integral God-love demands too an integral work for the sake of the Divine in yourself and in all creatures. The ordinary man does works in obedience to some desire sinful or virtuous, some vital impulse low or high, some mental choice common or exalted or from some mixed mind and life motive. But the work done by you must be free and desireless; work done without desire creates no reaction and imposes no bondage. Done in a perfect equality and an unmoved calm and peace, but without any divine passion, it is at first the fine yoke of a spiritual obligation, *kartavyaṁ karma*, then the uplifting of a divine sacrifice; at its highest it can be the expression of a calm and glad acquiescence in active oneness. The oneness in love will do much more: it will replace the first impassive calm by a strong and deep rapture, not the petty ardour of egoistic desire but the ocean of an infinite Ananda. It will bring the moving sense and the pure and divine passion of the presence of the Beloved into your works; there will be an insistent joy of labour for God in yourself and for God in all beings. Love is the crown of works and the crown of knowledge.

'This love that is knowledge, this love that can be the deep heart of your action, will be your most effective force for an utter consecration and complete perfection. An integral union of the individual's being with the Divine Being is the condition of a perfect spiritual life. Turn then altogether towards the Divine; make one with him by knowledge, love and works all your nature. Turn utterly towards him and give up ungrudgingly into his hands your mind and your heart and your will, all your consciousness and even your very senses and body. Let your consciousness be sovereignly moulded by him into a flawless mould of his divine consciousness. Let your heart become a lucid or flaming heart of the Divine. Let your will be an impeccable action of his will. Let your very sense and body be the rapturous sensation and body of the Divine. Adore and sacrifice to him with all you are; remember him in every thought and feeling, every impulsion and act. Persevere until all these things are wholly his and he has taken up even in most common and outward things as in the inmost sacred chamber of your spirit his constant transmuting presence.

* * *

'This triune way is the means by which you can rise entirely out of your lower into your supreme spiritual nature. That is the hidden superconscient nature in which the Jiva, a portion of the high Infinite and Divine and intimately one in law of being with him, dwells in his Truth and not any longer in an externalised Maya. This perfection, this unity can be enjoyed in its own native status, aloof in a supreme supracosmic existence: but here also you may and should realise it, here in the human body and physical world. It is not enough for this end to be calm, inactive and free from the gunas in the inner self and to watch and allow indifferently their mechanical action in the outer members. For the active nature as well as the self has to be given to the Divine and to become divine. All that you are must grow into one law of being with the Purushottama, *sādharmya*; all must be changed into my conscious spiritual becoming, *mad-bhāva*. A completest surrender must be there. Take refuge with Me in all the many ways and along all the living lines of your nature; for that alone will bring about this great change and perfection.

'This high consummation of the Yoga will at once solve or rather it will wholly remove and destroy at its roots the problem of action. Human action is a thing full of difficulties and perplexities, tangled and confused like a forest with a few more or less obscure paths cut into it rather than through it; but all this difficulty and entanglement arises from the single fact that man lives imprisoned in the ignorance of his mental, vital and physical nature. He is compelled by its qualities and yet afflicted with responsibility in his will because something in him feels that he is a soul who ought to be what now he is not at all or very little, master and ruler of his nature. All his laws of living, all his dharmas must be under these conditions imperfect, temporary and provisional and at best only partly right or true. His imperfections can cease only when he knows himself, knows the real nature of the world in which he lives and, most of all, knows the Eternal from whom he comes and in whom and by whom he exists. When he has once achieved a true consciousness and knowledge, there is no longer any problem; for then he acts freely out of himself and lives spontaneously in accordance with the truth of his spirit and his highest nature. At its fullest, at the highest height of this knowledge it is not he who acts but the Divine, the One eternal and infinite who acts in him and through him in his liberated wisdom and power and perfection.

'Man in his natural being is a sattwic, rajasic and tamasic creature of Nature. According as one or other of her qualities predominates in him, he makes and follows this or that law of his life and action. His tamasic, material, sensational mind subject to inertia and fear and ignorance either obeys partly the compulsion of its environment and partly the spasmodic impulses of its desires or finds a protection in the routine following of a dull customary intelligence. The rajasic mind of desire struggles with the world in which it lives and tries to possess always new things, to command, battle, conquer, create, destroy, accumulate. Always it goes forward tossed between success and failure, joy and sorrow, exultation or despair. But in all, whatever law it may seem to admit, it follows really only the law of the lower self and ego, the restless, untired, self-devouring and all-devouring mind of the Asuric and Rakshasic nature. The sattwic intelligence surmounts partly this state, sees that a better law than that of desire and ego must be followed and erects and imposes on itself a social, an ethical, a religious rule, a Dharma, a Shastra. This is as high as the ordinary mind of man can go, to erect an ideal or practical rule for the guidance of the mind and will and as faithfully as possible observe it in life and conduct. This sattwic mind must be developed to its highest point where it succeeds in putting away the mixture of ego motive altogether and observes the Dharma for its own sake as an impersonal social, ethical or religious ideal, the thing disinterestedly to be done solely because it is right, *kartavyaṁ karma*.

'The real truth of all this action of Prakriti is, however, less outwardly mental and more inwardly subjective. It is this that man is an embodied soul involved in material and mental nature, and he follows in it a progressive law of his development determined by an inner law of his being; his cast of spirit makes out his cast of mind and life, his swabhava. Each man has a swadharma, a law of his inner being which he must observe, find out and follow. The action determined by his inner nature, that is his real Dharma. To follow it is the true law of his development; to deviate from it is to bring in confusion, retardation and error. That social, ethical, religious or other law and ideal is best for him always which helps him to observe and follow out his Swadharma.

'All this action however is even at its best subject to the ignorance of the mind and the play of the gunas. It is only when the soul of man finds itself that he can overpass and erase from his consciousness the ignorance and the confusion of the gunas. It is true that even when you have found yourself and live in yourself, your nature will still continue on its old lines and act for a time according to its inferior modes. But now you can follow that action with a perfect self-knowledge and can make of it a sacrifice to the Master of your existence. Follow then the law of your Swadharma, do the action that is demanded by your Swabhava whatever it may be. Reject all motive of egoism, all initiation by self-will, all rule of desire, until you can make the complete surrender of all the ways of your being to the Supreme.

'And when you are once able to do that sincerely, that will be the moment to renounce the initiation of your acts without exception into the hands of the supreme Godhead within you. Then you will be released from all laws of conduct, liberated from all dharmas. The Divine Power and Presence within you will free you from sin and evil and lift you far above human standards of virtue. For you will live and act in the absolute and spontaneous right and purity of the spiritual being and the immaculate force of the divine nature. The Divine and not you will enact his own will and works through you, not for your lower personal pleasure and desire, but for the world-purpose and for your divine good and the manifest or secret good of all. Inundated with light, you will see the form of the Godhead in the world and in the works of Time, know his purpose and hear his command. Your nature will receive as an instrument his will only whatever it may be and do it without question, because there will come with each initiation of your acts from above and within you an imperative knowledge and an illumined assent to the divine wisdom and its significance. The battle will be his, his the victory, his the empire.

'This will be your perfection in the world and the body, and beyond these worlds of temporal birth the supreme eternal superconsciousness will be yours and you will dwell for ever in the highest status of the Supreme Spirit. The cycles of incarnation and the fear of mortality will not distress you; for here in life you will have accomplished the expression of the Godhead, and your soul, even though it has descended into mind and body, will already be living in the vast eternity of the Spirit.

'This then is the supreme movement, this complete surrender of your whole self and nature, this abandonment of all dharmas to the Divine who is your highest Self, this absolute aspiration of all your members to the supreme spiritual nature. If you can once achieve it, whether at the outset or much later on the way, then whatever you are or were in your outward nature, your way is sure and your perfection inevitable. A supreme Presence within you will take up your Yoga and carry it swiftly along the lines of your swabhava to its consummate completion. And afterwards whatever your way of life and mode of action, you will be consciously living, acting and moving in him and the Divine Power will act through you in your every inner and outer motion. This is the supreme way because it is the highest secret and mystery and yet an inner movement progressively realisable by all. This is the deepest and most intimate truth of your real, your spiritual existence.'